D0209303

Hollywood Planet

Global Media
and the Competitive Advantage
of Narrative Transparency

Hollywood Planet

Global Media
and the Competitive Advantage
of Narrative Transparency

Scott Robert Olson
Ball State University

LEA LAWRENCE ERLBAUM ASSOCIATES, PUBLISHERS
1999 Mahwah, New Jersey London

Lawrence Erlbaum Associates, Inc., Publishers
10 Industrial Avenue
Mahwah, NJ 07430

Cover design by Kathryn Houghtaling Lacey

Library of Congress Cataloging-in-Publication Data

Olson, Scott Robert.
Hollywood planet : global media and the competitive advantage of narrative transparency / Scott Robert Olson.
p.   cm.
Includes bibliographical references and index.
ISBN 0-8058-3229-7 (alk. paper). — ISBN 0-8058-3230-0 (pbk. : alk. paper)
1. Mass media—United States—Influence. 2. Mass media and culture. I. Title
P92.U5044 1999
302.23' 0973—DC21
                                                                98–55063
                                                                CIP

Printed in the United States of America
10   9   8   7   6   5   4   3   2   1

Do

Kasia i Luczyna

Contents

Introduction:
Media and Cultures

What are the media doing to culture? The American film *Dirty Dancing* (1987), the tale of a summer romance between a rich guest at an exclusive resort and an across-the-tracks boy she meets there, was a big hit with teenage Hindus and Sikhs living in Britain. They saw in it a reflection of *Diwali*, the traditional festival of lights that celebrates the goddess Lakshmi (Gillespie, 1995b). Their parents, like the parents in the film, were somewhat aghast; the young people's restaging of the film's climactic dance number signified for the older generation the chaos of cultural pollution, but for the kids, the culture in the film was theirs already. Meanwhile, terrorists angered by U.S. policy detonate bombs in Planet Hollywood restaurants (Harris, 1998). American media are everywhere and responses to them are complex.

Scholars and politicians often proclaim that there is a fork in the road: tradition versus *Dirty Dancing* (1987); culture versus anarchy. Culture—anarchy is the dialectic that academics and politicians use to talk about the global media's effect on children and that Hindu parents use to talk about the Westernization of the Diwali festival. It has them wringing their hands. In this formulation, *culture* is everything good that we stand to lose and *anarchy* is what the mass media let loose on us. Setting culture against anarchy is not new, as anyone familiar with Matthew Arnold (1932) will recognize; he set culture against anarchy as the stuff we should preserve, "the best that has been thought and said." Such a formulation still suits admonitions that culture is fragile and has to be protected. A modern variant of Arnold is reflected in this statement on media flow from a United Nations Educational, Scientific, and Cultural Organization (UNESCO) Conference in the 1980s:

> Culture is certainly universal but we are careful not to reduce everything to the same level. ... The first cultural right is that of a people to take their own decisions. All our countries accept too passively a certain invasion of or submission to images produced elsewhere ... which inevitably wear away national cultures and transmit a uniform lifestyle which it is attempted to impose on the planet as a whole. (Forbes, 1988, p. 61)

As Ang (1988) indicated, "This cultural contamination is all the more threatening because it involves a sort of 'conspiracy' between internal and external forces" (p. 72). The same dialectic led to UNESCO's MacBride Commission report calling for a New World Information Order (NWIO, Hamelink, 1997) and to numerous subsequent attempts to keep the NWIO's spirit alive (e.g., Raghavan, 1995; Vincent, 1997). These reports point toward what seems to be a simple choice: We must choose culture, or we will have anarchy.

In part, because of these new world dreams, Arnold's (1932) idea of culture as being the cream at the top is a modernist dream mostly abandoned. Is any consensus on what is the best possible at the millennial fin de siecle? From the perspective of the 20th century's end, the notion of a single best culture seems quaint but impossible. After the horrible experiments in utopian culture that this century scarcely survived—many grotesque and cruel attempts at preserving "the best" that included National Socialism, Maoism, and Stalinism—the idea of ordaining certain artifacts to be the best seems futile and potentially dangerous. We are more content with pluralism than our modernist forebears.

So the option is not really between culture and anarchy, but rather between cultures and anarchy. We have not to choose between the one true and one false path but between many competing routes to paradise or perdition. There are plenty of cultures to go around. It is common to hear academic talk about Western culture, national culture, organizational culture, subcultures, cocultures, counterculture, media culture, pop culture, and internet culture. Indeed, there is now *The Dictionary of Global Culture* (Appiah & Gates, 1997) to offset the Arnoldism of projects like *Cultural Literacy* (Hirsch, 1988). Everything is culture. Culture is everything. Here, there are stark, real, and important choices.

This volume is essentially about the choice between cultures and anarchy, as well as the role that the international media play in coaxing us to one or the other. As television programs and films freely travel across national borders—from one cultural context to another—do they reinforce the difference or sameness of cultures? Is it possible that they do something else, something unrelated to reinforcing a dichotomy between difference or sameness?

The most common explanation about what media do to culture that is provided by media scholars is that international mass media embody a choice between indigenous culture and an imported (and probably American) culture, with the imported values and beliefs probably prevailing over time, resulting in homogenization. Given time, it is argued, this leads to *global monoculture*—a single set of shared values, beliefs, and behaviors imposed or accepted everywhere. Exposure to media causes this change. This tidy dialectic between indigenous and imported is clear and simple and therefore profits from Occam's razor, wherein the simplest explanation is assumed to be correct. It is nonetheless a poor description of what is really going on. Still, most scholars and elites tend to view the transnational flow of media as something both bad and urgent and that leads to a certain amount of tension within countries that import a lot of media. There is little consensus on what should be done about global media, although many approaches have been tried.

The film and television industry is not the only one in which one or a few countries are dominant. The United States dominates the aerospace industry much more spectacularly than it does that of the media. Heavy industrial hegemonies such as this seem less threatening, however, because they are not generally perceived to be the Trojan Horses that the media are. It is widely held, in the United States and abroad, that the media instill values, beliefs, and attitudes, and therefore, crouched inside "Walker, Texas Ranger" (CBS TV), or "Baywatch" (syndicated TV), or *Titanic* (1997) are devices that will turn viewers around the world (especially younger ones)—Japanese or Jordanian, Nigerian or Netherlander—into Americans. The fear is that as with Troy, indigenous culture will be destroyed by an enemy hidden behind a smile and a gift.

Consequently, a great deal of scholarly time, energy, and resources have been expended on trying to observe culture change due to media exposure. These studies have had varying success, and in some cases, have observed no behavior change at all. National strategies for dealing with media imports have often been based on cultivation studies of this type, on anecdotal evidence, or more likely, on no evidence whatsoever. These defensive strategies have been failing. National broadcasting systems almost everywhere are coming to look increasingly like the American commercial system; national film industries get increasingly smaller and, in some cases, die out. Simultaneously, however, "the distribution of media content throughout large territories has not always fostered cultural homogeneity" (Waisbord, 1998, p. 382).

Perhaps there is a question prior to, "What effect are these imported programs having?" that needs to be answered first: "Why are movies and television programs from the United States so dominant?" A few scholars have already tried to answer this question, but in most cases, they rely on purely economic or political explanations. Those studies are important contributions, but only go part of the way to explaining the imbalance; analogously, they are like trying to account for Japanese success in the automobile industry only in terms of U.S. and Japanese governmental policy, without consideration of such crucial factors as local taste, consumer perception, marketing strategies, currency exchange rates, and, most importantly, the attributes of the product itself.

In other words, consumers came, in many cases, to prefer Japanese automobiles because of certain properties those cars had or were perceived to have. This, more than any other factor, must account for their success: if consumers did not want them, for whatever reasons (including price, safety, styling, quality), they would not sell as well as they do. The same must be true of films and television programs: For the most part, their success is a function of their desirability, and their desirability is a function of specific qualities that buyers assign to them. To discover what these qualities might be, one has to look at audience expectations and responses and at the product itself. Looking at what the consumer expects and the actual way the product is used certainly reveals particular ways in which consumer desire is met with textual devices in a satisfying way either by a car or by the media.

This is not to say that the American media are in any way better than other media, just as it is problematic to say that Japanese cars are better than American cars. It is more meaningful to frame the difference in suitability to particular tasks. There is no meaningful and objective way of evaluating media or cars in this manner because such a qualitative evaluation is audience and consumer specific. Nor is American global success in the media inevitable or eternal; plenty of American films fail domestically and internationally, just as many models of automobiles fail to sell. Other national cinemas are capable of breaking through internationally, such as through the huge international box office receipts of the British film, *The Full Monty* (1997) or the Australian film, *Babe* (1995). Nevertheless, the American share of international film and television remains the lion's share. The reasons that share is so big need to be evaluated, systematized, and theorized.

Mattelart, Delcourt, and Mattelart (1984) and many others have lamented the absence of appropriate tools for analyzing international image markets. Luckily, however, there are methodological frameworks in place that enable such a project—they simply have not been put together before. Because this volume has, in a sense, a twofold purpose, it uses two methodologies from two fields frequently unrelated. In order to evaluate systematically American competitive advantage in the film and television industry relative to other nations, Porter's (1990) method is used. This ultimately proves better in understanding purely industrial products (e.g., photochemicals) rather than ones with overt cultural overtones (e.g., the media), so methods from cultural studies and reception theory are borrowed to fill in the gaps. These lead to the revelation that the American media form a fairly unique bond between text and audience, and this bond accounts, to a significant degree, for the dominance the U.S. media enjoy at this historical juncture. This volume then borrows methods from postcolonial studies to examine the viability of alternatives to this hegemony, mostly in the form of countervailing strategies and tactics.

In a nutshell, this volume's argument follows a simple structure. It first details the primary thesis, then demonstrates for the reader the magnitude of U.S. media success. It theoretically accounts for national advantages in different industries, showing how the United States has such a national advantage in the media. The argument then demonstrates what that advantage is—its strategy as displayed in media texts—showing examples of how that strategy has been deployed. Finally, this volume discusses social ramifications of this practice.

Chapter 1 of this text reviews the existing literature on global media and establishes the inadequacy of current theory to explain the phenomenon of relative American film and television hegemony. It then sketches a new theory—*transparency*—and relates it to the contention that the media are assembling a Hollywood planet.

Chapter 2 then looks at the current status of world media exports—who is exporting to whom—using current data culled from a number of sources. The picture that develops is in many ways a startling one: The United States has little serious competition in the production and distribution of films and little competition in the production and distribution of television programming. Some of these international markets, such as the European one, have limits on the amount of foreign programs that may be imported. Others take a free-market position, often seeming intoxicated with imported popular culture. These markets also widely vary in their ability to pay for imported media; consequently, pricing structures vary from place to place. Little unifies these cultures except for a popular interest in American media.

Chapter 3 proposes a partial explanation for American success in the media by making use of Porter's (1990, 1998) theory of competitive advantage and national clusters. The theory argues that four aspects of a nation—demand conditions, factors conditions, industry structure, and supporting industries—combine in unique ways to confer competitive advantage to some industries. This theory only goes so far in explaining the subtleties of demand conditions, however, particularly of how home demand anticipates international demand.

Chapter 4 tries to resolve the deficiencies of Porter's (1990, 1998) method by looking carefully and closely at the American home market. Of course, the attributes of transparent media indicate that they could be manufactured anywhere and yet, the United States seems particularly capable of producing them. This leads to a second question: "What is it about America that makes it so capable of producing exportable media?" This question is answered by and through observations of American culture made by de Tocqueville 150 years ago and Baudrillard more recently. From these, an image is developed of American culture as being ahistorical, nostalgic, hyperreal, melting pot mythic, conformist, speed-obsessed, primitive, spatial, abundant, and pragmatic.

The particular combination of demand, factor, rivalry, and supporting industry conditions, then, combine to make the United States particularly adept at manufacturing media that have competitive advantage. However, what about the other part of the formula: How do international audiences actually receive these media? More specifically, what makes them intelligible in such wildly different settings, let alone popular? Here, a new theory, *transparency*, is invoked by way of explanation.

The precise nature of *transparency*, and the mechanisms through which a media text exhibit it, are the focus of chapters 5 and 6. Blumenberg's (1985) theory of myths forms the basis for describing the elements of mythotype and the attributes of the iconic media that access it. It is argued in chapter 5 that these attributes include open-endedness, virtuality, circularity, ellipticality, negentropy, inclusion, verisimilitude, omnipresence, materialization, and production values. In chapter 6, the related phenomenon of *synergy*—merchandising and licensing, product placement, intertextuality, theming, and hyperreal environments—is shown to further enhance transparency.

Having examined the general attributes of transparent media, America's comparative advantage in producing them, and the world's demand for such output, this volume turns to some specific examples of movies and television programs that have shown transparency so as to analyze in some detail how transparency manifests itself in their case. This is done in chapter 7. Some of the specific examples to be analyzed are the films *The Lion King* (1994) and *Breaking the Waves* (1997) and the television programs "Walker, Texas Ranger" (CBS TV), "Neighbours" (Australian TV), and "Polski Zoo" (Polish TV). Some of the material about "Polski Zoo" was previously published in a different form (Olson, 1995).

Chapter 8 contemplates the effect that world dissemination of transparent products from particular cultures might have, returning to some of the questions posed at the beginning of this introduction: What are media doing to culture? Are they promoting difference or sameness? It also raises some questions about postcolonialism and transnational media flow. Is it correct to call this a form of colonialism? What economic impact does it have? What psychological and social effects does it have? What happens to the traditional and indigenous culture—does transparency allow it to continue in an altered state or does transparency replace it with some new, global culture? If identity emanates from culture, and culture is hybridized, is there anything left but chaos? Is the American domination of the media inevitable and do other cultures have any means to resist or reject it? This chapter particularly examines and systematizes the effects of international media on subalterneity and the subaltern strategies that are capable of directly countering and resisting cultural imports with their own tactics. Some cultures already engage in some of these strategies, but they could be much more widely used than they are now.

Many have directly and indirectly contributed to the development of this volume. It began to take shape at a conference on global communication in Plock, Poland several years ago, where Herb Dordick, Richard Pattenaude, Sarah King, Donald Cushman, and others gave useful advice on how to distill the argument. Andrew Moemeka, Ju Yanan, Serafin Mendez-Mendez, and Benjamin Sevitch steered me toward useful materials and ideas; Warren Vander Hill, George Clarke, and June Higgins provided the time, resources, and encouragement to make it happen. Ewa Wolynska helped with translation. David Morley has posed questions and indicated directions that have strengthened the project enormously. Fred Casmir provided invaluable insight on the chapter about subaltern resistance tactics, and my friends and colleagues in Poland, especially Marcelina Zuber and Jan Waskiewicz, have helped broaden my perspective. Pat Armstrong kept things working. The reviewers' comments were so invaluable that almost every one of them was integrated in the final draft of the volume, so I want to thank them. In addition, thanks especially to Jennings Bryant, Linda Bathgate, and Lori Hawver at Lawrence Erlbaum Associates, who gave such good direction.

As for Kelley, Katie, and Lucie, they have, as always, given the most—their time and affection. Hollywood is making the planet smaller, but I am still glad to have them close.

—*Scott Robert Olson*

1

Seeing Transparency

American mass culture did not even feel like an import ...
—*Richard Pells (1997, p. 205)*

Ours is becoming a Hollywood planet.

Tunstall (1977) proclaimed 20 years ago that "the media are American." Now, Tunstall (1995) is backing off a bit, seeing the possibility for other nations to be successful in the global media marketplace, but if anything, his earlier claim was somewhat timid: It is not that the media are American, but something much broader and more profound. Hollywood has conquered the world.

The evidence is staggering. Seventy-five percent of movie tickets sold in Europe in 1995 were to films made in the United States. This is up 34% from 10 years earlier. Thanks to the proliferation of satellite and cable, 70% of the movies shown on European television were also American ("Hollywood conquers Europe," 1996). Trends in other parts of the world are similar. Hollywood is everywhere, and there seems to be nothing outside of Hollywood, so "one question in every mind must be whether the geographical source of an individual's or country's media any longer matters" (Smith, 1995, p. 1). Even media made outside Hollywood have grown to have a Hollywood quality about them.

Swartzenegger, Stallone, Willis, and their coinvestors certainly call attention to this phenomenon by having named their successful restaurant chain Planet Hollywood. In its emphasis on the veneration of movie and television artifacts and the marketing of its brand name (rather than its menu), these restaurants claim to be little microcosms of a global obsession with media. They underestimate their own significance. The world is not a solar system of little Planet Hollywoods, but one Hollywood Planet. Hollywood is not a microcosm but the cosmos.

What does a *Hollywood Planet* mean? The traditional notion of global media, of course, is that if the planet is Hollywood, then a global monoculture—an American one—is taking root. This may be far too simple a conclusion, however. Among media theorists, a consensus is growing that this most fundamental assumption about transnational media is wrong. It may not be true that when the media from one culture are introduced into another, they force indigenous values and beliefs more in line with those that the media portray. The corollary of this assumption, and the source of its power, is that this infusion of nonnative values can be measured. This assumption and its corollary have guided academic research in this area for many years, and yet the results have been disappointing and inconclusive. The major failing of this approach is that it ignores essential work being done in postmodern and literary theory.

Examples of this mistaken approach to global media are easy to find. Kang and Wu (1995) and Kapoor and Kang (1995) are in good company. They wonder why it is that despite their elaborate methodology and attention to detail, they can find no changes in attitudes and beliefs among young people in India and Taiwan in spite of their recent introduction to extensive American television broadcasting. They wonder if they have selected the wrong sample or somehow asked the wrong questions: How could the effect of this new programming be so dramatically missed? In a sense they have asked the wrong question, just not at the level at which they suspect. They do not recognize their paradigm is in fact a theory that does not fit the evidence or that it is time for a new theory.

Why is it, then, that the television programs and movies produced in the United States are so dominant throughout the world, in places culturally similar to the United States as well as places that are vastly different, and so much so that many countries feel it necessary to severely limit their import, but measuring the media often shows that television and movies have little or no effect? American film and television "can be and are exported almost everywhere" (Dennis & Snyder, 1995, p. xii), so why is it that in Japan, for example, where they are voracious consumers of American cultural products, they consume them in a way that is entirely Japanese (Tobin, 1992; Yoshimoto, 1994), and audiences stay Japanese in the process? Indeed, although "the attractions of Western media at first seem overwhelming and transforming … people easily swim back to the surface of their lives" (Smith, 1995, p. 4). If the existing theory is wrong, a different theory should replace it by demonstrating more explanatory power with the data that has been gathered.

Perhaps the effect the media bring is of a type that has not been widely considered, one outside the dominant epistemology. Joseph Yusuf Amali Shekwo (1984), late social mobilization official from Abuja, Nigeria, told the story of how his people, the Gbagyi (often called *Gwari*), watched "Dallas" (CBS TV). He was intrigued by the popularity of this American program in such a different land, and knew that the traditional explanation for it—that people in the developing world were attracted to Western media because they emulated the Western lifestyle (e.g., Lerner, 1977; Schramm, 1964; de Sola Pool, 1977)—was naively incomplete. In talking to Nigerians who watched "Dallas," Shekwo came to the conclusion that although what was on the screen was more or less identical to the program that aired in the United States, they were not really watching the show in the same way that Americans were. Because of the way they watched it, they were watching a different show.

How could this be true? They were bringing to their understanding of American television a completely different set of cognitive assumptions, taxonomies, and background narratives. It became clear to Shekwo that what the Gbagyi saw in "Dallas" was not anything particularly American, but something more personal and more proximate—something indigenous. For example, his analysis revealed that the character of J.R. Ewing, the unscrupulous oil magnate played on the show by Larry Hagman, was perceived by the Gbagyi as having the same specific traits as Gbagwulu, a trickster worm from Gbagyi mythology. In a sense, J.R. acted as an archetypal surrogate for Gbagwulu.

Hardly any Americans and perhaps none of the "Dallas" production staff thought of J.R. in association with Gbagwulu (of whom they were no doubt unaware), so why is it that the Gbagyi make that connection? There are three possibilities. First, through some long forgotten act of diffusion, Gbagwulu has actually affected the evolution of American villain archetypes, just as African American slaves retained traditional African tales by evolving them into Brer Rabbit (Faulkner, 1977), so that J.R. is really a descendant (of sorts) of Gbagwulu. Second, the narrative archetype that J.R. embodies is so sufficiently encompassing that more particular archetypes and characters from other cultures can be projected into him, even if he did not descend from them. Last, there has been a little of both, a mix of diffusion and suffusion. In any case, the "Dallas" that the Gbagyi watched was theirs. There is an important difference, however, between the indigenous tale and "Dallas": The traditional stories existed primarily to satisfy spiritual and social needs; imported media may serve this need, but their raison d'être is commercial, what Schiller (1989) called the market criterion (p. 75).

The J.R.–Gbagwulu story is not an isolated phenomenon. Punjabi Hindu and Sikh families living in Southall, England see in the character of Mrs. Mangel, on the soap opera "Neighbours" (Australian TV) an embodiment of their cultural tradition of *izzat*, which is concerned with preserving honor and name through extensive familial control of social relationships (Gillespie, 1995a). Television watchers in Trinidad see in the soap opera "The Young and the Restless" (CBS TV) a manifestation of a defining national characteristic, *bacchanal* (Miller, 1995). Audiences everywhere see themselves reflected in films such as *The Lion King* (1994) or television shows such as "Walker: Texas Ranger" (CBS TV).

Consider the projective reception of *Titanic* (1997), a film that roared past the small list of films with revenues over $1 billion, earning at least $1.5 billion, and becoming the highest grossing film of all time, even adjusted for inflation. It was a different film to each interpretive community that viewed it. Japanese audiences reported an attraction to the cultural virtue of *gamen*—the ability to remain stoic in the face of adversity (Strom, 1998)—that they saw in the film. The film prompted such grief in Russian audiences that a national contest was devised for audience members to write a new, happy ending (Bohlen, 1998). The Chinese used the film as a challenge to develop the indigenous film industry (Eckholm, 1998). French cultural elites saw their own political consciousness reflected in the film (Riding, 1998). *Titanic* reminded Turkish audiences of their indigenous film *Bandit* (Kinzer, 1998). One Egyptian fan of the film declared to *The New York Times* that "it is not an American movie" (Jehl, 1998, p. AR 29). The Brazilian soap opera "Por Amor" incorporated scenes from *Titanic* (Sims, 1998). In short, *Titanic* was not one film but many depending on the interpretive community that watched it. One reporter covering the phenomenon said simply, "different countries have viewed the phenomenon of *Titanic* in their own ways" (Riding, 1998, p. AR 1).

To put it more theoretically, Jameson (1986) argued that all Third World novels are "national allegories," and Burton-Carvajal (1994) described certain first world cinematic texts as "allegories of colonialism." Given that texts lend themselves to a multiplicity of meanings and that particular readings of a text are privileged primarily through externally coded values and norms, is it possible that consumers in the developing world interpret imported American cinematic and televisual texts as national allegories too? This is a position somewhat consistent with Bhabha's (1994) and other postcolonial work, yet one commonly ignored in the study of media across cultures.

The dominant argument about the effect of global media on culture ignores the subtleties of Bhabha's observations, and instead goes something like this:

Major premise: Indigenous cultures are disappearing.
Minor premise: The reach of electronic media is now global.
Conclusion: The global media cause indigenous cultures to disappear.

This argument has several unexamined assumptions and consequently suffers from a post hoc ergo propter hoc fallacy. The following questions need to be asked:

- Are indigenous cultures really disappearing, or is something else happening to them?
- Are the media really causal in the process? If so, are they the primary causal agent that they are assumed to be?
- If they are the primary causal agent, what is the mechanism and effect of that agency?

Perhaps, despite alarms to the contrary, the world is not being melted down into a single, hegemonic, more-or-less American monoculture, even though American cultural products dominate the world. On the one hand, other production and distribution venues are developing (Tunstall, 1995). On the other hand, when one looks closely at the way that texts are read in specific cultures, rather than becoming overwhelmed by the astonishing magnitude of cultural exports alone, a multitude of differences and otherness emerges. György (1995) described the particular case of Ukrainians watching American media and noted that without an American cultural context, they are not watching the same program. Naficy (1996) showed how Iranian audiences made Hollywood films into indigenized hybrids. In both cases, imported media perpetuated rather than extinguished the Other. Despite its attempts, universality does not vanquish particularity (Yoshimoto, 1994), a claim generally borne out by history. Although readers around the world are increasingly gaining access to the same materials to read, they do not have access to the same ways of reading.

It is the thesis of this text that, due to a unique mix of cultural conditions that create a transparency, the United States has a competitive advantage in the creation and global distribution of popular taste. *Transparency* is defined as any textual apparatus that allows audiences to project indigenous values, beliefs, rites, and rituals into imported media or the use of those devices. This transparency effect means that American cultural exports, such as cinema, television, and related merchandise, manifest narrative structures that easily blend into other cultures. Those cultures are able to project their own narratives, values, myths, and meanings into the American iconic media, making those texts resonate with the same meanings they might have if they were indigenous. Transparency allows such narratives to become stealthy, to be foreign myths that surreptitiously act like indigenous ones, Greek gifts to Troy, but with Trojan citizens inside the horse. For better or worse, the transparency phenomenon facilitates the fragmented and incoherent beginnings of postcolonial culture. Hollywood studios have learned to profit from transparency and increasingly exploit it in the production of television programs and feature films.

The design of those media texts is driven, wittingly or unwittingly, by transparency. Consequently, as Smoodin (1994) pointed out, it is not nearly so important to understand what particular texts mean, as to ask "'who are these meanings available to?' and, related to this, 'how does meaning vary from audience to audience?'" (p. 17). By enabling different readings, by allowing and even encouraging subaltern perspectives, transparent media increase their market share. Paradoxically, however, in earning those additional revenues, they perpetuate indigenous culture in hybrid form.

It also does not mean that transparency is bereft of cultural consequences, that the global media have no effect. They do, but in a manner that differs from dominant assumptions in two ways: The process of cultural change is slower than generally assumed because it involves the accretion of new, transplanted images and consequently memories, and the process is causally the reverse of what is generally assumed—the indigenous culture actively reaches out, haggles (Naficy, 1996), and does not merely absorb in hypodermic, magic-bullet fashion some set of injected cultural values. The readings of a transparent text are indigenous, but the images and sounds are transplanted. Over time, these new images become familiarized, naturalized, and "real," just like those they replace. The result is something new, something interstitial, but not something American or Americanized.

PREMISES

Five premises lead to the conclusion that something like transparency must be present in the American media and that it can and ought to be observed and categorized. The first premise is that American media exports dominate the world media market. This initial premise stipulates, rather uncontroversially, that American movies and television programs are phenomenally successful internationally by almost any measure. The international market is a huge share of American movie and television profits, and more emphasis is being put by Hollywood into developing foreign markets. In fact, entertainment is the second largest U.S. net export, after aerospace ("The entertainment industry," 1989; Olson, 1993). Although other countries are also significant entertainment suppliers, the magnitude of America's dominance of this huge and important market is widely recognized and is almost beyond debate:

> From the point of view of competition, hegemony, and 'imperialism', [America] has certainly lost ground, but from the exponential point of view, it has gained some: take ... the worldwide success of *Dallas*. America has retained power, both cultural and political, but it is now power as a special effect ... It used to be a world power; it has now become a model (business, the market, free enterprise, performance)—and a universal one—reaching as far as China. The international style is now American. ... America has a sort of mythical power throughout the world, a power based on the advertising image ... (Baudrillard, 1988, p. 107, 116)

"Dallas" is a good example. As Ang (1985) pointed out, "Dallas" was viewed in 90 countries. With its huge volume and substantial economic significance to both the domestic and international media market, it is clear that the American media industry must be considered the major supplier of world entertainment.

A second premise is that the most common explanations for American media dominance and for the way audiences receive the media are incomplete. Frequently proffered explanations of U.S. television and film success are reducible to three basic perspectives:

1. The materialist explanation that American media dominate by sheer economic hegemony. In this model, the threat of U.S. media is primarily economic because it subverts the development of a domestic production capacity (see Mattelart et al., 1984; Schiller, 1969, 1989, 1995; Tunstall, 1977).

2. The traditional development model, which makes use of Lerner's (1977) want–get ratio (see also Lerner & Schramm, 1969), and which contends that American movies and television are popular because other cultures emulate the American lifestyle presented there. Although for Lerner and Schramm (1969), and other traditionalists, the emulation of U.S. culture

was desirable because it led to economic development and modernization, for cultural preservationists, it was undesirable because it subverted, even colonized, indigenous cultures.

3. The reader-response or reception approach theorized by Iser (1980) and Jauss (1982) and applied by Ang (1985) and others. It argues that audiences are capable of active and empowering readings of mass communication.

These three explanations are ultimately unsatisfying in explaining what has facilitated the American media's increasing dominance in world media because they fail to recognize what Bourdieu (1993) called "the objectivity of the subjective." Mattelart et al.'s (1984), McChesney's (1998), and Schiller's (1989) critical–materialist explanation was that the expanded presence and international role of multinational corporations and new media technologies that enable rapid and widespread dissemination of information lead to American dominance. Although these are certainly major factors, this explanation does not seem complete. Mustn't the success of the American media exports have something to do with the programs themselves? The materialist explanation is unfinished because it ignores the pleasure that American media certainly bring to many people (see Ang, 1985) or what Barthes (1977) and then Fiske (1987) called *jouissance*. Although it is true that American media are in many ways imperialist and hegemonic, most of the audience chooses to watch them. Governments would not have to regulate to limit their import unless there was sufficient domestic demand to warrant doing so; clearly, American culture "fascinates those very people who suffer most at its hands" (Baudrillard, 1988, p. 77). American media dominance cannot be explained, then, by simple imperialist models, and this approach is guilty of treating a complex human process in purely objective, material terms (see Bourdieu, 1993; Johnson, 1993). In more recent writing, Schiller (1995) recognized the need for incorporating audience behavior into his formulation of U.S. hegemony, describing an international "culture of contentment" whose attitudes and belief shape political and economic behavior (p. 469), a significant modification to his view of substructuration.

The traditional development explanation that the international community emulates America also fails to explain the global popularity of American media. On the one hand, it can scarcely be argued that the American media reflect any real American culture to emulate; "Dallas" or "Baywatch" are not representative of American norms and attitudes. On the other hand, cultures that are enamored with American media may be otherwise indifferent, or even repulsed by, the United States; it is possible to love certain things about American popular culture but be critical of American culture in general (e.g., the French relationship with the American cinema might fit such a description; the vacillations of their Ministry of Culture on this matter are documented in Schiller, 1989). Traditional development explanations underestimate the ability of persons within a culture to pick and choose and treat a complex human process in purely subjective terms (see Bourdieu, 1993; Johnson, 1993), ignoring the extent to which subjective and objective factors affect each other.

Although personal agency is important, it must be considered within its context. Cultural Studies is somewhat able to bridge the gap between objectivity and subjectivity by examining "the ways in which the culture industry, while in the service of organized capital, also provides the opportunities for all kinds of individual and collective creativity and decoding" (During, 1993, p. 30).

The third approach to international media popularity is also incomplete, but encouragingly focuses on audience reception of television and film. Most reader-response criticism and reception theory (Ang, 1985; Bacon-Smith, 1992; Fiske, 1987; Jenkins, 1992) does not systematically look at what viewers themselves are saying. Those scholars generally form the theoretical basis for which later experimental methods must be developed and the need for more studies of lived culture has been recognized (Harms & Dickens, 1996) and, to some extent, addressed.

So political economy, development theory, and reader-response criticism all fail to account for the breadth of American media dissemination. A fourth approach, *cultivation theory*, is less interested in why American media are popular than in how those media are affecting cultures. It has matured into a theory with a set of methodological tools, but this maturity has not produced a complete and convincing portrait of audience interaction with the media.

The basic contention of cultivation theory and its methodological off-shoot, *cultivation analysis*, is that the greater the exposure to the same media, the more the culture will become homogenized. Yet, although cultivation analysis has made important contributions to the understanding of media effects, it is as incomplete an understanding as political economy, development theory, and reader-response criticism, and one that is not well-suited to examining the subtleties of how identity is situated within culture or the interstitial nature of subaltern culture. The primary assumption of its approach is that although many different media affect social perceptions of reality, the omnipresence of television gives it a unique and preeminent role. This leads cultivation theorists to the conclusion that television's

> ... socially constructed version of reality *bombards* all classes, groups, and ages *with the same perspectives* at the same time. The views of the world *embedded* in television drama do not differ appreciably from images presented in other media, and its rules of the social hierarchy are not easily distinguishable from those imparted by other powerful agents of socialization. What makes television unique, however, is its ability to standardize, streamline, amplify, and *share common cultural norms with virtually all members of society.* (Morgan & Signorelli, 1990, p. 14; emphasis added)

Contemporary literary and semiotic theories indicate that this is a flawed formulation. The language of the quotation is revealing: it speaks of television "bombarding" audiences, denying the audience any active role in viewing; that bombardment is claimed to be of "the same perspectives," denying audiences a formative role in the creation of meaning. That meaning is "embedded" rather than projected and those embedded meanings apparently "share common cultural norms" with "all members of society," essentially denying different audiences the possibility of different understandings and responses and ignoring the possibility of polysemic texts. Morgan and Signorelli (1990) also wondered why some viewers are "most vulnerable to television's messages" (p. 21), language that resonates with hypodermic assumptions about media effects. To construct audiences as vulnerable is to attribute agency to the medium, not its consumer—audiences become objects rather than subjects. Cultivation analysis has little room for the idea of audiences clustered into interpretive communities.

It is small wonder, then, that cultivation analysis has produced incomplete and inconsistent results. As Morgan and Signorelli (1990) indicated, "the cards are stacked against finding evidence of cultivation ... Accordingly, we should not dismiss what appear to be small effects" (p. 20). Small effects are indeed what cultivation analysis has measured, and in the case of Kapoor and Kang (1995) and Kang and Wu (1995), no effects were measured at all, despite the researchers' best efforts to find some. This has led many scholars to conclude, as Waisbord (1998) had, that "regular exposure to media content that has originated in other nations does not seem to have undermined local distinctiveness" (p. 381). Perhaps cultivation analysis is poorly suited to international studies or perhaps it too closely equates exposure to consciousness and consciousness to identity (Waisbord, 1998). In either case, more ethnographically oriented research (e.g. Gillespie, 1995a,

1995b) confirms Bhabha's (1994) and others' theoretical contentions that culture is protean, interpretive, adaptive, resistant, and ultimately, resilient. In its most common manifestation, cultivation analysis assumes, and therefore discovers, that American media will render the world American, even when the evidence for that transformation is merely small effects. Other contemporary research seems to indicate that, although global cultural change is occurring, it is more likely that indigenous cultures will adapt the American media to their own purposes than for them simply to adopt wholesale American cultural values, beliefs, and behaviors. Although cultivation analysis recognizes that cultural differences will occur in response to the media, it maintains that the perspectives of the producers of that media, rather than that of its recipients, will dominate (Morgan, 1990).

To review briefly, the second premise underlying the argument in this text is that existing explanations of American media dominance and reception are incomplete, that the approaches used and conclusions gleaned from materialist–political economy, traditional development theory, reader-response criticism, and cultivation analysis are only stray pieces from a larger puzzle. A corollary to this second premise is that shared meaning across cultures is improbable and unlikely. Princeton University professor of history Robert Darnton (1994) noted that the inaccessibility of 18th century erotica to the modern reader is due to "the difficulty of 'getting' a culture that was fundamentally different from ours" (p. 72), but this is for early modern Western culture, a culture to which the modern West has a direct connection, and for a genre that persists. How much more difficult it is for meaning to move across cultures, for an Inupiat to understand Hausa poetry or vice versa. Shared meaning is even unlikely within a culture, as Derrida (1977), Foucault (1982), Hall (1980), and reception theories (Iser, 1980; Jauss, 1982) demonstrate.

A third premise is that the media texts themselves must provide at least part of the explanation for their global popularity. It is significant that some American media texts are internationally popular and others are not, a point lost on the materialist explanation of U.S. media dominance. "Dallas" was successfully exported throughout the world, but, despite attempts, "The Tonight Show with Johnny Carson" (NBC TV) was not. This indicates that although at least part of the explanation for the success of any text resides in the culture consuming it, another and perhaps more significant part resides in the text itself. This is particularly true given that certain texts are successful in so many different cultures; if the reason for the popularity of a text is found only in the culture, then why do so many cultures share such an interest in particular texts? Although "Dallas" was successful in Nigeria because of specific cultural attributes of the Gbagyi, Ibo, Fulani, and Hausa, perhaps even more of its success is due to the structure, images, and ideology of the text.

Not all scholars would support such careful analyses of media texts as a potential explanation of their power. One can identify many nontextual causes for the global preeminence of U.S. media: American foreign policy (see Pells, 1997), media pricing structures (which charge an African country 1/10 the price charged a European country for the same television program, e.g.), the accelerating conversion of national broadcasting systems to an advertising model (McChesney, 1997, 1998), the growth in satellite television and access to VCRs, the global spread of the English language (Pells, 1997), and other explanations. Many scholars warn against looking any deeper than these political and economic explanations. For example, Mattelart et al. (1994) cautioned that to do so is to miss the real cause:

> It is tempting to explain the success of American telefilms and series through their content and narrative structure, which is to try to find an answer to the issues raised by these programmes within the programmes themselves. This mediacentric tendency, which forgets that a television product emerges from a specific television set-up, itself the fruit of historical development, is the major weakness of most media sociology. (p. 90)

Although media texts alone do not hold the complete answer to their own success, neither does a careful examination of a media text preclude examination of the system that brought it into being. In fact, the purpose of this argument is to examine the interrelation between the text and the system as a means of explaining American media success. Furthermore, to consider only the system and not the text is like trying to explain why people like Monet's paintings only by looking at the brushes he used or the stability of his easel. Both textual and systemic approaches are necessary.

A fourth premise is that if the answer is in the text, then that is where one must look. Although this may sound obvious, the text is looked at too infrequently in the analysis of America's role in dominating world culture: Schiller's (1989) study of corporate control of world media, for example, never actually looks at the vehicle of domination, the television and movies themselves, and there are many others studies like it. Yet, if, as Bourdieu (1993) suggested, each work of art is "a manifestation of the field as a whole, in which all the powers of the field, and all the determinisms inherent in its structure and functioning, are concentrated" (p. 37), and if it is true that the best explanation for American media's global success is found in the movies and television programs themselves, then a close examination of them ought to reveal consistent attributes. This does not necessarily mean that all successfully exported programs share the same attributes and are consequently popular for the same reasons; it is possible, for example, that "Dallas" and "Dynasty" (ABC TV), another successfully exported prime-time soap opera, were successful for different reasons and in fact textual analyses reveal this to be the case (Ang, 1985; Gripsrud, 1995). In addition, it should not be assumed that the presence of particular textual properties guarantees export accomplishment. It does seem likely, however, that there is at least a pool of traits from which the American media draw. This presumption in and of itself is hardly controversial because it is consistent with any theory of national literature or cinema; if there is such a thing as a French novel, then there can be a French cinema, and if there is, it must have certain attributes that distinguish it from Russian or Japanese cinema. American cinema can be similarly distinguished.

It is important to remember that a text is not merely the mediated object, but rather the meeting of that artifact and the person who reads it. Consequently, any examination of texts that does not look at audiences is only partially formed. It is surprising how little this is recognized, but it is safe to say that the vast majority of those who theorize about the media do not look at specific audiences engaging with specific texts. Perhaps such theorizing is intended to point the way toward subsequent observational confirmation, but failing that, it is analogous to pre-Copernican notions of the movements of the spheres, where only the crudest observation confirms the theory. Happily, more researchers are now looking at what audiences actually do, applying ethnographic methodologies to the problems of texts. It is from this promising direction that this thesis proceeds. Among the media researchers establishing this method are Bacon-Smith (1992), Gillespie (1995a, 1995b), Jenkins (1992, 1994), Leuthold (1998), Liebes and Katz (1993), Naficy (1996), Waisbord (1998), and Wheeler (1998). Their writing suggests that although responses to media are overwhelmingly local and most media research ignores "the resiliency of local identity and cultural difference" (Wheeler, 1998, p. 359), these observations hold out the potential to extrapolate a theory of how local responses to media originate.

A fifth and final premise is that the international popularity of American media must find its genesis in American culture itself. This is a slightly more contentious premise because the linking of a text to the culture out of which it is born is difficult, problematic, and full of traps; nevertheless, products do seem to bear evidence of the culture that manufactures them (Porter, 1990, 1998). Every text is poured out of three crucibles: the author, the culture, and the technology of its production. The study of the first of these is appropriately called *authorship study* and approaches the text in search of the distinguishing characteristics placed there by the human agent of its creation (see Caughie, 1981), although isolating an individual creator is of course problematic (see Bourdieu, 1993). This is as true of a film—even though it is created by a group of people—as it is of a poem; for example, films directed by Woody Allen are all presumed and perceived by film scholars to have something in common.

The easiest way to study the second of these, the cultural crucible, is through genre studies, because genres inculcate what is present across many texts significant to a particular culture, undergirding the authorship of each text. A genre reveals what is ideologically, morally, and narratalogically important to the society that gives birth to it. In every text, there is a tension between genre and author: The genre anchors the text to the culture, insuring it will be meaningful, whereas the author makes certain aspects of it unique. The text that tends to the generic extreme will seem predictable, even boring, to most readers because it adds little new to cultural narrative convention—it will seem like a rehash of familiar situations and characters. A literary example of the generic extreme is a Harlequin romance novel, and a cinematic example is a serialized movie Western; these narratives hold few surprises for those familiar with their narrative devices. The text that tends toward the authorial extreme will seem unpredictable and incomprehensible to most readers because it adds so much that deviates from narrative convention. A literary example of the authorial extreme is *Finnegan's Wake* (Joyce, 1982), which essentially creates its own unique language, and a cinematic example is *Un Chien Andalou* (1928); readers or viewers find such narratives difficult because they lack a reference point, something familiar.

The third crucible in any act of narrative creation is the text itself, particularly its unique technological properties. The book *The Shining* (King, 1978) is not the film *The Shining* (1980). Of course, in addition to the technological differences there are also different authors in conflict here. Stephen King did not direct the film, which was directed by Stanley Kubrick, who is widely regarded by cinema scholars to have a distinctive style. It is the difference in technology that best explains the difference between this book and film, however, because different media have such different properties, not only of transmission, but of audience reception (Ellis, 1992).

These technological differences, were what led McLuhan (1964) to conclude that author and genre do not matter at all in the shadow of technology, because "the medium is the message". Although McLuhan's contention remains debatable, it is clear that when technology triumphs in the text, such as in a 3-D movie where it dictates everything from the story itself to the *mise-en-scène*, both author and genre usually lose.

These three crucibles—author, genre, and technology—give the text its shape. All of them can be linked to culture to one degree or another: The author is the product of a culture and chooses to convey the narrative in a particular language; the genre is a formative part of the culture as well as its product, and if one subscribes to narrative theory, it *is* the culture (see Coste, 1989; also Lakoff, 1987); technology also has cultural causes and effects. With the exception of genre, making these connections is difficult, however: The extent to which personal agency is socially created or the extent to which the technology of High Definition Television (HDTV) can be said to be Japanese or American is not known. This becomes a complex and subtle problem when considering the global media. For example, although the American media may not dominate every television market, in many cases, markets are dominated by locally produced programs that "[copy] the American series" (Tunstall, 1995, p. 8), embodying and replicating an essentially American genre. China is trying to do something like this now by engineering its own version of a Mickey Mouse character ("Mickey Mao," 1996).

Still, given America's unique ability to produce globally ubiquitous programs, there ought to be a connection between its store of textual formulae and the culture that produced it. Porter (1990) observed that certain societies are better at producing certain products; although he only briefly examined the entertainment industry per se, his method applies there as it does to automobiles or microwave ovens. Porter's approach involves analyzing how the four elements of his national competitive advantage diamond are manifest in a particular national industry: These include *factor conditions, demand conditions, supporting industries,* and *strategy, structure, and rivalries.*

Porter's method does not work unless the properties of the product and its market are fairly well-understood. Unfortunately, little scholarship has been done on the textual reasons behind American media hegemony. The few books that even peripherally consider it are rather old. Ang's (1985) *Watching Dallas* is useful but is 10 years out of date; it was criticized for its ad hoc methodology, its focus on pleasure instead of meaning, and for considering the case of only one television program in one particular nation state. Schiller's (1989) *Culture, Inc.* shared a deficiency of much of the neo-Marxist literature: Although purporting to examine the American media, it never looked at the films and television programs themselves. Schiller's analysis of the political-economy of the television industry is useful, but it does little to explain the actual mechanism of the media he purports to study because it suffers from Bourdieu's (1993) objectivist fallacy. Perhaps one of the best books on international media use is one of the more recent ones: Liebes and Katz's (1993) *The Export of Meaning*, which situates American television in actual audience behaviors. The current study is in some ways an attempt to theorize on their observations, which are discussed at length in the next chapter (chap. 2).

A few more recent books do a better job of applying contemporary theory to transnational media. Shohat and Stam's (1994) *Unthinking Eurocentrism: Multiculturalism and the Media* is an important study of postcolonial media and provides a good deal of useful data for the study proposed here. Its focus is not, however, primarily on narratology and textual apparatus. Gillespie's (1995b) *Television, Ethnicity, and Cultural Change* is particularly interested in resistant and recombinant readings, but her scope is narrower than the one proposed here. She primarily focused on the use of transnational media by South Asians in London.

Tunstall (1977) updated his seminal *The Media Are American* into a new edition (1994) that included a new foreword. His central argument was that the media themselves embody Americaness, in "the same way that spaghetti bolognese is Italian and cricket is British" (p. 13). Mattelart et al. (1984) did extensive work on the political and economic aspects of the international media; their most relevant book for this project is *International Image Markets*, which advocates abandoning the concept of cultural imperialism of the sort Schiller (1989) used in favor of a more complex approach that recognized greater subtlety and interstitial dialectics in the behavior of national markets and industries. They recognized textual reasons—the symbolic dimension—as part of the formula of American success, but did not focus extensively on the text from an audience-use perspective.

Other existing books are even further away from postulating an inclusive theoretical explanation of American success at media exporting: Skovmand and Schrøder's (1992) *Media Cultures: Reappraising Transnational Media* is a useful and important collection, but attempts no inclusive theory about media exporting; Featherstone's (1990) *Global Culture: Nationalism, Globalization, and Modernity* examines globalization in its broadest sense, without specific consideration of the role that the media play in the process; Schiller's (1969) *Mass Communication and American Empire* is out of date; Himmelstein's (1984) *Television and the American Mind* does not consider the export of American media; Allen's (1995) *To Be Continued...: Soap Operas Around the World* and Gripsrud's (1995) *The Dynasty Years: Hollywood Television and Critical Media Studies* provide useful data, but no general transnational theory; Smoodin's (1994) *Disney Discourse* spends little time on international aspects, and what time it does spend is mostly descriptive; and Bhabha's (1990) *Nation and Narration* focuses on literature rather than media, as does his *The Location of Culture* (1994) for the most part. In short, the apparatuses of America's global film and television success are in need of further study.

Such a study is urgently necessary because major world treaties like the North American Free Trade Agreement (NAFTA) and the General Agreement on Trade and Tariffs (GATT), not to mention issues of national and cultural sovereignty, hinge on understanding how the American media function in an international context. If American media dominate the world market, existing explanations for this dominance are incomplete, the media texts must provide at least part of the explanation for their own global popularity, looking in the text can elucidate particular general attributes, and these attributes can be traced to the American cultural crucible, then the success of the American entertainment industry can be systematically studied and at least tentatively accounted for using an approach like Porter's (1990). Much of the intercultural, ethnographic, and economic empirical data for such a study has already been collected. What remains to be done is to synthesize that data and suggest what they mean from the standpoint of recent media, semiotic, and cultural studies theory. This is not an easy thing to do because "no simple answer is possible ... Very divergent factors, including historical ones, contribute to this, and it seems almost pointless to try to examine the success of *Dallas* without taking into account the wider social context of the postmodernist media culture" (Ang, 1985, p. 5). Placing American media in that wider social context is the next step. The primary contention of this work is that the existing data and a close examination of American media texts reveal that the most successfully exported ones are culturally transparent. Prior to offering that argument in detail, however, it is important to pin down the slippery meaning of *transparency*.

DEFINING TRANSPARENCY

The term *transparency* has been used differently by different media theorists. Baudrillard (1993) meant by it an absence, "disappearance and disembodiment" (p. 16), a similar sense to Virilio's (1991) "aesthetics of disappearance," in which small bits of time disappear. Ang (1985) meant by *transparency* something closer to, but not as encompassing as, the usage for this text: For her, it meant the visual media's use of a conventional style that seems natural, that has the "illusion of reality" (p. 41), and consequently, allows viewers to project themselves easily into the narrative. In the context of this analysis, the term *transparency* is used more literally, in its most traditional sense of "appearing through"—not invisible but hypervisible. (In this sense, Baudrillard, 1993, and Ang, 1985, are really talking about opaqueness, something in the text that cannot be seen.) The *transparent* is diaphanous, luminous and lucid, penetrating, and clear, both in its literal sense of enabling something to be seen through and its figurative sense of the understandable manifestation of meaning.

Transparency is the capability of certain texts to seem familiar regardless of their origin, to seem a part of one's own culture, even though they have been crafted elsewhere. The commercial advantage to a movie or television program of this type is that it has the potential to garner a large global market; a film of narrow interest to a particular culture or subculture, a film that would seem inaccessible or incoherent to some segment of the world's population, in short, a film that lacks transparency has much more limited commercial possibilities. Given the tremendous costs of producing a feature film, culture factories like Hollywood increasingly rely on international distribution to make films profitable and have consequently toiled to increase the exportability of their product. Producing films with intercultural appeal is not an easy thing to do even for Hollywood.

Hollywood does not hold a monopoly on the production of transparent texts, and in specific media domains, other culture factories are dominant: Britain is unrivaled in exporting pop music; India and Hong Kong are exceptional exporters of feature films; Brazil excels at producing and distributing soap operas; and Japan controls the computer game market. To some extent, every text has some measure of transparency because external social determinants are necessarily refracted in any process of reading or viewing (Johnson, 1993). Where Hollywood is unrivaled, however, is in the creation of *synergy*—an industry term that means the coordinated marketing of a single concept across manifold media platforms, product merchandising, licensing, spin-offs, and simulated environments. Outside of Hollywood, rare is the sort of strategic commercial coordination behind the simultaneous release of *Jurassic Park* (1993), its affiliated dinosaur toys and human action figures, games (both traditional and computer), the tie-in with a McDonald's promotion, licensed clothing, candy, and television specials about the making of *Jurassic Park*, not to mention the theme park ride. In the end, *Jurassic Park* and its by-products are estimated to be worth over $1 billion worldwide, making it not only one of the biggest films in history, but essentially an industry unto itself. In order for it to have succeeded in communicating with such a large audience across so many different nations and cultures, *Jurassic Park* must possess some level of transparency; such successful global synergy would otherwise be impossible.

Jurassic Park is unique, but it epitomizes a trend in media programming design and distribution. Because American film and television are phenomenally popular throughout much of the world, many countries seek to limit their import. The disagreement between France and the United States over American cultural exports became a major stumbling block to the negotiation of the GATT treaty in 1993 (Cohen, 1993; Moerk & Williams, 1993; Williams & Dawtrey, 1993). France was understandably sensitive because *Jurassic Park* had outgrossed a domestic production released the same day (Cohen-Solal, 1995). Bettelheim (1977) noted that the greatest human need is for meaning; the GATT debate would not exist if there was no chasm in France and elsewhere between one audience, those who want to see the imported media because they are somehow meaningful to them, and another audience, those who do not want the first audience to see imported media because they believe such media espouse undesirable meaning. Despite protestations, however, the integration of American media into world culture has been so complete that it has come to be regarded as "'natural,' no longer an intrusion that provokes dismay or opposition" (Schiller, 1989, p. 123).

What enables meaningful crosscultural transparency is that audience members, acting in interpretive communities that exchange and reinforce meaning, perceive or read (i.e., actively engage and interpret) the media differently based on their own cognition, culture, and background narratives. This is not a new concept, but has been of interest to media scholars for at least 10 years, often with the "Dallas" television program as the catalytic object. There are several possible explanations for how transparency allows a text to generate different meanings in its audience, but they can be approximately categorized into two theoretical camps: On the one hand, there is negotiation theory, primarily associated with Hall (1980) through his theory of negotiated codes and oppositional decoding; on the other hand, there is polysemy, an approach advocated by de Certeau (1984) and Fiske (1987, 1996). The fundamental distinction between these two approaches is that negotiation is inherently dialectical, presuming two or three meanings, a few inferred and one implied, with the production of a synthesized meaning. *Polysemy*, however, presumes that the text is capable of implying, and the reader capable of inferring, a much broader range of meanings; the process is less like negotiation than like selecting from a smorgasbord.

Hall (1980) argued that every act of communication must go through a process of encoding and decoding in order for it to be transmitted. When this is applied to the mass media, it can be seen that certain interests naturally tend to be encoded in the transmitted text, particularly the interests of advertisers, media conglomerates, and the powerful institutions to which they cater. This is what Hall called the *dominant code*—the code that is intended. The audience most likely decodes media messages using this dominant code, especially if their producers encode them skillfully, and this encourages audience decoders to behave in the prescribed manner, for example, to buy the product advertised. Members of the audience are not limited to this response, however. They may also negotiate their decoding or oppositionally decode. The negotiated code occurs when audience members accept the basic legitimacy of the hegemonic capitalist system that created the message, but nevertheless interpret the message in a manner different from the intended meaning. Oppositional decoding occurs when members of the audience reject not only the message, but also the system that created it and interpret the message in a manner critical of its originator.

Hall's approach to negotiated meaning has been applied to the crosscultural understanding of media and even to "Dallas." Liebes (1988) studied how "Dallas" was perceived by an international audience, accurately concluding that "it cannot be taken for granted that everybody understands the programs in the same way or even that they are understood at all" (p. 277). Meaning of television programs is, for Liebes, constructed within interpretive communities, but all programs seem to permit diverse readings. Ultimately, however, this argument relies on the traditional notion that television programs "infiltrate into the culture" (p. 278), a process contradictory to true transparency and reception theory, where it would be more accurately argued that the culture infiltrates the television programs.

Ang (1985) hinted at polysemy in documenting how "Dallas" was received and interpreted by Dutch viewers. Ang's explanation for their attraction to the program centered on the pleasure this soap opera afforded them, but a pleasure that was generated in different ways. For some, the text was pleasurable program centered on the pleasure this soap opera afforded them, but a pleasure that was generated in different ways. For some, the text was pleasurable because they enjoyed the costumes and the settings; for others, pleasure came from the twists and turns of the plot; still others got pleasure from projecting themselves into the characters. This led Ang to conclude that "each has his or her own more or less unique relationship to the program" (p. 26). Yet, despite these differences in reading, these viewers had a great deal in common: gender, nationality, and language. The most interesting implication of this was not examined by Ang: if understandings of "Dallas" greatly vary within a culture, then how much must understandings vary between cultures?

Schiller (1989) was critical of Liebes' and Ang's style of audience-response media study. His argument with it had four components:

1. Audience-response theories ignore social factors external to the consciousness of a single audience member but that are nonetheless powerful conditioners of the manner in which they will interpret what they see, factors such as economic class.
2. These theories are unrealistic in their attribution of active, involved, and pluralistic readings of television and movies to an audience that is actually quite passive.
3. Audience-response theories make use of questionable methodology and overly subjective interpretation of data.
4. These theories ignore the massive and monolithic coordination and control that corporations exert over the production and dissemination of media programming.

Consequently, for Schiller (1989), although audiences are capable of diverse readings, they rarely assert this capability because "their capacities are overwhelmed" (p. 156). Schiller's criticisms are apt, but do not necessitate an abandonment of audience-response methodologies. Instead, a modification of these theories is possible so as to take into account social and economic factors. This would constitute an overdue resolution of a serious conflict between the critical and hermeneutic schools of media study.

Ultimately, negotiated meaning theory fails to answer the question that is the primary focus of this text: What is it about the American media that make their programming so adaptable to other cultures? This is not an empirical question, but a semiotic one: It has to do with the structure of the text itself, the images it uses, the type and relationships of the characters, and the way in which an individual narrative fits into the overall narrative parallel and contradictory readings, and consequently the text that must be studied to find answers.

Polysemy is the most persuasive explanation for why American media are so transparent. Fiske (1986, 1987) did not take a truly global perspective on polysemy and did not feel that texts were open to an infinitude of meanings. In an acknowledgment of Hall (1980), he argued that certain meanings are given preferentiality, but texts are nonetheless capable of creating a great many meanings. For Fiske (1987), polysemy is the result of several textual devices, each of which opens the text up to alternative reading. These devices include irony, metaphor, jokes, *contradiction* (by which he meant the resistance of various elements in the text to a tidy resolution), and *excess* (by which he meant *hyperbole*, as in the over-the-top indulgence of wealth on "Dallas" or *semiotic excess*, the presence of too many signs in any text for their meaning to be controlled).

Whereas negotiation is a process of an audience, polysemy is the properties of the text. Another useful term more descriptive of a process resident in the reader or viewer is *eisegesis*—the antonym of exegesis. Whereas in *exegesis* the reader draws meaning out of the text, in *eisegesis*, the reader puts personal meanings into the text. Traditionally, and particularly in the area of Biblical scholarship, eisegesis has been considered an improper method, a fallacy, and a misreading. Yet, eisegesis is clearly consonant with contemporary theories and methods of literary criticism and textual interpretation. Two entire schools of critical interpretation–reception theory (Iser, 1980; Jauss, 1982) and reader-response criticism (Fish, 1980; Tompkins, 1980)—are eisegetic, and Bloom (1975) argued that all reading is actually *misprision*, misreading. Indeed, rather than eisegesis being a fallacy, it seems that denying its role in the production of meaning is the real fallacy. So, the presence in a text of transparency enables polysemy, which enables eisegesis, which gives the text the illusion of indigenous meaning.

Not all texts are equally polysemic, however, and just as O blood can be used by someone with AB blood, but not vice versa, so are the texts born of certain cultural industries more polysemic than those born of others. Visual polysemy exists within a defined band that includes various possible readings constructed within the dominant band, other readings that are oppositional or resistant, and still others that are simply misreadings. Most alternative readings are neither subversive nor oppositional, but are nonetheless different. Judging from its global omnipresence, and the relative lack of media flowing the other way, the American media seem intrinsically polysemic.

Merging polysemy with transparency resolves many of the contradictions and conflicts between the reader-response and critical schools of media study. Polysemy is a middle ground between critical analysis, such as Schiller's (1989), and audience-response analysis, like Ang's (1985), because it recognizes the audience's role in the consumption and understanding of texts, but also acknowledges that this is conditioned by external social factors internalized by each audience member, such as culture, race, class, and gender. Transparency is a further resolution of these two schools of thought, because it acknowledges both the deliberate corporate design and intention that guides the design and production of media programming, but also acknowledges the audience's ability to project meaning into these same programs, to adapt them to indigenous needs, as postcolonial studies (Bhabha, 1994) and other approaches indicate. Each of these functions is compatible with transparency, because each serves a different need of the text: The program designer's need for capital is satisfied by a program that does well internationally, and the emotional needs of the audience find fulfillment in its narrative.

If the polysemy of the American media account for their international success, then another question must be raised: What is it about these movies and television programs that makes them polysemic? This is a complex question, and one with no simple answer, but one that is examined in detail throughout the rest of this volume. Answering it requires examining the media texts themselves.

MEANINGFUL ARCHETYPES

Polysemy is not boundless because culture inhibits the possible range of readings. Even those whose acts of interpretation diverge substantially from the norm, such as those diagnosed as schizophrenic, decipher and depict their experiences within culturally bounded linguistic and narrative parameters. Meaning resides in and is conferred by the language and narratives themselves, and consequently, is an inescapable context. The form that meaning takes is relevant to understanding not only how it is conferred, but how related, corollary forms can seem to convey different meaning in different contexts. The most common and time-tested form of meaning is myth, which can be either ancient or modern. The human need for myth has not waned in the face of Enlightenment scientism (Blumenberg, 1985).

Myth is a system of signification that has authority, credibility, and a claim to truth (Lincoln, 1989). In other words, *myth* is a form of speech that is respected and believed, although not necessarily as fact; myth possesses the literary truth of the parable or aphorism, not the documentary truth of a newspaper. For Barthes (1972), myth is *metalanguage*, "a second language, in which one speaks about the first" (p. 115), a level of signification once removed. It is a contention here that polysemic forms act transparently as if they were *mythotypes*, latent archetypal needs that act as the architecture of manifest historical myths, the human longings that encompass and undergird all myths.

Myth and meaning are inextricable. Can meaning resist myth? In other words, is it possible for meaning to be conveyed in language itself, without mythic insinuation or resonance? Not for Barthes (1972).

> Myth is always a language-robbery ... Is there no meaning which can resist this capture with which form threatens it? In fact, nothing can be safe from myth, myth can develop its second-order schema from any meaning and, as we saw, start from the very lack of meaning. (p. 131)

All communication has at least some mythic component, and the more successful it has been in conveying meaning, the more likely it is that myth has been extensively invoked. Cinematic and televisual language is almost always mythic, although the displacement of the myth can be at different levels of remove; that is to say, its mythology can be latent or manifest.

It is important, then, to understand what myths are and how they function in order to understand international media, not so much because media programs retell national myths, but because they function as myth. It is precisely because humans have such a need for meaning that insures that it is frequently entrusted to the simplest and most accessible narrative forms. For Bettelheim (1977), this form is the fairy tale, which he saw as capable of conveying truths great and deep:

> Through the centuries (if not the millennia) during which, in their retelling, fairy tales became ever more refined, they came to convey at the same time overt and covert meanings—came to speak simultaneously to all levels of the human personality, communicating in a manner which reaches the uneducated mind of the child as well as that of the sophisticated adult. Applying the psychoanalytic model of human personality, fairy tales carry important messages to the conscious, the preconscious, and the unconscious mind, on whatever level each is functioning at the time. (pp. 6–7)

What are the conveyers of fairy tales in the modern age if not television and the movies? This is explicitly so with media aimed at children, which often animate the very tales Bettelheim cited (e.g., Snow White, Goldilocks, Cinderella, Sleeping Beauty, Aladdin, Beauty and the Beast, etc.) and with which so many children, at least in the United States, spend so much time. Given that tales such as these form a child's language, his or her sense of narrative coherence, and his or her general outlook on the condition of society and nature, it is not surprising that, as Bettelheim suggested, they continue to have meaning for adults within the same culture: For the adult, these stories are reiterative and reinforcing of what has already been learned and is still believed. Because the most basic function of the media is reinforcement (Klapper, 1960), television and film narratives targeted at adults never stray very far from the fairy tales aimed at children. The farther they stray, the less familiar, less accessible, and less coherent these narratives become. In a sense, myth functions like genre, as Frye (1957) demonstrated; more accurately, genres are rearticulations of basic mythic tropes. The 1998 film *Ever After* ... , a postmodern retelling of the Cinderella story rated PG-13 in the United States and therefore aimed at teenagers and young adults rather than small children, is just one example.

One of the reasons that myth is so powerful is that it is inclusive; whether it be in the form of allegory, analogy, or fable, the reader senses from myth that it is speaking directly to him or her, that it has something relevant and useful to convey. Barthes (1972) characterized this function of myth from a personal perspective, stating that "it is I whom it has come to seek. It is turned towards me, I am subjected to its intentional force, it summons me to receive its expansive ambiguity" (p. 124). This is because myths "tell the truth" (Eliade, 1954, p. 46), at least in the sense that truth is understood within a particular context. How could it be otherwise, because it is they who have been seen as the developmental catalyst and benchmark of truth through the ages? As Lincoln (1989) showed, however, this is an elastic truth, as adaptable to progressive or revolutionary agendas as to reactionary ones.

If the meaning found in media programming is comparable to the meaning found in myth, there ought to be a morphology to the media narrative that is analogous to the morphology Propp (1968) delineated for the folktale. Propp taxonomized the internal structure of fairy stories—the components, relationships, and motifs out of which they were constructed. Although tales have superficially different settings and characters, for Propp:

> the names of the dramatis personae change (as well as the attributes of each), but neither their actions nor function change. From this we can draw the inference that a tale often attributes identical action to various personages.

> This makes possible the study of the tale according to the functions of the dramatis personae. (p. 20)

This also made possible Propp's lengthy and detailed articulation of the structure of the archetypal tale, one in which the functions of characters are stable and constant and in which the sequence of functions is limited.

If, as Lincoln (1989) asserted, contemporary culture transmits meaning via the authority, truth, and credibility claims of modern mythologies, then the vehicle for their transmission—the mass media—must possess meanings comparable to that of Bettelheim's (1977) and a morphology comparable to that of Propp's. Media certainly provide the sort of ritualized experience Eliade (1954) saw as essential to the creation of a personal projection into mythic time. This does not mean that myths or media rituals are universal; quite the contrary, it means that myths and rituals are particularized, but grow out of a human need for myth that is essentially the same everywhere. Universal human needs, then, may constitute an underlying structure to the iconic narrative, analogous to the underlying structure that Propp (1968) documented, which could therefore be examined and catalogued. A media morphology would not only be a descriptor of cultural norms and beliefs, but the architecture of narrative exportability—the structure of ubiquity. Such a structure would allow narrative particulars—names and characteristics of the dramatis personae, settings, moral lessons, all traditional and significant to the culture in question—to be projected onto the transparent narrative architecture. The indigenous narrative is merged with the supposedly alien, transparent narrative and J.R. is Gbagwulu because media consumers continue to need the social and psychological satisfactions of mythic storytelling.

The use of myth itself does not confer transparency; in fact, the use of particularized myth may do the opposite. *Ulysses* (Joyce, 1961), for example, is a displacement of myth, but is far from transparent, in spite of the possibilities it presents for polysemy. Joyce developed a specific mythic architecture for the novel, an endoskeleton, that is available only from other texts, but without which a close reading becomes exceedingly problematic (see Parr, 1961): For example, the chapter titles (e.g., "Telemachus," "Nestor," and "Proteus") do not appear in the novel itself but are nonetheless essential to a close and comprehensive reading of it. Although not precluding alternative mythic interpretations, this endoskeleton had the effect of prescribing a dominant reading along the lines Hall (1980) articulated for the popular media. Negotiated or oppositional readings, such as trying to project Beowulf or Gilgamesh into *Ulysses* rather than Odysseus, are problematic given the specificity with which the text identifies itself internally and externally with a particular structure. The popular media rarely have this problem because they rarely prescribe the dominant mythic meaning by invoking the displaced myth itself.

Clearly, then, it is not possible to discuss some universality of myth that is encoded in American media and then decoded elsewhere. The world does not share a single myth system, mythologist Joseph Campbell's musings to that effect notwithstanding. Therefore, attempts to explain American media success in terms of mythic displacement are doomed to failure. Something else is going on: The American media do not so much encode myth as become (or function as) myths themselves. They embody something prior to myth that enables them to satisfy the need for myth. Although authorial intention does not define the nature of a literary act, it is clear that some of the leading Hollywood media producers believe they distill, displace, and display mythic archetypes. Steven Spielberg and George Lucas are perhaps the best examples. Their use of mythic displacement ranges narrowly from the overtly manifest to the slightly less manifest, particularly in their work together, which explicitly mine Western mythology (e.g., the Ark of the Covenant in *Raiders of the Lost Ark,* 1981; the Last Supper and Holy Grail legends in *Indiana Jones and the Last Crusade,* 1989). There are more subtle displacements, however. In the opening sequence to Spielberg's "Amazing Stories" (NBC TV), a McLuhanesque history of storytelling technology unfolds, culminating in a visual metaphor equating television with a prehistoric shaman. Lucas' *Willow* (1988) is a virtual catalogue of Western myth. Lucas has tried to foreground the Arthurian subtexts to his *Star Wars* cycle (1977, 1980, 1983), so much so that Joseph Campbell videotaped his series *The Power of Myth* (PBS TV), in the library of Lucas' Skywalker Ranch and dedicated an entire episode to the displacement of mythic archetypes in the three films.

Such deliberate intention is not the only wellspring of mythic displacement, of course. Myth permeates culture almost by definition, so much so that it is inescapable. Lucas and Spielberg do not need to announce the mythic substructure to their work; what choice did they have? Their great accomplishment, and the accomplishment of others like them, resides not in their use of myth per se; myths are culture-specific and are consequently not particularly transferable to other cultures. On the contrary, their global intercultural success can best be attributed to their ability to reduce myth to its prior elements, elements that like those on the periodic table are recombinant and universal. Their success does not lie in regenerating a particular myth, but in transgenerating a new, elemental one. This can best be called a *mythotype* because it transcends any particular myth. Ang (1985) was only half correct when she said that "Dallas" developed "into a modern myth" (p. 2); what also happened was that a modern mythotype developed into "Dallas."

The discussions of media enculturation in Asia, which found the introduction of television to have no effect (Kang & Wu, 1995; Kapoor & Kang, 1995) indicate that existing theory does not describe the relation between American media and their international audiences. Yet, the data seem to confirm perfectly the theory of media transparency: There is an effect to the American media, but it is not to project American values; quite to the contrary, American media are now cleverly designed so as to reinforce existing values. This results in interstitial readings and polyglot cultures, but not monoculture. The media are not so much catalysts as catalyzed. Actual media producers have abandoned the want—get ratio of traditional development theory (Lerner, 1977; Lerner & Schramm, 1969; Pye, 1986; Schramm, 1964). They no longer need to create a market for American products, because they can design products that act as though they are indigenous. Polysemy is built in. All that is ultimately necessary is selling the product and that is better accomplished without having the burden of transforming the culture first. "The Other" has become just another commodity to sell.

This is not to say that the presence of American television has no effect. It does have a very powerful effect, but not in the way often presumed. It is as if Schramm is remembered, but Klapper forgotten. Klapper (1960) did, after all, demonstrate that the predominant effect of the media was reinforcement. It may initially seem peculiar that the media of one culture can actually reinforce the values and beliefs of another, but not if one considers the possibility that those alien media may contain a narratology and apparatus designed for exactly that purpose.

There is but one Larry Hagman, and only one multichaptered "Dallas" text, but apparently there are many J.R. Ewings. Indeed, "Dallas" represents American cultural hegemony, the export of a particular economic and political perspective, the channeling of money from throughout the world into Hollywood, and the potential seed of cultural change. Yet, these oversimplify: If crude monocultural colonizing tactics were the sum total of what "Dallas" is, it would not be so successful; in essence, there has to be more to "Dallas" than these intentional functions. It must have a corollary potential that allows it to become so widespread, so successful. Without such stealth, it could not bring about a monoculture, nor promote a particular worldview—its audience would not allow it. "Dallas" must have significance in all its contexts. Without the appearance and accessibility of indigenous meaning, it would be of no interest. It would be unintelligible. To convey meaning, it has to be understandable and coherent on local terms, although in hundreds of particular local ways that by their sheer number suggest its creators cannot control or intend them. It must be crossculturally polysemic, enabling hundreds or thousands of eisegeses.

Somehow, Lorimar Productions, the producers of "Dallas," did not need to do extensive research on traditional Gbagyi mythology for J.R. to be Gbagwulu. Somehow, J.R. is not only Gbagwulu, but also Hermes, Brer Rabbit, Winnebago Hare, Prometheus, Coyote, Picaro, Reynard, Circe, Loki, Iago, Karagös, Felix Krull, Dakota Spider, and Jacob. Somehow, "Dallas," together with many other Hollywood media creations, is transparent. That transparency forms the tectonic plates of a Hollywood planet.

2

Modes of Reception in World Media Markets

We move into an economy where sitcoms replace iron and steel as principal products, and where fun is not merely big business but seemingly the only business.
—O'Brien (1997, p. 14)

It is widely known that Hollywood media have a worldwide audience and that the flow tends to be one way: 200,000 hours of American exports compared to 20,000 hours of British and French exports according to the United Nations Educational, Scientific, and Cultural Organization (UNESCO); (Mattelart et al., 1984). In financial terms, in 1992, there were $3.7 billion worth of American media exports to Europe in comparison to only $288 million in European media imports to the United States (Pells, 1997); the disparity is still greater to other parts of the world. Hollywood had revenues of $215 billion in 1996, an increase of 475% over a 20-year period; this growth (almost 25% a year) is double the growth of the U.S. economy as a whole ("Entertainment has become," 1997).

Worldwide, audiences are 100 times more likely to see a Hollywood film than see a European film ("Home alone in Europe," 1997). Hollywood satisfies 70% of international demand for television narrative and 80% of demand for feature films ("Star wars," 1997). In Britain alone, 93% of the feature films are American and 75% of broadcast airtime is consumed by American programming, the same proportion as in the rest of Europe (by comparison, U.S. prime-time television has only 1% imported programming, and that appears on cable or public television; Pells, 1997). All this success has escalated the entertainment industry to become the United States' second largest export ("Entertainment has become," 1997).

The reception these media receive in different cultural contexts is scarcely understood. The television program "Dallas", for example, is perhaps the most successful transnational television program in history. Chapter 1 raises two simple questions about it and other media texts: Can "Dallas" mean the same thing to a Nigerian or a Pole that it means to its American audience? If not, what is it about "Dallas" that allows it to be received by these audiences in different ways?

These are complex questions and to understand them fully, one must examine the full extent of American media hegemony. This chapter examines the evidence of three contentions central to a reception orientation to transnational media: diverse readings of simple media texts are possible; diverse readings of exported media are occurring throughout the world; and many of the readings of imported media texts reflect an indigenous decoding. This examination reveals that purely materialist explanations of media dominance do not provide a complete picture.

The prevalence of Hollywood media in the world marketplace is significant. There are other nations that are net exporters with the films they produce; India is the best example, with a huge film infrastructure and decades of successful exporting. Yet, all but a few of these films are distributed only in the developing world, where ticket revenues are relatively small; the rare Indian film that plays in wide release in Europe or America is usually marketed as an art film. In fact, in the first world market, Hollywood films and television have no serious competition. In terms of revenues, although the United States accounts for only 5% to 6% of the world's production of feature films, 15 years ago it claimed half of the world's box-office revenue (Mattelart et al., 1984) and that proportion has grown. In France, once a cinematic stronghold in its own right, Hollywood now claims 60% of box-office revenues, and in Great Britain, it claims 95%; the result has been a ninefold decrease in the size of the European film industry since 1945 ("Home alone in Europe," 1997). In terms of television production, some countries import as much as 80% of their programming from the United States (Mattelart et al., 1984).

There are, of course, a number of ways to account for the predominance of the American media. As mentioned in chapter 1, the most common method attempts to make use of critical political–economy analysis. This approach argues that the success of U.S. media abroad is primarily due to economic and political reasons, not cultural ones. For example, Schiller (1989) argued that the economic capacity of the American media industry dwarfs and subverts any indigenous production; countries simply cannot afford to compete. Consequently, the apparent preference of international audiences for American media is nothing more than a lack of choice; had there been greater economic vitality in the indigenous film industry, or any other industry as the argument goes, these films would inevitably be preferable to imports.

Scholars are increasingly questioning the extent of the legitimate application of a political–economy approach, however. Although the political–economy approach has significant explanatory power, it ignores and even denies the actual relationships that exist between audiences and texts. Even if it is true that audiences have limited access to non-U.S. films and television, political–economy cannot account for why some films connect with audiences and others do not. The American media export machine is gargantuan, but even it cannot force audiences to see movies they have no interest in. Culture, too, plays an important role in the international success of American film and television.

The notion that cultural factors may be working in connection with political and economic ones may not seem all that controversial, but in fact, the relation between Cultural Studies and political-economy has been a tense one. Garnham (1995), for example, argued that Cultural Studies is illegitimately divorced from political–economy; that it is really the same thing with an inferior and naive methodology. Grossberg (1995) countered that Cultural Studies is very much a separate field and approach and that the study of culture is as important to understanding the social function of media texts as is the study of the economy, perhaps even more so. The two approaches have been growing apart, with the Cultural Studies approach ascendant.

One of the more important components of Cultural Studies methodology is the ethnographic study of reception, how particular audiences receive particular texts. In general, this methodology repudiates the traditional communication model of the audience as a passive receptor of media programming (e.g., Lasswell, 1927; Schramm, 1949), replacing it with an image of the audience as active, involved, and dynamic. Building on the idealist philosophy of reception, theorists Iser (1980) and Jauss (1982), reception-oriented cultural studies scholars, examined the specific meanings that specific audiences, even specific audience members, generate and extract from the media they consume. Such an examination contradicts political–economy assertions that textual analysis and audiences do not matter: When all is said and done, meaning only exists at a nexus of text and reader.

THEORIES OF READING

In Jauss (1982) and Iser (1980) can be found the genesis of contemporary audience theory; they are themselves descendants from the hermeneutics of Hans-Georg Gadamer (1986). Jauss (1982) was primarily interested in the psychological differential between what a reader expected from a text and the pleasure (or discomfort) that they actually received from reading it, a phenomenon he called the *horizon of expectations*. Iser (1980) examined the *implied reader* implicit in every text, and the implications this reader has for the author, the text, and the real reader. Neither Jauss nor Iser concerned themselves with mass media texts per se, but their approaches to literature have legitimized subsequent media theories.

The most paradigmatic model of reading, at least from the standpoint of media criticism and Cultural Studies, is de Certeau's (1984) concept of *textual poaching*. De Certeau envisions reading (and many other activities of daily life) as a kind of semiotic theft: Meaning is coaxed out of consumption by consumers "in innumerable and infinitesimal transformations of and within the dominant cultural economy in order to adapt it to their own interests and their own rules" (p. xiv). Whatever meaning might have been intended for a consumer product (e.g., a media text), members of the audience project their own meaning onto it, coopting it, and in a sense, stealing it away from its owners. Just as a rabbit poached from royal land, cooked, and eaten by a peasant thief is coopted and put to a purpose for which it was not intended, so is a media text poached by its active audience and reshaped to and comprehended within their own intentions. Whereas the producers of a media text have a strategy (e.g., "buy this product"), viewers can have their own tactics (e.g., "this is a great advertisement, but who in their right mind would buy that junk?"). Pleasure is stolen rather than exchanged.

Cultural Studies was quick to exploit de Certeau's model and apply it to particular text–audience interactions. Bacon-Smith (1992), for example, studied the many ways women poached meaning from episodic television, particularly the series "Star Trek" (NBC TV). Of particular interest to her, and perpetually annoying to owner of the "Star Trek" franchise, Paramount Studios, is the fan culture that creates its own unlicensed "Star Trek" magazines, short stories, and comics. This includes unauthorized, but apparently meaningful, homoerotic fiction about Kirk and Spock, two characters on the show. The copyright holder sees this use of the characters as a kind of larceny, but the heterosexual women who write and read it feel entitled. Jenkins (1992) attempted a broad theory to explain media poaching. His interest is in what he called *participatory culture*—the ways in which such monolithic and seemingly unidirectional communications as television programs are actually sites of manufactured meaning. The audience Jenkins is interested in is the one that:

> differs from the [culture] fostered by the educational system and preferred by bourgeois culture not simply in its object choices or in the degree of its intensity, but often in the types of reading skills [it] employs ... [it] constructs [its] cultural and social identity through borrowing and inflecting mass culture images, articulating concerns which often go unvoiced within the dominant media. (p. 18, 23)

Even within a culture, then, there are different levels of reading and different ways to engage a text: Witness gay readings of "Dynasty," which tended to regard Alexis as a character who stretched and defied the boundaries of gender (Schiff, 1985). There can be little doubt that there are more striking differences between cultures. The process of decoding a media text, as in decoding any message, has a cultural bias.

INDIGENOUS DECODING

The theoretical framework of active media consumption proposed by Jenkins (1992) and Bacon-Smith (1992) enable a consideration of how different cultures might read media programming differently. Because texts can be decoded in different ways, to what extent can culture (or other factors) systematically account for the differences? Scholars examining the media in the communication field and in other disciplines associated with cultural studies are increasingly turning their attention toward the interactions between certain texts and certain audiences, hoping to assemble a picture of how texts and cultures interact.

Perhaps Liebes and Katz (1993) conducted the most interesting and rigorous study of this type. Although they do not use Jenkin's poaching concept in regard to television viewing, they do reveal empirically distinct variations in the ways in which audiences from different cultures, and even audiences within cultures, perceive media texts. They assembled focus groups from a variety of cultural backgrounds and conducted controlled viewings of a few episodes of "Dallas," then questioned the group using a set of interview guidelines and a questionnaire about what they had seen, how they interpreted it, and how they felt about it. "Dallas" may seem the most simplistic of texts, but they found that it provoked a significant diversity of interpretations and reactions. They attributed these differences to culture.

The cultural groups that Liebes and Katz (1993) tested separately and repeatedly were Americans, Moroccans, Palestinian Arabs, Russians, and residents of Israeli Kibbutzes. They found marked differences in the perceptions these groups had of "Dallas" that extended along several different poles. Arab groups and Moroccans seemed to have the most linear perception of the narrative; both groups tended to see each "Dallas" episode as a closed text, rather than the open, serialized, segmented narrative that Americans perceive it to be. Russians, on the other hand, were entirely thematic in their perception and retelling, mostly interested in what they took to be the program's implicit ideologies. Russians also seemed to engage in the most critical and analytical reading of the text. Americans tended to be cool, detached, and referential in their reading, most similar to the Kibbutzniks. Each group tended to relate the narrative to indigenous storytelling forms, which yielded interesting results because many of these cultures have nothing like a soap opera genre; somehow, though, the "Dallas" text encourages such comparisons.

All of these groups had very different perceptions of the narrative value, morality, and ideology of "Dallas." Arabs tended to see it as a parable of the moral degeneracy of modernism; Russians as an exercise in the politics of capitalism; the Japanese as an allegory for the decline of American economic preeminence; Americans as a lesson in how wealth fails to bring happiness; Moroccans as an aphorism that wealth itself is evil; and the Kibbutzniks as evidence that all Americans are unhappy (Liebes & Katz, 1993). Given these differences, it would be easy for any reader to privilege their own reading and declare the others to be wrong, but clearly the text itself is enabling these different perspectives, so how can any one be truly privileged? Interestingly, it is the Americans themselves who are the least likely to think anything serious can be learned or said about "Dallas" (p. 120); this media product of the American culture factory is taken more seriously abroad than at home.

Although Liebes and Katz (1993) have been the most systematic and quantitative in their approach to global audiences for transnational media, there have been numerous worthwhile qualitative studies that illuminate other aspects of global audiences and their patterns of reception. Allen (1995) found that the American soap opera "The Bold and The Beautiful" (CBS TV) had huge audiences in Italy, Egypt, and Greece, where it had bigger ratings than it does in the United States. Another American soap opera,

"The Young and the Restless," has been not merely successful, but transformative in Trinidad. Miller (1995) showed that its popularity there is due entirely to an indigenous cultural criterion that it serendipitously manages to address: This he summarized with the calypso term *bacchanal*, which simultaneously means scandal, confusion, and bringing the truth to light. Because "The Young and the Restless" has particular elements that correspond to the indigenous notion of bacchanal, the program is viewed not only as though it were indigenous, but realistic, although:

> it is clear that the "realism" with which it is identified has little to do with the environmental context of domestic presentation; the scenes cannot look like Trinidad. Realism rather is based on the truth of the serial in relation to key structural problematics of Trinidadian culture. It is the realism of myth. (Miller, 1995, pp. 219–220)

This American soap opera, it seems, is paradoxically a manifestation of Trinidadian myth, and this accounts for its popularity. Of course, the makers of "The Young and the Restless" could not have consciously and deliberately tried to integrate Trinidadian mythology and culture in the show they produce any more than director James Cameron could have included bits and pieces for every culture around the globe where his film *Titanic* (1997) was a hit. Consequently, it is not a matter of the Trinidadian people finding something that is hidden inside, but of them projecting some part of themselves. A similar phenomenon was observed by Hodge and Tripp (1986), who noted that the Gary Coleman character on "Diff'rent Strokes" (NBC TV) was seen by Australian aboriginal children as one of them–an aboriginal.

Such projection does not work equally well with all texts, yet American texts seem particularly adept at encouraging it. Disney is perhaps the best at exporting media that is read as though it were indigenous. Yoshimoto (1994) contended that:

> Americans see the popularity of their culture abroad as a sign of their popularity and superiority; moreover, that popularity makes Americans believe that every foreigner potentially wants to become an American (p. 191).

Yet, this is a mistaken understanding of that popularity. Yoshimoto (1994) showed that Tokyo Disneyland is not read, used, or perceived by the Japanese to be a particularly American institution; rather, they see it as Japanese. Although Tokyo Disneyland has many of the same features as Disneyland in California, there are many subtle differences that transform the experience to an indigenous one for the Japanese visitor, but to which other visitors are blind. Disneyland fits into the building style and conventions of *ikoku-mura*, or the "foreign villages" found in Japan, large scale replicas of actual foreign towns, designed for entertainment. "To the extent that it perfectly fits in with the nativist discourse valorizing the selective hybridity of Japanese culture, *Tokyo Disneyland is in fact one of the most powerful manifestations of contemporary Japanese nationalism*" (Yoshimoto, 1994, p. 197, emphasis added). In other words, nothing is more Japanese than Disneyland.

Because of global ubiquity such as this, Disney easily lends itself to comparisons of media reception. These theme parks are just one example: A strict political–economy perspective would be hard pressed to account for Tokyo Disneyland's success as just described in the face of Eurodisney's quasifailure; the same economic factors were marshaled in each case. Clearly, audience reception needs to be taken into account in explaining their different profit margins. Different receptions of Disney film exports have also been well-documented. Burton-Carvajal (1994), for example, showed how the films in Disney's Latin American trilogy (*South of the Border*, 1941; *Saludos Amigos*, 1943; and *The Three Caballeros*, 1945) are read differently in the United States than in the countries they depict: What may have been intended as tribute is often read as expropriation or colonialism. Cartwright and Goldfarb (1994) argued that Disney films that were read as pure entertainment in Latin cultures were read as intercultural training films in the United States. The more recent global success of *Aladdin* (1993), *The Lion King* (1994), *Pocahontas* (1995), and *Mulan* (1998) indicate that Disney has grown sophisticated at opening texts up to indigenous readings.

Not all transnational successes are American, however. The Australian soap opera "Neighbours" was quite successful in the United Kingdom, in large part because of historical similarities between those two countries; it was less successful in other markets, such as the United States (Crofts, 1995). Brazil, Mexico, and Peru all successfully produce and export soap operas, many of them to the Spanish-language market in the United States. India and Hong Kong are successful exporters of motion pictures, and of course, Great Britain and France still produce international box-office hits.

Nevertheless, few transnational media exports match the American ones for versatility, ubiquity, and sustainability. Latin American soap operas have one distinct difference from Americans ones: the former generally have narrative closure (i.e., eventually, they come to an ending). American soap operas are, invariably open—they need never end (Allen, 1995; Hagedorn, 1995). Many media products from other nations are virtually unexportable. For example, "Coronation Street" (BBC TV), a 35-year-old phenomenon in British broadcasting, has found no significant foreign market, partially because a sense of place is so important to its discourse (Geraghty, 1995). The Welsh soap opera"Pobol Y Cwm" (S4C TV) is even less exportable for linguistic reasons and for its abiding concern toward defining Welshness (Griffiths, 1995). A television series like "The Ramayan" (Doordarshan TV) from India would have extremely limited appeal to a non-Hindi audience, who would lack the most rudimentary cultural knowledge to comprehend its discursive structure, use of narrative time, and characterization (Lutgendorf, 1995).

Indigenous readings of media programs, then, may be quite different than the readings given back home, which may themselves be diverse. Openness to varied readings is a distinct advantage to those trying to sell programs internationally. An examination of the global media market reveals the extent to which the U.S. industry has been successful at this.

THE GLOBAL MEDIA MARKET

Careful analysis of the international film box office reveals the hegemonic extent of the success of the U.S. film industry. A consideration of the global reception of American media cannot be based merely on data reflecting export volume, but on data reflecting import reception, data that reveal how different countries and cultures consume American media in different ways. One reliable source of such data is gross weekly box-office revenues for selected international markets. Within each market, two useful bits of evidence can be examined: one is a purely quantitative measure of the proportion of successful films in that market which are imported (specifically, from America, but imported from anywhere else as well); the other is a more qualitative measure of the type of film likely to be successful in that market as observed over time (e.g., what genres tend to be popular, which stars seem to have a regular audience, which countries of origin are the most popular, etc.). Each of these methods reveals important aspects of the international movie market; together, they lay a foundation for more substantive analysis of particularly successful texts.

A quantitative analysis of the international movie marketplace is fairly easy to synthesize. The following figure (Fig. 2.1) reveals the mean number of American films in the top 10 films each week in selected countries from

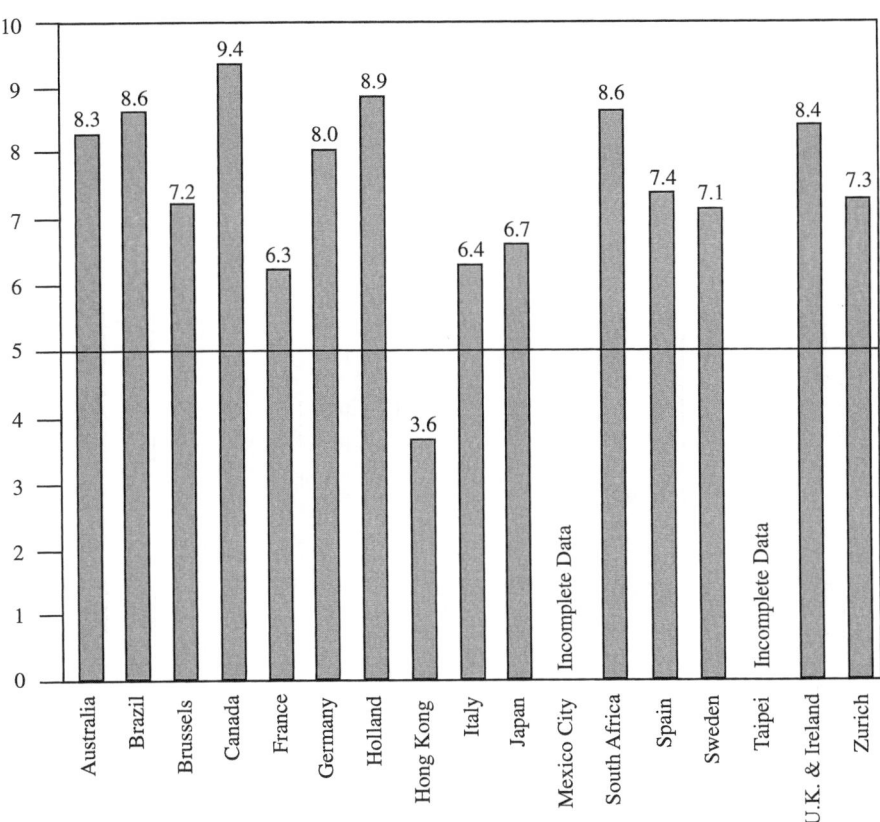

FIG 2.1 Mean number of top ten films at the domestic box office that were of American origin, by selected countries and cities, December 1993–July 1995. Data assembled from weekly box office figures. Source: "International box office," *Variety*, December 1993 to July 1995.

December 1993 to July 1995 as determined by gross weekly box-office revenues ("International box office," 1993, December 13 through July 17, 1995). Similar data are found for the period July 1995 through April 1996 (see Fig. 2.2).

As might be expected, Canada had the largest proportion of American films: Nine and a half out of the top 10, over time, were imported from the United States. Even France, with its ambivalent tendencies toward Ameri-

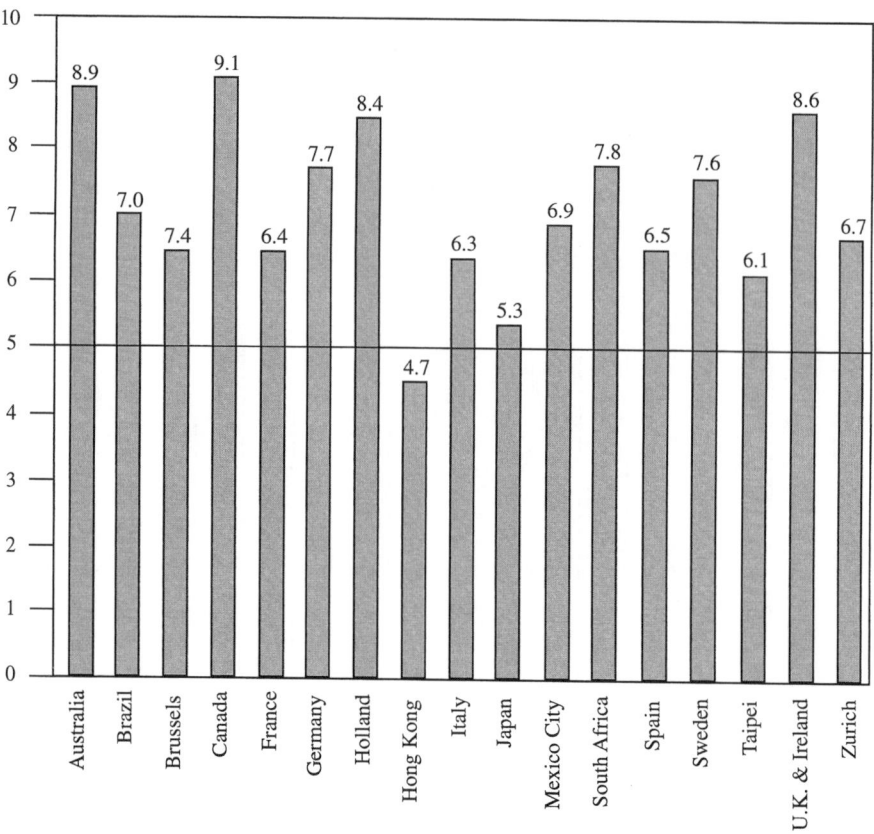

FIG 2.2   Mean number of top ten films at the box office that were of American origin, by selected countries and cities, July 1995–April 1996. Data assembled from weekly box office figures. Source: "International box office," *Variety*, July 1995 to April 1996.

can culture, consistently has 6 of its top 10 films imported from the United States. Interestingly, of these major markets, only Hong Kong is a net exporter.

The impression that these data give is one of American box-office dominance: In every European market, and in Australia, South Africa, Brazil, Mexico, Taiwan, and Japan, more than one half of the top 10 films from 1993 to 1996 were American origin, leaving far less than half to be distributed among all other film-producing nations, including the host nation itself. As might be suspected, the top two or three films in any country at any time are almost always international blockbusters, such as *Jurassic Park* (1993) or *Titanic* (1998), and these are almost always of U.S. origin.

What of the non-American movies that are successful in the international marketplace? Often, they are *favorite children*—products of the home film industry that do moderately well in that market for a short time, but have limited export potential to other developed countries, particularly when crossing linguistic boundaries. During the week ending September 20, 1995, for example, *La Ceremonie* (1995, Film Elysee) was number two at the French box office and number three in the Brussels box office, but did not make the top 10 anywhere else (Groves, 1995). That same week, *Menino Maluquinho* (1995, O Filme) was number eight at the Brazilian box office but did not make the top 10 elsewhere. At the same time, *Waterworld* (1995, Universal), an American film, was the top grossing film in Australia, Italy, Japan, and Spain, was the fourth top grossing film in Mexico, was number six in Hong Kong, and number seven in the United Kingdom and Ireland (Groves, 1995, September 25). It had not yet been released in most of the other markets.

Using a reception approach, it is clear that each market has its own peculiar tastes, but somehow, many of these tastes help make American films a success there. In roughly descending order of acceptance of American media, these markets are Canada, Holland, Brazil, South Africa, the United Kingdom and Ireland, Australia, Brussels, Sweden, Japan, Italy, France, Poland, and Hong Kong. They are all quite different, but they have the U.S. media in common. A close examination of these markets reveals the extent to which they are different in their cinematic tastes, different in their selections for reception, but unified in acceptance of American films.

Canada

About 9 1/2 of the top 10 films in Canada, over time, are imported from the United States. It comes as no surprise that Canada has the largest proportion of U.S. films in its top 10 box-office successes: As far as the media are concerned, Canada and the United States have come increasingly to act as a single market (Olson, 1993). Its film marketplace operates very much the same way the U.S. market does, embodying the cross-fertilization of cultures that define the interrelated histories of these two countries. Canada has been successful at exporting talent to the United States that is then co-opted by Hollywood (e.g., Jim Carrey or John Candy). Many popular American television shows are actually filmed in British Columbia as a cost-containment measure, signifying a further blurring of the distinction between what is American and what is Canadian. Canada's indigenous film industry has suffered as a result of this, however, so that the few non-American films in the Canadian top 10 are international hits like *Four Weddings and a Funeral* (British, 1994).

Holland, Brazil, South Africa

It is initially a bit surprising to note that Holland is almost as receptive to American cinema as is Canada: Fully, 9 out of the top 10 pictures there, over time, are U.S. imports. It might seem that an anglophone country would be more receptive, but there are many cultural reasons for its situation. Holland has a very limited domestic film production capacity, and it has a history of receptiveness to American media, as Ang (1985) pointed out in her study of the impact of "Dallas" there. Still, there are occasional domestic successes, such as *Flodder 3* (Holland 1995). About 8 1/2 of the top 10 films in Brazil are American in origin; Brazil is more linguistically isolated than many of the other countries on the list, given that it could only naturally export to Portugal. Yet, although the indigenous film industry creates hits only infrequently, the indigenous television industry is one of the world's most successful exporters of soap opera programming (Allen, 1995). South Africa has produced only one international film hit (*The Gods Must Be Crazy*) and 60% of its broadcast programming is imported, mostly from the United States (Mokone-Matabane, 1995).

The United Kingdom and Ireland

Given the common cultural heritage between the United States and Great Britain, it might seem surprising that Holland, Brazil, and South Africa actually import more U.S. film entertainment. This is at least in part due to the relative (if struggling) vitality of the British film industry, which can still produce international hits now and then, like *Four Weddings and a Funeral* (1994) and *The Full Monty* (1997). The British industry should be concerned, however, that its successes have generally led to a talent drain: For example, the costume dramatists of Merchant-Ivory Productions were recently bought out by Disney, and Hugh Grant, British star of *Four Weddings and a Funeral*, has moved to Los Angeles.

Australia

From a political–economy perspective, Australia is perhaps more like the United States than other countries on this list, but it is not the most similar in its cinematic viewing habits. Australia has a fairly successful and competitive film industry that has served up several hits, only a few of which have played the art house circuit to which foreign films in the U.S. market are usually consigned. Perhaps the most notable of these are the *Mad Max* trilogy and the *Crocodile Dundee* films, all of which feature an Australian variation of the generic Western hero, making them appeal to a wide international audience for such films. Australia has had its share of art house releases as well, notably the early films directed by Peter Weir. Weir subsequently went to Hollywood. The serious slant of Australian feature film exports has been modified in the 1990s by a string of modest international comedy successes, including *Babe* (1995), which featured a talking pig, and *Muriel's Wedding* (1995); (Shenon, 1995).

Sweden

About 7 out of the top 10 films in Sweden are imported from the United States. Its box-office taste tends, over time, more toward comedy (*Ace Ventura: Pet Detective*, U.S., 1994; number one the week ending June 9, 1994), art films (*Short Cuts*, U.S., 1994, number five the same week), and melodrama (*The Client*, U.S., 1994; number one the week ending August 11, 1994) rather than toward the action adventure films that predominate most other international markets, but this still leaves many American films from which to choose. Sweden has managed to continue its domestic production of feature films, albeit with less success than was common in the golden age of Swedish cinema. Occasionally, and unusually in the European market, an indigenous film can often hit number one at the box office, such as *Yrrol* (Sweden, 1994), which was there for 2 weeks in November, 1994 (Groves, 1994). *Yrrol* has limited export potential, however, and has not turned up in the box-office figures for any other country.

Sweden is not the only Scandinavian country to import significant amounts of Hollywood films. The proportion of imported films, and of the success of American imports, is even more remarkable in Finland than it is in Sweden (Kivikuru, 1995). The indigenous film production capability in Finland is miniscule, although some pop music is produced indigenously.

Japan

Japan's taste in American cinema has its similarities to and differences from the U.S. market. U.S. and international hits like *True Lies* (U.S., 1994), *Mrs. Doubtfire* (U.S., 1994), and *The Lion King* (U.S., 1994) were all number one hits in Japan, but so were American products such as *Major League 2* (1994) and *Wyatt Earp* (1994), which were disappointments at the U.S. box office ("International box office," 1995c). Between 3 and 4 of the top 10 films each week, over time, at the Japanese box office are not American, but almost all of these are indigenously produced; there appears to be little taste in Japan for French, Italian, or any other cinema.

Such importing has had a powerful effect on the Japanese film industry. Japan has historically had four great film production studios—Shochiku, Toho, Toei, and Nikkatsu. The last of these has closed. Toei branched into other ventures, such as commercial real estate, as a means to stay afloat. Toho cut back on production and only makes a few films a year, maintaining operations primarily through the distribution of foreign films. Only Shochiku bears a resemblance to its film studio past, and it is branching into direct broadcast satellite as a means to bolster a flagging market. Part of the problem is that the Japanese box-office for theatrical films is only one tenth of its size in the late 1950s ("The silver scream," 1997, p. 51).

Italy

The Italians have perhaps the most international film marketplace, with films from throughout Europe and the United States moving up and down in box-office receipts and comfortably mixed in with the occasional Italian production. Their tastes, it seems, are fairly eclectic, but tend less toward action–adventure films than the other major markets. For example, the French–Polish film *Trois Couleurs: Rouge* (1994) was at the top of the Italian box office for several weeks ("International box office," 1994a), a feat unmatched elsewhere (although the film was an international success, even in the United States), and remarkable given its lack of an indigenous connection. The domestically produced *Il Postino* (1994), a modest international hit that played on the American art cinema circuit, did not match *Trois Couleurs'* accomplishment in Italy. At other times, as many as 5 indigenous productions were in the top 10 ("International box office," 1995a), including *OcchioPinocchio* and *Miraculo Italiano*. *Nell* (U.S., 1994) and *Pret-a-Porter* (U.S./French, 1995) were bigger hits in Italy than they were domestically. As for television, Italy is a major importer of American programming, importing 21,000 hours in 1982 alone (Mattelart et al., 1984).

France

Although the French are rightly proud of their indigenous film industry, they still import 6 1/2 of their top 10 films over time from the United States. It is for this reason, perhaps, that they entered into a major trade war with the United States in the name of French cultural survival. This conflict nearly prevented international agreement on the GATT in 1993 (Cohen, 1993)—the French insisted on strict quotas on how many non-European films can be imported into the European Union (EU), but the United States, predictably, backed a free-market position. In fact, the French government was far more adamant about protecting itself from imported culture than from almost every other kind of product. Although there is a fairly strong indigenous film industry, one that still produces the occasional international hit, France is, like the rest of Europe, overrun with imported American films. They are more likely than most, however, to have a significant proportion of the top 10 locally produced: The week ending June 7, 1994, for example, had *Grosse Fatigue* (French, 1994) at number one, *La Reine Margot* (French, 1994) at number three, and *Les Patriotes* (French, 1994) at number four. Number two that week was not American either, but the British *Four Weddings and a Funeral* (1994); ("International box office," 1994a). The most similar European box office to France is Brussels, which also had *Grosse Fatigue*, *La Reine Margot*, and *Les Patriotes* in its top 10 that week; they did not make the top 10 in any other market ("International box office," 1994a). Perhaps sensing that the exportability of French films is dwindling, however, the French production company Gaumont recently began to produce films in the English language (Williams, 1994).

Broadcasting has also been a site of French cultural self-defense. Its national statute Article 24, for example, requires no less than 60% of fictional programming to be French productions or coproductions (Mattelart et al., 1984). Changes in programming distribution, however, such as satellite and cable television, make the principle behind and implementation of laws like Article 24 almost impossible (Tunstall, 1995).

Poland

Poland is a film-loving country and has a distinct history of producing unique and exportable films with relative freedom, even under communism, with the one exception being the period of martial law (Michalek & Turaj, 1988). It is no surprise, then, that a remarkable 93 different films were playing in Warsaw during a sample week in 1994, and of these, about two thirds were imported from America. Yet, in addition to such contemporary American films and international hits as *Krol Lew* (*The Lion King*) and *Milczenie Owiec* (*The Silence of the Lambs*), were revivals of *Nashville* (U.S., 1985) and *Taksowkarz* (*Taxi Driver*, 1976), which are rarely screened in cinemas in the United States anymore. The rest of the Polish movie market was made up of indigenous and other international productions, such as *Czetery Wesela I Pogrzeb* (*Four Weddings and a Funeral*; Britain, 1994) and numerous French films ("*Na ekranach*," 1994). Like the Italians, Polish tastes tend to be international.

Hong Kong

As far as the film marketplace goes, Hong Kong is the antithesis of Canada in terms of its tastes and spending habits. Hong Kong has one of the most vital indigenous film industries in the world, and as a result imports very little from the rest of the world (and exports rather successfully). The week ending December 8, 1993, for example, fully 8 of the top 10 films were indigenous, with titles like *The Tai-Chi Master* (Hong Kong, 1993, number one that week), *Ghost Lantern* (Hong Kong, 1993), and *Eight Hilarious Gods* (Hong Kong, 1993); (Groves, 1993). The two films that were not indigenous, yet ranked in the top 10 that week were *M. Butterfly* (U.S./Canada, 1993; number five that week and a film with Chinese subject matter) and *Sleepless in Seattle* (U.S., 1993; number six that week). Number one that same week in Brussels, France, Germany, Helsinki, Holland, Italy, Madrid, Sweden, the United Kingdom and Ireland, and most of the rest of the world was *Aladdin* (Disney, 1993), which did not even make the top ten in Hong Kong (Groves, 1993).

The most successful motion pictures in Hong Kong tend to have heavy doses of action, adventure, and violence (for example, number one the week ending May 25, 1994 was *Chinese Torture Chamber Story*), so it follows that imports with similar qualities would do well there, and they do. *The Mask* (U.S., 1993), *Die Hard With a Vengeance* (U.S., 1995), and *Batman Forever* (U.S., 1995) have all been number one films in Hong Kong ("International box office," 1994b; "International box office," 1995b; "International box office," 1995c). Nevertheless, Hong Kong remains the most resistant to imported media of the major markets and its own international export prospects are encouraging. U.S. demand for action pictures has brought some Hong Kong films to the American market, and films like *Supercop* (1993), dubbed into English and released in the United States a few years after its release in Hong Kong, have had some international success.

Hong Kong is in many ways the most serious competition to Hollywood, and is often called *Dongfang Haolaiwu*, the Hollywood of the East. The world's most popular movie star, Jackie Chan, worked there but has made a transition to Hollywood. Hong Kong is responsible for a prodigious output of films and dominates the Asian market, particularly in South Korea and Japan. It is, in fact, the second-largest film export market. Textually, Hong Kong films are often described as part of a "comic-book aesthetic ... a cinema of incessant action, eye-popping effects, and cartoon-like violence" (Dannen, 1995), although the genre of comedy was, by the late 1990s, the most popular there (Lau, 1998). The effect that the transfer of Hong Kong's administration from British to Chinese control will have on the Hong Kong film industry is unclear, but many industry leaders, including John Woo, the preeminent director of Cantonese action films, have left for Hollywood. Like Chan, Woo has made a successful move to Hollywood, and has made successful U.S. films like *Face Off* (1997).

More important than the fact that all these movie marketplaces import a lot of American movies and television is that they are quite different in the mix of movies they prefer, in how they tend to rank them with their ticket purchases, and in which non-American films they prefer. In general, most of the same American movies turn up on their hit list, but they will not follow the same path up and down; also in general, the non-American films in any country's top 10 tend, with a few exceptions, to be indigenous or in the native language. Beyond that, however, there are few tendencies; each market is distinct and there are many distinct subcultures and cocultures in each of these nations that create their own unique markets.

There have certainly been non-American international blockbusters, but these are few and far between. The most significant one of the past few years is *Four Weddings and a Funeral* (1994, Rank/Polygram), a certifiable international hit of British origin that was a hit in the United States as well. What is most interesting about *Four Weddings and a Funeral* is how it stands out: It is not an action–adventure picture, contains no A-list talent, has a relatively small budget, and is not American. *Four Weddings and a Funeral* is an exception that proves the rule, however, and the general prospects for European film production and export are not nearly so bright. European revenues from European-produced films have dropped sixfold from a high of nearly $3 billion per year in 1955 to around $500 million today; at the same time, the United States share of the European market has grown to over $2 billion, four times the current combined share of France, Germany, Britain, Italy, and Spain ("European films: Gumped," 1995).

Television exports follow a similar pattern. "Dallas" (see Ang, 1985) has not been the only internationally successful program exported from the United States; "Dynasty," "The X Files" (Fox TV), and especially "Baywatch" (syndicated TV) have all been big international hits. Whole cable channels have been successfully exported: For example, in 1994, MTV India was added to MTV Europe, MTV Brazil, MTV Asia, and all the other MTVs (da Cunha, 1994). The American media have a global omni-presence.

SYNTHESIS

Why are American films and television programs so successful in the world market? Liebes and Katz (1993) eschewed materialist and deterministic explanations in favor of the sort of textual explanations that are increasingly accepted by media scholars. They concluded that:

> the universality, or primordiality, of some of [the American media's] themes and formulae … makes programs psychologically accessible; the polyvalent or open potential of many of the stories, [increases] their value as projective mechanisms and as material for negotiation and play…. (p. 5)

Liebes and Katz perhaps oversimplified how the media function, however. To suggest that cultures throughout the world can relate to the American media because they share some universal or primordial narrative, some essentialist myths (they go so far to suggest the Biblical narrative in Genesis), is too reductionist, rather Jungian, and basically unnecessary. In fact, it undercuts their own argument that cultures read texts differently.

Cultures throughout the world may not share narratives, but persons in those cultures share the human experience, and it is this that provides a way to account for particularly successful narratives. Every human knows what it is to laugh, cry, wonder, and participate. These emotions do not always lead to the same myths, or even the same mythic structures, but they do inevitably lead to some myth, to some narrative. Films and television programs that engage these emotions most directly, most undiluted by cultural encrustation, are the most likely to seem familiar and archetypal, not because they correspond to indigenous mythology, but because they are premythic.

Lacking a reading context, like a myth system, means imported media make no sense or contradictory sense. György (1995) described how Ukrainian audiences gave a completely different reading to CNN coverage of American military pilot Scott O'Grady's escape when his plane was shot down than did American audiences. Whereas Americans treated it as a story of courage, fortitude, heroism, and determination, Ukrainians—whose daily lives resemble the emergency condition O'Grady found himself in—saw CNN's coverage as self-indulgent and myopic.

Nationalist media, like the Welsh soap opera "Pobol Y Cwm," are primarily concerned with questions of ethnic and national identify, or, as Griffiths (1995) pointed out, concerned with establishing what a culture is not in order to establish what it is. American media seem to have a diametrically opposed narrative strategy: to avoid any indication of what a culture may not be so as not to call the question of what culture is. Because difference is constructed in archetypal rather than cultural terms in many American media exports, the narrative can almost always have a sense of familiarity, of déja vu, because nothing is there to the contrary. Whereas "Pobol Y Cwm" embodies locality, topicality, and specificity, movies like *The Lion King* (1994) or television programs like "Walker: Texas Ranger" embody universality, eternality, and generality. The nationalist narrative has a limited international appeal because, in Gillespie's (1995b) words, "certain cultural knowledge is assumed" (p. 372); the American export assumes nothing.

It should not be assumed that America is any more homogeneous in its reading than the rest of the world, either. As Gates (1995) pointed out in his analysis of African American and Anglo-American receptions to the O.J. Simpson trial:

> It's a fallacy ... to equate shared narratives with shared meanings. The fact that American TV shows are rebroadcast across the globe causes many people to wring their hands over the menace of cultural imperialism; seldom do they bother to inquire about the meanings that different people bring to and draw from these shows. ... A similar thing happen[s] in America: the communal experience afforded by a public narrative (and what narrative more public [than the O.J. Simpson trial]?) was splintered by the politics of interpretation. (p. 62)

Narratives construct but do not constrain, consign, or confine meaning. The global village may be tuned to the same broadcast, but its villagers are not seeing the same broadcast.

What all this means is that although political and economic explanations provide pieces of the puzzle, it is impossible to understand the global media marketplace without careful consideration of the texts themselves and the ways audiences read them. Examining these readings is just a starting point, because it only examines differences, and only on national levels, ignoring the complex variety of tastes that exist within any market. Two additional types of studies can help in this regard. One comes from the narratological, textual study tradition of film and television, and these have, happily, become more common in recent years. A second type is more rare: studies that compare how different cultures read particular texts. These too are growing in number thanks to collections like those by Allen (1995) and Smoodin (1994). Where theoretical work most needs to be done, it is not being done at all—at the nexus between these two approaches. The question this yet-to-be-done theoretical work would need to address is simply stated, but methodologically complex: what is it about certain narratives that allows them to be easily read in different ways by different cultures? To put it another way, how do narratology and polysemy intersect? Only when this question is answered, and combined with economic and political explanations, would a full picture of the apparatuses of American cultural exporting be available.

Materialist explanations for the global success of the American media stress the prevalence of English in the world, America's dominance in world markets, and the lower cost of importing films and television compared with producing them locally. These certainly explain part of the international successes of *Jurassic Park* (1993) or "Baywatch," but fail to explain why some succeed while others fail, let alone how audience taste affects selection. The reason that "Dallas" flopped in Japan while succeeding almost everywhere else is not merely a question of political–economy—there is a cultural dimension as well. Many scholars worry that the global dominance of American media transforms indigenous culture into something American, but the data indicate a simultaneous and countervailing effect: whether or not these texts are transforming indigenous cultures into something American, those audiences are transforming the texts into something indigenous.

It is clear, then, that the United States has established itself as the most powerful player in the world media marketplace, if not in terms of the quantity of exports, then certainly in terms of box office receipts. Why the

United States? Why not Japan or someplace else instead? Porter (1990, 1998) provided the most systematic method available for answering these questions. Its careful application points to specific areas of American competitive advantage. That advantage is what has made this a Hollywood planet.

3

Competitive Advantage and the Media

The cultural heterogeneity of the U.S. domestic market has probably also helped to make the marketing of almost any American cultural product quite easy.
—*Gripsrud (1995)*

That the United States dominates the international production and distribution of motion pictures and television programs is clear; the industry also has a dominating effect on the U.S. economy, where it has become the second largest export, generating annual revenues of $215 billion ("Entertainment has become," 1997). This dominance raises several questions that need to be considered in assessing the ongoing significance of the American media in the international consumption of entertainment: Is American media dominance inevitable due to certain conditions intrinsic to the United States economy, political structure, and social organization? What specific factors contribute to the relative hegemony of the United States in this arena? Will the American media always have this superordinate position?

There are many ways to approach these questions; given their complexity, they almost insist that many approaches be used. Explanations for U.S. media dominance can be political, economic, social, or cultural; in fact, all of these domains work together to play a role. As just mentioned, almost all analyses to date can be roughly clumped in either the political–economy camp (Mattelart et al., 1984; Schiller, 1989), the development camp (Lerner & Schramm, 1969; Schramm, 1964), the textual camp (Ang, 1985; Liebes & Katz, 1993), or the cultivation camp (Gerbner, 1993; Morgan & Signorelli, 1990). As has been shown in chapter 1, none of these approaches is wholly satisfying. An integrative approach needs to combine elements of each, while adding the important theoretical framework provided by *man-*

agement theory—a discipline that seeks to explain why organizations choose the strategies they do, and how the efficacy of these strategies can be measured and evaluated. Such a framework is important because, ultimately, the configuration of the international film and television marketplace comes down to particular production and distribution firms following particular strategies to particular results. None of the four common approaches alone provides any insight into this crucial aspect of global media. Another approach is needed, one that integrates aspects of these four while adding other dimensions.

Is it important that a national cinema or broadcasting system have competitive advantage? In other words, what does it matter if the movies or television programs from a particular country are only viewed internally and have no export value? There are certainly many alternatives to international distribution, including strict self-reliance, state control of industry, and protectionism, and in some cases, these have been successful (Mattelart et al., 1984). Nevertheless, there are many reasons why competitive advantage matters a great deal and must be taken seriously: In terms of economies of scale, successful international distribution generates revenues that enable further domestic production; a strong cinema and television industry employs many more people than a weak one and helps support the development of related industries. In cultural terms, a weak national cinema will most likely lose domestic audience over time to further imports, therefore losing the ability to communicate with the national population itself; furthermore, the lack of international distribution deprives a culture of its ability to communicate who and what it is to other countries and cultures.

PORTER'S DIAMOND

To analyze the behavior of these media production and distribution firms, there is no better framework than the one provided by Porter (1990, 1998). Porter attempted to account for the relative strengths that certain countries exhibit in certain industries: Swedish strength in mining equipment, Japanese strength in consumer electronics, or Italian strength in ceramic tiles, for example. It is Porter's argument that specific factors present in the nation combine to enable preeminence, to give that nation a competitive advantage. These factors may be the availability of natural resources, of favorable regulatory policies, of a uniquely educated and configured workforce, of unusual industry structure, of blind serendipity, or of something else. These factors combine in a fortuitous way to make such a nation a:

home base for successful global competitors in a particular industry. ... The home base is the nation in which the essential competitive advantages of the enterprise are created and sustained. It is where a firm's strategy is set and the core product and process technology (broadly defined) are created and maintained. (p. 19)

He used this home base concept to characterize the growth and sustainability of a variety of industries in several Eastern and Western countries.

This is not to say that nations have some sort of generalized and deterministic advantage that enables them to do well in whatever industry they choose; he was not saying, for example, that the British are industrious and frugal and therefore successful at whatever they do. There have been plenty of such theories in the past that attributed inherent industriousness to Northern European nations, implying that they are somehow better able to manufacture and compete, no matter what the product, because of an implicit cultural work ethic. This bespeaks at best xenophobia and at worst racism. Such an approach is incompatible with Porter's; no nation can be successful at everything because the unique cultural and material attributes found in each nation positions it to be better able at some tasks than others. The very elements that make the Swiss good watchmakers, for example, might make them poor steel manufacturers. Nations are neither good nor poor competitors per se, but create an environment in which specific industries might prosper.

Often, this prospering is a result of what Porter (1990) called *factor-based competitive advantage*. This results from an abundance of cheap labor or natural resources. Although this might account for some instances of competitive advantage (he gave the example of Korea, p. 11), it is rarely a sustainable advantage, because lower cost labor or more abundant resources can frequently be found elsewhere (in China). So, low-cost inputs alone cannot account for ongoing competitive advantage; the high cost of labor and materials in Germany and Sweden seem to preclude them from competitive advantage, but they are world leaders in automobiles, lenses, X-ray equipment and steel, mining equipment, and refrigeration, respectively. Furthermore, and unlike industry leadership based on low-cost inputs, Germany and Sweden have had sustained leadership in these areas for many years.

The alternative to *low-cost input manufacturing*, which allows a firm to compete by presenting a lower cost product, is *differentiation manufacturing*, in which the product, although more expensive, has attributes that make it more desirable to its buyers than its lower cost competition; in a sense, differentiation uses marketing to confer a difference that is not all that substantial (Williamson, 1994). These attributes include "product quality, special features, [and] after-sale service" (Porter, 1990, p. 37). This differentiation approach has typically been the route to sustainable advantage and certainly characterizes the appeal of the American media: Hollywood films and television have little factor-based advantage of this sort due to huge production costs, yet are differentiated in such a way in the marketplace that they have an inherent desirability. An important question, and one to be considered here, is how the American home base helps create that differentiation.

Porter (1990) was specific about how a home-base competitive advantage comes about. Accepting Vernon's (1966) theory that initial home demand helps encourage sophisticated design and manufacturing for export, Porter wonders what mechanisms created and sustained home demand and what other factors were significant. Unfortunately, Porter provided a very limited methodology for analyzing home-base demand, a defect that becomes a serious flaw when considering cultural products like television programs or movies.

Advantage is largely a product of the scope particular firms choose for competition, and this selection is itself a result of innovation. For Porter (1990), innovation has several causes: new technology, changing consumer needs, development of new segments in the industry, changing cost of production, and government regulation or deregulation. To capitalize on one or more of these is to find a way to lower costs or differentiate, and hence, increase market share or enable high-end pricing (Kozminski & Cushman, 1993). These innovations are also available to international competitors, at least in principle, so they alone do not explain how certain nations can be consistently successful in certain industries. In fact, while these factors can bestow industry leadership, they alone are not the formula for sustaining a leadership position.

Sustainable competitive advantage for a home base derives, instead, from what Porter (1990) called the *diamond* of four interrelated national attributes: *factor conditions, demand conditions, related and supporting industries,* and *firm strategy, structure, and rivalry* (p. 71). These attributes, which combine in a unique way in every nation, create opportunities for differentiation and innovation. Due to their particularity, they essentially encourage and support national success in certain industries, while making success unlikely in others. Although a nation may not always have unique determinants of this type, "national advantage arises when the system is unique" (p. 147).

Factor conditions are the basic elements and raw materials of production that a nation has at its disposal. Countries inherit or must create these factors. They include the labor force, natural resources, infrastructure, capital, and knowledge (Porter, 1990, p. 75). Obviously, these attributes vary extensively from country to country, but this variance does not confer competitive advantage. Gaining competitive advantage from factor conditions involves using them in the most efficient manner possible.

The second facet of Porter's (1990) diamond, demand conditions, describes the nature and extent of the home market for particular products and services. Usually, it is the home market that gives rise to particular product differentiations; "A product's fundamental or core design nearly always reflects homebuyer needs. All these considerations make proximity to the right type of buyers of decisive importance in national competitive advantage" (p. 87). Some of these home-base oriented differentiations will foreshadow and in a sense create international demand, providing "a window into the most advanced buyer needs" (p. 89) and conferring on the original a significant competitive advantage. Frequently, national passions—such as the Japanese enthusiasm for electronic miniaturization—act as important demand conditions. A further qualitative aspect of home demand is the extent to which it already has been internationalized, either because its own composition is rather international (i.e., Hong Kong) or because it is in a position to influence international tastes (i.e., France). In addition to these qualitative factors, the volume of home demand is also significant; some home bases are large enough to form a huge share of the potential international market (i.e., the United States), whereas others will ultimately be rather small shares (i.e., Singapore).

The third aspect of Porter's diamond is the system of *related and supporting industries* found in the home-base country. No product is conjured out of thin air, but must rely on natural resources, suppliers, subassemblers, distributors, and other companies in a value chain that Porter (1998) called a cluster. Each of these companies is part of a necessary but distinct industry and without them the nation would not have particular dominance in one area. Porter (1990, 1998) used Italian success in the footwear industry as an example: Italy is also noted for its excellent design firms and for the production of high quality leather and the machines needed to process it. Each of these separate industries helps to support the footwear industry. It is difficult to envision how Italy's footwear industry could be successful without them. Related industries, which are not suppliers per se, can also be beneficial because they use similar inputs, so that manufacturing can be coordinated with other industries. For example, Porter (1990) mentions that Germany is strong in chemicals and printing ink; although these neither compete with nor supply each other, they do make use of similar technologies and resources, thus helping to strengthen each other's position. Also in Germany, Daimler-Benz has a successful relation with supporting industries that further its own success ("Le Défi Américain, Again," 1996).

Firm strategy, structure, and rivalry are the final facet of Porter's diamond. This has to do with the way in which firms in a particular country organize themselves and compete with each other and how the resultant structure and competition can lead to global predominance. As shown elsewhere (Olson, 1996), organizations can take on a number of different organizational structures: Weberian hierarchy (where communication is top-down), Theory Y and System IV (where communication flows between organizational levels), the Matrix model (where communication is omnidirectional), and others. Which of these structures is deployed has to do with *fit*, the appropriateness with which they match the national culture and industry. For example, Disney's unique corporate identity (Auletta, 1996) has contributed to its ongoing success because of a good fit between culture and product. The structures that are chosen can differ considerably from industry to industry and country to country, however, so there can be no one correct option. For example, the loose and flexible matrix structure of Gore Associates would not work well at Disney or in a military organization. The choice of structure can strongly affect the nature of domestic competition and therefore affect international strength and competitive advantage. Strong domestic rivalry can also contribute to competitive advantage, Porter (1990) argued, because if the strongest competitors are at home, then success abroad comes more easily. He argued that Japanese success in audio equipment, for example, results in part from the fact that there are 25 domestic competitors in that industry, yet relatively few competitors elsewhere in the world.

These four sides to the diamond—factor conditions, demand conditions, related and supporting industries, and firm strategy, structure, and rivalry—combine in unique ways in different national contexts, conferring home-base advantages to particular nations in particular industries at particular times. For Porter (1990), this accounted for Danish success in dairy products, Korean success in automobiles, and British success in auctioneering. These advantages are by no means immutable; indeed, the United States has lost its home-base advantage in several industries since the 1970s, the automobile industry being the most obvious example.

How does that erosion of advantage occur? Porter (1990) articulated several ways in which a nation can lose its competitive advantage: the deterioration of factor conditions; changes in demand conditions that make the nation a poor predictor of international tastes—either because they grow dissimilar to global consumers or lose their sophistication; quality erosion in supporting industries or the lack of new supporting industries; inflexibility; and faltering home-base competition (pp. 166–169). Several of these were operative in the case of the decline of the American automobile industry and in the decline of every national industry, according to Porter.

In addition, these four components of Porter's (1990) diamond are not created equal, but confer competitive advantage in varying measure:

> Two elements—domestic rivalry and geographic industry concentration—have especially great power to transform the "diamond" into a system, domestic rivalry because it promotes upgrading the entire national "diamond," and geographic concentration because it elevates and magnifies the interactions within the "diamond." (p. 131)

These help insure that competitive advantage is a dynamic system: Domestic rivalries can disappear if one of the competitors falters, which can then dissipate geographic concentration, as can downsizing and outsourcing. In short, advantages held today may be gone tomorrow, and in any case, should never be regarded as inherent and inevitable in particular nations. The shifting of competitive advantage is, after all, the wellspring of history itself.

Porter (1990) applied his diamond analysis to 10 nations and over 100 industries in order to develop a general and theoretical view of the relation between nations and industrial success. This means that of necessity, and in spite of the fact that he provided excellent case studies, Porter inevitably supplied a gloss: No industry or nation is examined in extensive and sufficient detail to fully illuminate his theory. It has been for others to take on the task of actually applying this approach to particular industries in particular nations in order to assess its explanatory power. The implication of Porter's diamond for international competition in the television and film industries has been one of those unfinished tasks.

MOVIE AND TELEVISION'S HOME BASE

Porter (1990) said little about the film and television industries per se, except to note that the United States possesses a competitive advantage in these areas, as well as the related areas of advertising and computer software, which help in cross promotion. The actual and systematic application of his method to the American media industry is a task that has not been previously undertaken. In order to adequately assess the explanatory power of Porter's method in relation to international competition in the television and film industries and the role of the United States in that competition, the specific criteria of factor conditions, related and supporting industries, firm strategy, structure and rivalry, and demand conditions need to be applied to it in depth and detail.

Factor conditions are a big part of American success in the film and television industry, but are not the crucial part. The skilled labor force available to film and television production and distribution is extensive, and scores of universities and colleges throughout the country turn out more than the needed number of qualified writers, producers, directors, actors, specialized accountants, and other personnel the industry needs. Well-developed film and television intern and apprenticeship programs further reinforce the base of skilled labor. The telecommunication and transportation infrastructure in the United States is currently sufficient to support this information-intensive industry, and given widespread American access to the Internet, it is only likely to get better. Adequate investment capital continues to be available with entertainment companies remaining popular on Wall Street. The collective knowledge base of film and television aesthetic conventions, formulae, and production practices that are shared by Hollywood with the American people are without equal and reinforced by a steady diet of inside the media broadcast programs (i.e., *Entertainment Tonight*), magazines (i.e., *Entertainment Weekly*), and dedicated cable TV channels (i.e., *E! Entertainment*).

Another aspect of Porter's (1990) method, related and supporting industries—is also important to the competitive advantage of the United States in the film and television industries, so much so that Porter himself remarked on it as a prime example of the phenomenon:

> The concentration of rivals in movie and television production in Hollywood has led to the growth of a thriving and highly specialized group of supplier industries, ranging from special effects firms, to costume designers, to firms providing production insurance. Their quality and proximity to the studio only enhance Hollywood's competitiveness. (p. 139)

In fact, and as any visitor to Los Angeles has noticed, the whole metropolitan area is largely dedicated to the media industry or its suppliers in one form or another. That a feature film like *Armageddon* (1998) can rely on a dependable and competitive supply of studio space, specialized photographic equipment, optical and digital special effects firms, postproduction houses, film laboratories, writers, and acting talent, all within commuting distance of each other, is invaluable to its success.

This industry system and geographic concentration further benefit Hollywood's film and television industries. The United States is the world leader in film stock manufacturing; in fact, it has about 82% of the world market share in this area (Porter, 1990, p. 509). This is part of a value system of film and television suppliers, distributors, and theater chains that is unsurpassed and largely centered in Southern California and New York City. Their geographic and cognitive proximity fuels a creative and financial synergy that enhances Hollywood differentiation.

Porter (1990, 1998) called the domestic system of sophisticated suppliers, producers, and distributors a *cluster* and saw advertising and software development as two of its components. Advertising has always been extremely important in the broadcasting industry, because "there remains a deep coherence between American series and advertising" (Mattelart et al., 1984, p. 97) in the form of program structure, scheduling, and flow. The eventual significance of the software industry to the film and television industry can only be guessed at, but the huge volume of CD-ROM and website tie-ins to other media spectacles hints of a profound convergence of these industries yet to come. The United States also possesses significant world market share in the manufacture of cinema cameras, film projectors, photochemicals, exposed film plates, newspapers, periodicals, prerecorded CDs, audio cassettes, and discharge lamps and bulbs (Porter, 1990, p. 517).

Firm strategy, structure, and rivalry are also significant to the success of the American film and television industry. Certainly, the sophisticated use of marketing in the United States has contributed to overall industry shape. The United States has had commercial broadcasting from the beginning, whereas in many countries, it is a relatively new phenomenon, giving the United States a significant headstart (Mattelart et al., 1984). Furthermore, structural conditions within the industry lend it strength, such as:

> high production and technical standards, an efficient marketing system, professionalism, the power to impose block bookings, the mastery of adventure and action genres, carefully planned scenarios, their rapid rhythm, the star system, the long-established entertainment tradition in the United States, etc. All these elements bear witness to an industry which has developed a commercial model of entertainment without equal. (p. 93)

Although they did not feel these to be the only structural factors encouraging American success, Mattelart, Delcourt, and Mattelart felt them to be significant ones.

Porter (1990) did not have enough to say about U.S. demand conditions. He did mention that the United States was the first mass-consumption society, that it had significant postwar affluence that shaped sophisticated consumer demand, abundant leisure time, and that it has tended to prefer disposable products (pp. 299–301). An absence of European products after World War II pulled American manufacturers into international distribution markets they had not seriously needed, considered, or planned on. The prevalence of English as a first or second language throughout much of the world also relates to American home-demand success (p. 302). America's history and ethnic composition as a nation of (mostly) immigrants certainly also helped internationalize home demand (p. 304). Pells (1997) saw the heterogeneity of the United States as a primary factor in American global media success:

> The domestic market was a laboratory for and a microcosm of the world market. On the other hand, the Europeans, operating for the most part in countries with homogeneous populations, had no incentive to communicate with a multicultural audience and were thus ill equipped to compete in the international arena. (p. 209)

Such domestic demand shaped the sort of programs American media producers created and prepared them well for global competition.

Television, in particular, was important to the development of American home demand, because commercial television began in the United States with a philosophy of private ownership of the media that had always been in place. Advertising on television and radio had been relatively unregulated. According to Porter (1990), the combination of these factors meant that "American companies developed unique skills in image building for mass-consumed products" (p. 300).

This is essentially all that can be said about American home demand for film and television using Porter's method alone. Clearly, this is not enough: Demand conditions are perhaps more important in cultural industries than in other ones because the product itself is such a close and careful barometer of the culture. Consequently, a detailed and elaborate consideration of American home demand must be undertaken using methods that Porter had not used himself, namely, a Cultural Studies approach. This is be undertaken in chapter 4.

SUSTAINABLE ADVANTAGE?

America's recent and current dominance of the world media market is not necessarily permanent, and some already see evidence of its decay (Mattelart et al., 1984; Tunstall, 1995). What, then, would it take for the United States to lose its competitive advantage in the film and television industries? One of the following five things is necessary:

1. Factor conditions supporting the film and television industry would have to deteriorate.
2. There would have to be significant changes in demand conditions that would make the United States a poor predictor of international tastes—either because it fell out of synch with international tastes or because its audiences became a lot less sophisticated.
3. Supporting industries would have to erode in quality or the film and television industry would need to evolve in a direction that required supporting industries that were unavailable to it.
4. Firms in the industry would have to become too inflexible to deal with changing international demand.
5. Home-base competition would have to falter, most likely through the disappearance of sufficient, substantive players in the industry.

How likely are these changes to occur? Could factor conditions deteriorate to the point that it significantly eroded U.S. home-base advantage? To some extent, they already have. Film and television production costs, especially labor, have proven cheaper in other countries, so many "Hollywood" television shows have actually been filmed in Canada (including "The X-Files" and, ironically, "NYPD Blue," (ABC TV), leading Groen (1995) and others to speak of Canadian media exports to the United States. This exodus is due largely to the relatively high cost of labor in Los Angeles and New York City; that same labor, however, is the among the best trained in the world, meaning that although some programs are shot in Canada, the majority are still made in greater Los Angeles. Furthermore, although shooting might occur in Canada or elsewhere, all other aspects of preproduction and postproduction generally remain in California, maintaining the essentially American quality to these shows: Consequently, "The X-Files" can scarcely be considered a Canadian television show.

Whether or not there would have to be significant changes in demand conditions that would make the United States a poor predictor of international tastes—because it fell out of sync with international tastes or because its audiences became a lot less sophisticated—is subject to debate. Porter (1990) argued that "no longer is America the nation that always foreshadows the world market. No longer is America so consistently the home of the world's most sophisticated buyers" (p. 522). This he attributed to what in the late 1980s appeared to be America's declining relative affluence and increasing ability to tolerate shoddy product quality or service. He acknowledged, however, that in certain domains, American sophistication remains high. Because Americans continue to "celebrate entertainment and leisure" (p. 525), they are extremely savvy when it comes to the media, and are intolerant of media products which fail to reflect the latest technology or social trends. Given America's ongoing obsession with the media, the United States is likely to continue producing interested, sophisticated, and demanding audiences for film and television products.

Because of the tremendous demand for their services, the extent to which they actually drive the sorts of productions that are undertaken and so, lead innovation, and the American dominance in related tertiary industries like advertising and software development, it is unlikely that supporting industries could erode in quality or the film and television industry would evolve in a direction that required supporting industries unavailable to it. Furthermore, firms in the American film and television industry are likely to remain flexible enough to deal with changing international demand; their shape and employee roster has always been among the most protean of any major industry.

Perhaps the most likely source of weakness is the fifth. Home-base competition could falter, due to the disappearance of sufficient, substantive players in the industry through mergers and acquisitions. Concentration of power in the media industry has been an ongoing phenomenon in the 1990s, creating gargantuan megacorporations like Disney–Capital Cities–ABC and Time-Warner–Turner, but these are not necessarily improvements over the separate entities they bring together. In fact, these mergers might severely limit the competitive advantages of their constituent pieces by becoming unwieldy, something "too big, too centralized, too intent on asserting managerial control" (Auletta, 1996, p. 28).

In order to remain competitive, firms in an industry must engage in six strategies according to Porter (1990). They must: "sell to the most sophisticated consumer;" "seek out buyers with the most difficult needs;" "establish norms of exceeding the toughest regulatory hurdles or product standards;" "source from the most advanced and international home-based suppliers;" "treat employees as permanent;" and "establish outstanding competitors as motivators" (pp. 585–586). The American film and television industry does an excellent job at all of these with the exception of treating its employees as permanent, where it has a terrible record. Perhaps this very lack of employment stability is part of the industry structure, however; Hollywood is such a small town that employees discharged by one studio quickly find employment at a competitor, leading to a cutthroat mentality that makes the industry even more fiercely competitive. A good example is the firing of Jeffrey Katzenberg by Disney CEO Michael Eisner: Katzenberg immediately established a new studio, Dreamworks SKG, with friends Stephen Spielberg and David Geffen, vowing to compete directly with Disney in the production of high-quality animated entertainment. This, no doubt, only sharpened Disney's resolve; they quickly (but temporarily) hired Creative Artists Agency CEO Michael Ovitz as Disney President and then purchased the ABC television network. Katzenberg countered by changing the release date of Dreamworks SKG's computer animated film *Antz* (1998) to a month before Disney/Pixar's similarly themed *A Bug's Life* (1998). The skirmishes continue.

Despite these potential pitfalls to ongoing American success in the media industry, one must conclude that in the near future it will still retain its power. Yet, Porter's (1990) method remains an incomplete explanation of how that power works. One failing of Porter's method is that it ultimately glosses over the most significant but subtle aspect of national home-base demand—the culture itself. It is understandable why Porter almost completely neglects this in his examination of national industries: He is not a Cultural Studies specialist and can hardly be expected to analyze anything so complex in such a broad study of so many nations and so many firms; furthermore, for most industries—from dishwashers to milled steel—the cultural particularities of any one home-base nation do not really matter all that much. This is not so for the film and television industries, however: They are culture itself, a creation of culture that engages in cultural creation in a constant and inseparable cycle. Tastes are served and created by movies and television, so this aspect of home demand must be considered in detail.

It is clear, then, that "the first test of the 'universal value' of American programmes is carried out within the country itself" (Mattelart et al., 1984, p. 99). The next logical question seems to be: What is it about American home demand that gives luster to the duller facets of Porter's (1990) diamond and allows us to connect the American audience with the international audience via specific and demonstrable aspects of the text? The answer to that question requires an examination of American culture itself. American home demand can then be seen as the solid core of a Hollywood planet around which the molten mantle flows.

4

The Culture Factory

America is, therefore, just another brand name.
—*Yoshimoto (1994, p. 195)*

Porter's (1990, 1998) analytical approach to competitive strategy goes a fair way toward explaining the success of the United States in the global media market. Yet, Porter does not adequately explain the qualitative aspects of home demand, its cultural identities. Such omission necessitates an examination of the unique aspects of American culture as they relate to home demand; to do so is to provide a more sophisticated explanation of how success comes to the United States in the film and television industries.

American home demand may be the most important single aspect of American success in the media, but the domestic audience is complex. Dwelling on demographic data, which tend to particularize and empiricize rather than generalize and evaluate, is the wrong avenue. It is clear how relying strictly on demographic data and not a Cultural Studies or semiotic approach can go wrong in this regard. Robert Reich (1990), a former U.S. Secretary of Labor, tried to define American core business attributes when he asked, "Who is Us?" He did not come up with much of an answer; being concerned with economic policy, not semiotic structure, he saw only the lack of an American corporate identity.

So, what can be said about U.S. home demand, about the expectations, psychographics, and sophistication of the American media audience? Instead of using demographic data, a more interpretive approach is needed: An approach that meaningfully asks about the essential nature of American national identity as it relates to establishing American competitive advantage in the global media. There are several ways to do this.

However, any such approach is not easy. As Bhabha (1994) and Spivak (1995) showed, cultural identity is difficult, even impossible, to define, given its protean nature and tendency to define identity in terms of otherness: "Here is what we are not" rather than "Here is what we are." Still, there is a commonsense belief, and a correct one, that to be Iranian is not the same thing as being Irish, Indian, or Indonesian. How can those differences be characterized? The solution that is adopted here is to make Spivak's, "What we are not" paradox work in favor of the argument, by letting American home demand be defined by those who see it most clearly—outsiders.

It is natural that outsiders would have the clearest vision in this regard. The United States is noted for being inward looking, and the creative people behind the American media do not seem to care much about the rest of the world, even though that is where much of the profit is. According to Dennis and Snyder (1995), "For the most part, the American media are parochial. Not since their beginnings in colonial times have their form and outlook been knowingly influenced by the world outside. For the most part, they are native-born and native-grown" (p. xi).

Yet, in spite of this parochialism, or perhaps because of it, American media have tremendous appeal internationally. "Beverly Hills 90210" may not seem much like the real America to Americans, but it says volumes about the United States to Swedes or Russians. Liebes and Katz's (1993) study of "Dallas" showed how this can take place. What is it, then, about the provincial, inward-looking American audience that helps them anticipate and mimic international demand, providing the film and television industries with a home base consumer who enhances their competitive advantage? Those attributes make the United States the culture factory that it is.

Two outsiders in particular have made prescient, lasting, and incisive observations about the United States as a cultural entity, one while observing it in the early 19th century as a fledgling democracy, the other while touring it in the late 20th century as a hyperreal, postmodern culture factory. Alexis de Tocqueville and Jean Baudrillard have America in common. Their observations, which agree on many counts, attempt to define the essential properties that constitute American culture. These observations provide an invaluable framework for understanding the nature of American home demand for the media and, consequently, for America's home-base competitive advantage in the film and television industry.

The observations that follow can in no way be taken as the totality of American home demand, nor do they speak for all media consumers. These are the dominant demands of the largest audience, consistent with Porter's (1990) methodology. Other American audiences demand other things from the media, with varying degrees of success. These parameters, however, define the fundamental demands that shape American films and television, filling in the gaps in accounting for American competitive advantage.

DE TOCQUEVILLE'S AMERICA

The attributes of America that form the crucible in which American media are wrought are too numerous for a comprehensive consideration, but there are particularly dominant traits of American culture worth considering insofar as they affect the exportability of its media. In 1835, de Tocqueville (1945a, 1945b) identified several significant aspects of American culture from the perspective of a European and most of these still apply.

Perhaps the most salient of de Tocqueville's observations is that the media in the United States at that time—newspapers, mostly—had as their foremost concern pleasing their readers, an obsession with satisfying audience tastes that is still a defining aspect of the American media (Dennis & Snyder, 1995). The American media are first and foremost about giving audiences what they want (as opposed to what they need or what elites feel they need). This is evidenced in particular by the obsession of the U.S. broadcasting industry with ratings data: shares, Homes Using Television (HUTS), overnights, sweeps, and so forth. This was well-parodied on "Max Headroom" (ABC TV), a television series in which broadcasting executives watch ratings data and make programming changes, from millisecond to millisecond, in the hope of best pleasing fickle and fleeting audience tastes.

This is not the only observation of de Tocqueville's that needs consideration, however; several others are worth noting as they relate to American home demand for the media. Specifically, de Tocqueville observed the following in the United States:

- Moral certitude (1945a, p. 46).
- A contempt for the theory of the permanent equality of property (1945a, p. 53).
- "Few ignorant and at the same time so few learned individuals" (1945a, p. 54); in other words, an encompassing intellectual median.
- A belief in personal autonomous agency ("everyone is the best and sole judge of his [sic] own private interests," (1945a, p. 67).
- Legalism (p. 73), which is to say a predilection toward the use of the legal system to solve disputes.

- A press that favors advertising and trivialities instead of a passionate examination of current issues (p. 192) and that panders to audience emotions (1945a, p. 194).
- A mistrust of social authority (1945a, p. 198).
- "An irritable" patriotism of "great transient exertions but no continuity of effort" (pp. 251, 253); in other words, intensely passionate but transitory nationalism (1945a).
- A rhetoric extolling freedom of opinion, but constructed within very narrow parameters of tolerance, parameters that act to silence many opinions before they have been uttered (1945a, pp. 274–275).
- A preoccupation with commerce and practical matters instead of science, art, or literature (1945b, p. 38).
- "A taste for the tangible and the real, a contempt for tradition and for forms" (1945b, p. 42).
- A focus on gratifying the body instead of the mind (1945b, p. 46).
- Audiences that are easy to please (1945b, p. 64).
- Self-obsession (1945b, p. 77).

To a large extent, these conclusions remain descriptive of an America more than 150 years older than the one which de Tocqueville observed.

How has each of these manifested itself in the American media audience? Each seems to have its place, observable either in audience behavior or the media themselves. Moral certitude, for example, is a common aspect of American media programming. Levy (1995) argued that in American television, for example, the identities of the protagonists and the antagonists are never in doubt (e.g., Darth Vader wears black and Luke Skywalker wears white), and that, like an Aesop fable, programs must hold a suitable lesson for the audience at their conclusion.

Contempt for the theory of the permanent equality of property is directly manifested in the laws and policies governing allocation of the airwaves by the Federal Communications Commission (FCC). Although in most countries, there is an enduring sense that the airwaves are a national resource that belong to all citizens, and therefore there are policies in place that insist on broadcasting in the public's interest and for the public good, in the United States, the airwaves are overwhelmingly licensed to commercial companies for their own profit via entertainment programming. There are few programming requirements a broadcaster needs to fulfill to retain its license and the trend has been mostly toward deregulating the few policies that still exist. Most Americans neither question, nor think to question, this broadcasting structure for reasons de Tocqueville identified 100 years before the advent of broadcasting, a belief that property is private and unequal allocation of it is not only tolerated, but encouraged.

"Few ignorant and at the same time so few learned individuals," or the encompassing intellectual median, is another feature of American culture that affects its home-base advantage in media production. As Mattelart et al. observed (1984), European class structures and reinforcement of "high culture" have profoundly affected the way European film and television systems have been organized. In short, European media have helped propagate art, literature, and music, whereas the American media have concentrated on entertainment and commerce. Because ratings are essentially the exclusive driver of programming in the United States, broadcasters argue with some justification that Americans get what they want and want what they get. American popular culture is decidedly middle class.

Belief in personal autonomous agency also manifests itself in American media programming. Levy (1995) noted that in the United States, choice is regarded as a birthright, necessitating the huge selection of cable channels or the number of screens in a multiplex theater that Americans enjoy. It is axiomatic of film and television plot structuring that protagonists must also be confronted with a profound choice at the climax of any good script, a confrontation with their own past or inner self that they either overcome or to which they succumb. Their choice then resolves the essential conflict of the narrative: The correct choice leads to a happy ending and the incorrect one leads to a sad ending. The pattern is formulaic: Contentment for choosing to stay with an estranged husband in *Peggy Sue Got Married* (1986), reconciliation by choosing to defend a spouse in *Die Hard* (1988), or the loss of everything beloved through a failure to abandon criminality when the chance was given in *Godfather III* (1990) are all manifestations of the formula.

As previously mentioned, the audience's own interest in choice is evident in multiplex theaters with 20 screens, homes with 60 or 70 different cable or satellite channels, and video rental and sales outlets on every other street corner. The extent to which these offer a real choice is debatable, of course: The multiplex shows almost no independent or foreign films, and Bruce Springsteen complains that his television has "57 channels and nothing on." There remains, however, the perception of choice, which is what the audience seems to want.

Legalism, the predilection to the use of the legal system to solve disputes, is among the most common themes, and is clearly evident in the many lawyer and courtroom programs found on American television, including "L.A. Law" (NBC TV), "Civil Wars" (ABC TV), "Law and Order" (NBC TV), "Murder One" (ABC TV), "The Practice" (ABC TV), "The People's Court" (syndicated), "Judge Judy" (syndicated), and even a dedicated cable network, Court TV. American audiences were captivated by the legal minutiae of the O.J. Simpson trial and Clinton impeachment hearings. Films are similarly obsessed with laws and legalism, as exemplified by *Legal Eagles* (1986), *Adam's Rib* (1949), and the series of movies based on John Grisham novels, such as *The Client* (1994) and *A Time to Kill* (1996).

It has been extensively discussed elsewhere that the American press seems to favor advertising and trivialities instead of a passionate examination of current issues (two classic examples are Boorstin, 1978 and Tuchman, 1978). Similarly, the argument is often made of television news that it panders to audience emotions, a phenomenon particularly evident on tabloid news program such as "A Current Affair" (syndicated), "Hard Copy" (syndicated), "American Journal" (syndicated), and "Turning Point" (ABC TV) and many talk shows, such as "Oprah" (syndicated), "Montel Williams" (syndicated), "Sally Jesse Rafael" (syndicated), "Jerry Springer" (syndicated), "Ricki Lake" (syndicated), and others. This style of reporting seems to have a spillover effect, particularly into ratings-conscious local news programs, which increasingly promote and headline tabloid-style stories over traditional hard news. Reality television is primarily about feelings.

Certainly, American feature films and network television programs attempt to deliver a few clear, simple feelings. Contemporary films are often built around a plan to instill one or two emotional states in the audience: to thrill them, make them laugh, or make them cry. Uses and gratifications theory (Berger, 1982) helps explain, in part, the power of this approach: Audiences knowingly consume the media precisely in order to attain emotional states they already desire before seeing the film—they know that *Armageddon* (1998) will thrill them before they see it and know that *Titanic* (1998) will make them cry. Cawelti (1976) argued that this essentially contractual understanding between the makers of popular culture and their audience is the raison d'être of formulaic fiction.

The mistrust of social authority is found less on the television networks than in films. Villains are increasingly crafted in media narratives as corrupt U.S. government officials or even a government-within-the-government, as in *Outbreak* (1995), "The X-Files" (Fox TV) or *The X-Files* (1998); the heroes are portrayed as freedom fighters working against the government. Rather than fanning the flames of social contempt, however, these examples seem more like the fire's reflection on the wall: The David Koresh standoff in Waco, the Freemen secession in Montana, the reassertion of the Republic of Texas, and the bombing of the Oklahoma City federal building bespeak the deep contempt of authority that de Tocqueville observed and that still characterizes an important aspect of American culture.

This suspicion of the government seems to run contrary to the irritable patriotism that de Tocqueville observed, but in fact, they are expressions of the same thing: a ferocious dedication to the idea of "America," but a profound conviction that the government, although democratically elected, does not (and in some cases, cannot) reflect the will of the people. This is, of course, paradoxical: If America is its people, and its people democratically elect a government, how can that government be fundamentally anti-American? Yet, that is the essence of a belief held not only by isolationist reactionaries, but also by many middle-class Americans. Indeed, the Republican, Democratic, and Reform (Perot) Parties all adopted anti-government rhetoric in their 1996 platform out of the belief that a failure to do so would cost votes. Bill Clinton, a Democratic U.S. president, vowed that with his presidency, the era of "Big Government" begun with FDR would be over. It manifests itself in the bivalent sentiments demonstrated in many films, including *Independence Day* (1996). Whereas this film is bluntly patriotic (including flag waving, a lengthy Declaration of Independence speech to a cheering world, a new Monroe Doctrine, and the patriotic reference in the film's title itself), its only human antagonist is a member of the President's cabinet who maintains a deep government secret that cost millions their lives.

de Tocqueville also identified a rhetoric extolling freedom of opinion in the United States, but one constructed within very narrow parameters of tolerance, limitations that act to silence many opinions before they have been uttered. The clearest example of this is the self-censorship resulting from the threat of subsequent punishment created by the first amendment to the U.S. Constitution. Although the U.S. Constitution prohibits prior restraint of any media message except where it poses a clear and present danger, civil law allows anyone who feels that they have been libeled or defamed to seek compensatory and punitive damages. The threat of such suits often structures the nature of what is produced, distributed, and seen: For example, it limited the distribution and recognition, and nearly resulted in the destruction of *Citizen Kane* (1941) and more recently, it delayed an interview with a former tobacco company executive critical of that industry from appearing on "60 Minutes" (CBS TV). The net result of these statutes is that they make lawyers de facto gatekeepers at news and other media organizations, reinforcing American legalism. Audiences feel they have free access to all possible opinions, yet what they actually receive is rather limited.

A preoccupation with commerce and practical matters instead of science, art, or literature can be found everywhere on television, from local news segments on how to choose a good doctor to cooking segments on morning talk shows. The industry calls this *"news you can use."* Even public television, which is ostensibly higher brow than its commercial cousins, remains practical: How-To programs such as "This Old House" (PBS TV), "The Victory Garden" (PBS TV), "Hometime" (PBS TV), "The New Yankee Workshop" (PBS TV), and "Wall Street Week" (PBS TV) far outnumber the ballets and operas it broadcasts. Media texts often have titles that refer to their practicality, such as "Home Improvement" (ABC TV) and *How to Make an American Quilt* (1995).

Commerce is as important as practicality. Indeed, British cultural critic Levy (1995) noted that putting commerce before art is perhaps the single most defining aspect of American media: "Commercials are king, and must be placed in the king's position" (p. 120). Guests on late-night talk shows freely discuss that their sole motivation to appear on the program is to plug (i.e., to promote) a new movie or series. Americans are so aware of and comfortable with the commercial nature of the media that they find humor in it: In *Wayne's World* (1992), for example, Wayne and Garth rapidly display a succession of products and product logos, sophomorically declaring that their movie would never "sell out." Funnier even than their silly hypocrisy is the rather sophisticated hypocrisy of the filmmakers who, by using real products and logos (e.g., Nike) rather than invented ones, manage to fan commerce in the face of the audience even as they make fun of the cinematic practice of doing so. The same is true of television. Boorstin (1978) convincingly argued that Americans not only like television commercials, but also may prefer them to the programs themselves. Certainly, commercials during the Super Bowl or the Atlanta Olympics were awaited with as much expectation as the athletic competition. Even presidential nominating conventions have been turned into infomercials (Kelly, 1996).

The taste for things tangible and real, as opposed to traditional and formal, is embodied in many ways in American audiences and movies. Cohen-Solal (1995) remarked on the American cinema's obsession with gadgets and devices at the expense of history and sociology in her interesting comparison of the simultaneous Paris release of *Jurassic Park* (1993) and the French film *Germinal* (1993); despite excellent reviews, a magnificent cast, and a home-base advantage, *Germinal* lost to *Jurassic Park* at the box office. An interest in things being real is found in the litany of television movies and feature films that claim to be "based on a true story," such as *The Billionaire Boys Club* (NBC TV) and *Dead Man Walking* (1995).

A focus on gratifying the body instead of the mind is evidenced by the visceral intentions of the American cinema and television corpus. Levy (1995) described American television as a form of "worship at the altar of beauty" (p. 122), and programs like "Charlie's Angels" (ABC TV), "Dynasty", "Beverly Hills 90210", "Melrose Place" (Fox TV), and especially "Baywatch" (syndicated TV) make the point well. De Tocqueville declared that Americans cared nothing for tradition; what they admire instead are youth and youth culture. The popularity of plastic surgery among aging Hollywood stars and the near-total absence of elderly characters on television and in the movies are two sides of the same coin.

That American audiences are easy to please has been axiomatic for media scholars and television programmers until quite recently, when a different model of the audience emerged, one that would seem to contradict Tocqueville on this point. The picture of the American audience developed by Bacon-Smith (1992), Fiske (1987), Jenkins (1992), and others reveals an extremely active, engaged, intelligent, and in some cases obsessive group. "Star Trek" fans, or *trekkers* as they call themselves, are the best example of a discerning, difficult to please, and possibly over-the-top audience that contradicts de Tocqueville. This media obsession of American audiences is itself the subject of knowing parody in the media, as in the "Saturday Night Live" (NBC TV) sketch in which William Shatner, the actor who played Captain Kirk on "Star Trek", tells his fans to "get a life," or more darkly, in Stephen King's *Misery* (1987), a novel that bespeaks an author's anxieties about keeping his demanding—even dictatorial—audience happy.

It is essentially true that the American media are self-obsessive, and that Americans are primarily interested in things American. Few non-American protagonists outside the James Bond and Mad Max franchises have much long-term hope for box-office success in the United States, and attempts to create new franchises in feature films based on British television series "The Saint" (1997), "The Avengers" (1998), and "Dr. Who" (Fox TV) failed. Films like *Independence Day* (1996) depict a world in which only Americans have any ideas, wherein other nations are content to await American leadership, and which only the United States can save from annihilation. Foreign films are often entirely remade for American audiences, such as the recreation of the French film *La Cage aux Folles* (1978) as *The Birdcage* (1996) or of *Trois Hommes et un Couffin* (1985) as *Three Men and A Baby* (1987). NBC coverage of the 1996 Olympics in Atlanta, although widely criticized for airing only those events in which the United States won medals, nevertheless garnered record ratings (Lexington, 1996)—apparently, it gave the audiences what they wanted.

Nostalgia is another example of America's inward-looking nature, with Disney serving as the prime example of its potentialities. Disneyworld, for example, reconciles "an ideal past with a real present" (Marin cited in Wilson, 1994, p. 122). Celebration, Florida, Disney's real estate development project, is a hodgepodge of housing and public building styles culled from an idealized sense of the American past more likely to be found in a Disney film than in the historical records: "The buildings seem vaguely familiar, like the sort of small-town architecture that is found across America—or used to be, for this looks, at first glance, like a nineteenth-century downtown, and actually recalls Disneyland's Main Street U.S.A." (Rybczynski, 1996, p. 37).

What, then, can be concluded about American domestic demand for the media using de Tocqueville's observations? Although American audiences are extremely diverse and contradictory, some generalizations are possible (especially because they embrace, embody, and encompass the diverse contradiction). American audiences expect the media to try to please them. They prefer movies and television programs that deliver moral certitude, where good and evil are set in clear contrast and with an important moral lesson to be learned. They accept without question the private ownership of the media for profit making. As a group, they prefer middle-class ideology to be embodied in films and television rather than the alternatives. They need to feel that they have a choice in the media they consume and that protagonists in movies and on television similarly have choices. They find the legal system entertaining. They prefer media that deliver a few clear, simple, predictable feelings to those that deliver complex and confusing ones. They like media that are simultaneously patriotic and critical of authority. They believe in openness and tolerance, but in fact, receive and expect little of it from the media. They have an interest in practical matters. They are accepting of and even have affection for the commercial nature of the media. They like stories in the media to be tangible and ostensibly real. The physical beauty of things and people is important to them. They are sophisticated, discerning, and extremely demanding in what they watch. Finally, they prefer watching programming about America than about other nations.

These are only a few important aspects of the home audience that shape the condition of its demand, however, and their application has been limited. A more contemporary perspective, used in tandem with de Tocqueville's analysis, provides a more comprehensive picture of American home demand. Jean Baudrillard provides such a perspective.

BAUDRILLARD'S AMERICA

French philosopher and sociologist Jean Baudrillard (1988) self-consciously replicated de Tocqueville's methodology and analysis 150 years later with some similarities and some differences. Like the America de Tocqueville observed, Baudrillard's America is conformist (pp. 9, 92); vulgar and banal (pp. 89, 94); self-obsessed to the point of autism (p. 20; this contention is explored more fully in de Certeau, 1984); new (p. 23); pragmatic (p. 75); "factitious," which is to say that "America believes in facts ... in the total credibility of what is done and seen" (p. 85); *materializing*, namely interested in rendering into a physical existence rather than a purely formal one (p. 79); and advertising-oriented: "the American flag itself bears witness ... not as a heroic sign, but as the trademark of a good brand" (p. 86). These all closely coincide with many of de Tocqueville's observations just mentioned.

Yet, Baudrillard (1988) also saw things in America that de Tocqueville did not see, probably because there have been some changes, but also because of the sort of observer Baudrillard was. These other attributes describe an America that is:

- Unpretentious (p. 93).
- Hyperreal (p. 4).
- Obsessed with speed, which leads to emptiness, forgetfulness, superficiality, and pleasure (pp. 5, 6, 8, 10, 53). In some cases, the acceleration is to such a degree that things must be instantaneous (p. 37).
- Primitive (p. 7).
- Spatial: Similar to Turner's (1962) frontier thesis, Baudrillard sees the geography of absence as perhaps the single greatest physical determinant of American cultural identity (pp. 70, 81).
- Abundant (p. 30).
- Ahistorical: "It lives in a perpetual present ... created in the hope of escaping history, of building a utopia sheltered from history" (pp. 76, 80).
- Utopian (p. 90).

These aspects of American culture function in ways rather different from what de Tocqueville described and are each worth examining in detail. They are both a result of and a contributor to American media culture and as such, form further important components of American home demand.

The lack of pretension that Baudrillard observed is in some ways similar to de Tocqueville's observation that in the United States, there is neither a wealth of highly educated people, nor a plague of uneducated ones, but a great mass in the middle. This certainly breeds the sort of anti-intellectualism in the United States that causes George Bush, Michael Dukakis, and Bill Clinton to play down their Ivy League school credentials in a way that a French politician never would. It also leads to television programming and filmmaking that has no pretense of being art, content to reveal itself for the commerce it most certainly is. Whole cable channels are dedicated to 24-hour, tollfree shopping. Infomercials pitch products with only the thinnest veil of being something other than an advertisement. Television broadcasts with any artistic ambition are inevitably relegated to low-rated public television; art films hardly make it to the multiplex.

Hyperreality is of primary interest to Baudrillard (1988) and is his most essential conceptual framework. Media technology and corporate strategy in the 1990s are converging in a way that makes hyperreality increasingly more tangible and omnipresent, in such a way that not only can media fictions pass through to this world, but also that the audience can pass through into the media world. Historical distinctions that have been drawn between the world of storytelling and the real world are increasingly problematic, nowhere more so than in the United States.

At least since Descartes (1641), the dominant paradigm for human interaction with the world has been governed by foundationalist presuppositions that the body and the mind are distinct, that the world is knowable and objectifiable, and it is knowable through subjective processes such as observation and experience. This is now being debated in the natural and social sciences, fueled by the late Kuhn's (1970) observation that scientific inquiry is governed by paradigm and by the *Heisenberg principle* (1958), which argues that the act of observation modifies the thing observed. The Cartesian sense of a real world has become more problematic, less monolithic, and less comforting as a result. Consequently, the term used to describe the unmediated, actual, "authentic" (Jones, 1993), and natural environment will be put in quotation marks (i.e., "real") to signify the tentative nature of the concept itself relative to human models of it, per Kuhn (1970) and Heisenberg (1958).

Nothing has contributed more to this paradigm shift than the American mass media, which have been creating alternative realities since Edison's (1897) first experimental films. As Baudrillard (1983) and others (e.g., Eco, 1986) noted, the media have become so pervasive that they not only challenge, but also supersede the possibility of direct contact between human cognition and actual things, replacing the potential for perceiving "reality" with a succession of simulations instead, a *hyperreality*. This term has both the senses of "above reality" and "excessive reality," as it describes a cultural environment so impregnated by the media that representations come to dominate, obfuscate, and even efface the things they represent. Because *culture* is "the production and circulation of symbolic meaning" (Garnham, 1987) and "TV *is* American culture" (Thorne, citing D. Lavery, 1994, p. 6), the manipulation of hyperreal signs are a major component of postmodern culture. Even organized religion has become hyperreal, with multimedia, feel good, pop-culture churches growing up everywhere (Trueheart, 1996).

The 19th and 20th centuries have seen the coinage of numerous terms to describe the tentative relation between language and the world: the term *impressionism* was used for those works of art that examined the subjective manner in which the objective world is known; Levy (1936) used *surreality* to describe situations in which signifiers are unasserted, unconscious, and unnatural, yet rife with latent meaning, such as in a dream; Barthes (1972) saw myth as the second-level signifier in a first-level sign, one step removed from a natural signifier–signified relationship. Such examinations of the tensions between representation and the thing represented revealed:

> a new awareness of an other, more real world, which was separate from the world we superficially accepted. No object was complete in itself and nothing was what it seemed. The mimetic relationship had been severed ... Today, the referent of the creative act is not an object which mimetically relates to the world and has been materially formed by the standards set by the rules of aesthetic taste; it is the byproduct, in whatever material form, that results from the subjective state of individual creativity itself. (Shottenkirk, 1994, p. 46)

Representations, in other words, are removed from the objects they are purported to represent; Magritte's "Ceci n'est pas une pipe" is a modernist embodiment of this semiotic conundrum (see Foucault, 1982).

Baudrillard's (1983) hyperreality extends this removal of the sign from the subject ad infinitum: For him, media culture created an environment so saturated with signification that signs only signify other signs, with no possibility of connection to the real. Eco's (1986) use of the term *hyperreality* also included a sense of excessiveness that he embodied in the parallel aspects of vivid representations acting not only as "the real thing," but also as somehow "more" (p. 7). Consequently:

> to speak of things that one wants to connote as real, these things must seem real. The "completely real" becomes identified with the "completely fake." Absolute unreality is offered as real presence ... The sign aims to be the thing, to abolish the distinction of the reference, the mechanism of replacement (p. 7).

The signifier not only becomes real, but also steals from the original its claim of authenticity.

Whether we accept Baudrillard's or Eco's definition, it is clear that American cinema and broadcasting, in particular, are hyperreal in their constant recapitulation of familiar tropes. New successful films and television programs are often recombinations of old successful ones:

> A film like *Raiders of the Lost Ark* is a condensation of all the adventure films, whereas *Dallas* articulates the western, the soap opera and the family saga. In its time, the educational series *Sesame Street*, which appeared on most of the world's television screens, skillfully relaunched the aesthetic, programme styles and formats overwhelmingly experienced in commercial television. (Mattelart et al., 1984, p. 95)

Independence Day (1996) is another good example of this hyperreal recombination. Its plot line, characters, and sets are a veritable catalog of science fiction films, including gooey antagonists (from *Alien*, 1979), surprising side effects of alien surgery (from *The Thing*, 1982), a gung-ho kamikaze American (from *Dr. Strangelove*, 1963), space-age aerial dogfights (from *Star Wars*, 1977), friendly and troublemaking computer software (from *2001: A Space Odyssey*, 1968), and human victory thanks to unforeseen infection (from *War of the Worlds*, 1953), with characters from non-genre films, such as *An American President* (1995), thrown in for those with shorter memories or other generic tastes.

Hyperrealism is a tangible and popular manifestation of postmodernism (Olson, 1987). The extent to which postmodernism serves the commodification of culture has been well-documented (Jameson, 1991; Lyotard, 1984). The hyperreal aspect of postmodernism has occasionally been examined as a contribution to commodification (Baudrillard, 1981, 1987), but not so far as it contributes to the exportability of American media. Disney is perhaps the company that best exemplifies these American attributes. As Wilson (1994) noted,

> the object is to transform the product—or in this case the corporate image—into a symbol of particular cultural values or norms. With Disney, such values are easy to identify: patriotism, family life, and free enterprise, together with the corporate logo, form the story of the inexorable triumph of American society. (p. 126)

Hyperreality and postmodernism, overlapping cultural phenomena, together define, in a way few other concepts do, a *fin-de-siècle* America and as such, American home demand for the media.

Another of Baudrillard's descriptors of the American audience is its obsession with speed. This is true to such a strong extent that there is even a film titled *Speed* (1995). The instantaneousness of American culture frequently perplexes international visitors. Born in part of their love affair with automobiles, many Americans do not like to queue, want to get their meal a few moments after they order it, and want to eat it in their car while driving to work, play, or shopping.

Of course, this need for speed manifests itself in the relationship between audiences and their media. Frozen TV dinners, common in the 1950s and 1960s, were perhaps the first expression of increasing time spent with the television by saving time somewhere else; of course now, in many households, every meal is spent watching television, because there is a television in many kitchens now. Many movie theaters allow the purchase of tickets in advance from home by the telephone. Pay-per-view options on cable television save viewing time by allowing viewers to avoid a trip to the video store or theater. This is even evident in computer media, where single speed CD-ROM drives are quickly outdistanced by double speed, quad speed, 8x, 24x, and then DVD drives. All of these social phenomena are mirrored by the ever-faster pacing of Hollywood feature films, particularly action films. Films more than 20 years old are frequently accelerated by as much as 20% when shown on American television to better suit the attention span and pacing expectations of modern audiences (and to make room for more commercials). One of the by-products of such speed is forgetfulness (Baudrillard, 1988), which in turn contributes to the nostalgia previously discussed and the ahistoricism that is later discussed.

Primitivity is another trait of the American cultural landscape according to Baudrillard (1988). By this, he meant that there is a fundamental barbarism to the structure of American social interaction. This is obviously visible in the level of violence frequently found in popular American films, a level matched only perhaps by certain action films from Hong Kong. Republican presidential candidate Bob Dole praised the healthy American values displayed in films like *True Lies* (1994), an action film with a huge body count and abundant carnage. In the debate about appropriate programming for television, greater concern is expressed in America about exposure to sexual material than to violence—the exact opposite of complaints is found in Europe. The appetite for violence found in the media is also manifest in politics, where in many states a strong support for capital punishment is a *sine qua non* for every candidate.

America has a lot of space, and Baudrillard (1988) would agree with Turner (1962) that such space is a defining element of American culture. In fact, Baudrillard saw the geography of absence as perhaps the single greatest physical determinant of American cultural identity. The relation between space and the American media audience is manifest in several ways, most having to do with distance or scale. Multiplex theaters are often far away from urban centers, placed instead out near exurban strip malls that go on almost indefinitely. This necessitates the use of a car to get there, which in turn necessitates gigantic parking lots. The multiplex itself is often huge, both in terms of its lobby and number of screens. American cable television similarly has enormous space, in most cases 60 or 70 channels, with the promise of hundreds more very soon. The love of open spaces manifests itself as well in the genres Americans developed and prefer, particularly the Western. Slotkin (1992) showed that the Western genre remains to be one of the defining aspects of American culture.

Such open space is closely related to the abundance that Baudrillard (1988) also observed in the United States. America's wealth is not what it was in the years following World War II, but the sense of plenty—manifest most explicitly in the American holiday of Thanksgiving—still shapes American culture. The wealth displayed on television programs like "Beverly Hills 90210" reinforce the sense of abundance that is also manifest in the preference for gas-guzzling cars, the continued growth of casinos, and the success of state lotteries and Powerball. Abundance also leads to excessive consumption and waste.

Another thing wasted is history. Baudrillard (1988) called the United States ahistorical because "it lives in a perpetual present … created in the hope of escaping history, of building a utopia sheltered from history" (pp. 76, 80). A desire to escape history can be a powerful motivator in the arts and business: In *Ulysses* (Joyce, 1961), for example, Stephen Dedalus tells his headmaster that "history is a nightmare from which I am trying to awake" (p. 34). Due both to its geography and national consciousness, America has avoided having this nightmare.

The Walt Disney Company attempted, perhaps unsuccessfully, to capitalize on American ahistoricism by planning to build an American history theme park called Disney American History near Washington, D. C. The park was intended to teach Americans about their own history, while entertaining them as well. Criticism from Civil War scholars concerned about the park's proximity to historical sites led Disney to shelve the project. Yoshimoto (1994) called Disney's brand of history "packaged history" (p. 186). Perhaps a better term for the American relationship with history is not so much "ahistorical," but "heritable," oriented to heritage—declaring faith in the past rather than accounting for or ignoring it (Jenkyns, 1998).

The last of the American attributes identified by Baudrillard (1998), *utopianism*, is enduring even in the face of postmodernity, although usually utopianism and the postmodern zeitgeist are incompatible. Certainly, one of the most significant expressions of American utopianism is its enduring belief that it is an ethnic, religious, and racial melting pot, or at worst a salad bowl—the tension between these two metaphors is explored in films like *Higher Learning* (1994) and *Lone Star* (1996), which although critical of racial intolerance, remain nevertheless optimistic about diversity serving as a solution rather than a problem. *E pluribus unum*. America's diversity cannot be disputed and the film industry was shaped and built largely by immigrants (Wasser, 1995). Ethnic and national diversity, brought about through immigration, slavery, an indigenous population, and domestic birth trends, is a significant aspect of American home demand for media texts. In fact, American media were themselves the by-product of and response to this diversity from the beginning:

> Very early in its history, the United States was confronted with the problem of unifying its population of immigrants and various ethnic groups. This problem, which had haunted it since the Civil War, was to find its solution in mass culture. The comic book, then the western and now TV series like Kojak and Dallas have powerfully contributed to weld Americans into a nation. (Mattelart et al., 1984, p. 99)

As a state that is not (or was not) really a nation in an ethnic or linguistic sense, the United States gave rise to a practical solution, a way of defining what America was and is, and in a Foucaultian (1965) sense, these images would be absorbed and accepted by the people and enacted by them as its agents.

Utopianism is also exhibited in the American attempt to build from scratch perfect communities, an ancient European dream unrealized and abandoned there. Walt Disney was a futurist and utopian, and his ultimate vision of the future is now manifesting in the Disney company's aforementioned real-estate development project, Celebration. Whether Celebration fulfills its promise remains to be seen:

> ... much of the public assumes—or at least hopes—that a Disney town will be a perfect town. "It's one of my fears," says Todd Mansfield [executive Vice President of Disney Imagineering], who is himself going to build a house in Celebration. "We have people who have purchased houses who think they're moving to Utopia." (Rybczynski, 1996, p. 39)

In its unbridled postmodernism, the Walt Disney company differs from über–modernist Walt Disney in many ways; Celebration is, for the company, less an experiment in social engineering than a cheap, effective, and efficient development of land near Disneyworld that was unsuitable for theme park uses. Yet, for its settlers, Celebration holds the naive promise of a community free of social strife, a quest as old as the American Revolution.

To sum up, Baudrillard (1988) added several dimensions to the America that de Tocqueville described. For Baudrillard, American audiences lack pretense; live in a hyperreal environment; crave speed; enjoy primitive (even barbaric) forms of entertainment; are accustomed to open space and abundance; lack a historical memory or historical outlet on human affairs, especially their own; and believe that America can be, and maybe has been, a utopia. These factors combine with the ones de Tocqueville identified to give a more-or-less comprehensive image of the unique, defining attributes of American audiences compared to audiences in other parts of the world from a cultural studies perspective. This is by no means a comprehensive list; indeed, in defining a culture, the adjectives are infinite. America has numerous cocultures that exist in and around it as well and as many interpretive communities as there are television programs. These generalities form the starting point for considering a few aspects of American home demand that reach across many audiences and their reception patterns. In order to understand American competitive advantage in the film and television industries, it is important to see how these attributes of home demand affect the process of manufacturing the media.

HOME-DEMAND CONDITIONS

That the American audience for media products is in some ways different from other international audiences has been established. A question remains, however: How do these demand conditions shape the American media text in a way that gives the United States competitive advantage in the film and television industry using Porter's (1990, 1998) methodology?

de Tocqueville's and Baudrillard's lists can be synthesized into a single composite image, depicting an audience composed of members who are morally certain, middle brow, individualistic, legalistic, mistrusting of authority yet patriotic, practical, actively engaged with the media, self-obsessed, hyperreal, primitive, ahistorical, utopian, and who crave speed, open space, and abundance. The synthesis also reveals a media system that promotes private property, embraces advertising and commercialism, and extols yet constrains free speech. If America's second most important export product is its popular culture, these attributes are in part the source of the same sort of comparative advantage that state-of-the-art factories provide the automobile industry.

These factors confer competitive advantage. Porter (1990) said that home demand confers an advantage when it is large enough to be a significant part of the world market, when it is advanced or sophisticated in a way that leads to a desirable differentiation of the product, and/or when it anticipates or creates international demand. Home demand that does all three of these can be a source of considerable strength, and the American audience for media products actually provides an advantage in each of these three ways. It is a large audience, a significant percent of world market share, and it has a voracious appetite for the media—Americans watch a great deal of television in particular. There is sufficient economy of scale in the home market alone to generate a huge amount of movies and television for strictly internal demand.

The attributes that define the American audience, and that it wants to see manifested in its media, differentiate American films and television from other national media products. Differentiation means that American films do not look like French, Indian, or Brazilian films because the audience is looking for something else. *Raiders of the Lost Ark* (1981) is a good case study in how films produced in the United States are differentiated because of the audience. The moral certitude of American films, the extent to which the good guys and bad guys are clearly contrasted, differentiates them, to some extent, from the majority of European films; the Indiana

Jones films use Nazis as their villains in one attempt to polarize the moral nature of characters in the films. The individualism and self-reliance that audiences like to see in themselves is also exhibited in American films to a degree that differentiates them from other national cinemas; this is shown by Indiana Jones' boundless resourcefulness and ability to survive calamitous circumstances.

Other audience–text traits also differentiate the American text. The legalism or rule-following that interests American culture is found in the *Raiders of the Lost Ark* (1981) in the combating ethical codes of archeological exploration practiced by Jones and Belloq; rather than focusing on ambiguity, as might a European film, the American film is interested in right and wrong. Patriotism laced with questioning authority must seem a curiosity to international audiences, but even the all-American Indiana Jones succumbs to a secret government plot at the conclusion, as the Ark of the Covenant is relegated by disingenuous government bureaucrats to a cavernous vault. One would think the self-obsession of the American media would put off international audiences and to some extent it does, particularly with news programming; on the other hand, in fiction programming, it manifests itself as cocky self-assurance on the part of protagonists like Indiana Jones, a trait that some—particularly adolescents—find attractive. The primitive violence in films like *Raiders of the Lost Ark* also holds appeal for adolescent males around the world, a group sometimes known as *global teenagers* (Baker, 1989). The Indiana Jones movies are profoundly ahistorical, coopting historical places and people to fit into the fantastic narrative thread, such as when Hitler autographs Indiana Jones' map of the location of the Holy Grail at a Berlin Nazi rally in *Indiana Jones and The Last Crusade* (1989); such postmodern reinvention must seem a relief to some members of the international audience and a travesty to others. The ability of Indiana Jones to singlehandedly defeat fascism is an embodiment of a utopian ideal, the dawn of a better world, and although international audiences might be skeptical about the likelihood of that happening, they might nonetheless find its fictional realization interesting. Finally, the desire for speed (the rolling stone ball), the frontier (rapaciously borrowing from movie Westerns), and abundance (the golden Ark itself) combine with the other elements for a film that could only come from Hollywood.

Differentiation is not enough, however; it must be a differentiation that international audiences want. This brings up the third of Porter's (1990) criteria connecting home demand to international advantage: The American audience must, in some ways, anticipate and, in other ways, shape interternational demand for film and television programs. Because films like *Raiders of the Lost Ark* (1981) are squarely aimed at the great middle of American culture, they find the middle class of other cultures as well; it is there, perhaps, that the greatest similarities between cultures exists. The hyperreal and active engagement of American audiences with media texts encourages filmmakers to be ever more clever and postmodern in their constructions, keeping a step ahead of others. The love of private property, advertising, and commercialism in the American media anticipate the continual international erosion of national broadcasting systems in favor of American-style broadcasting. In some cases, and in some countries, the very Americanness of the media text might be part of its appeal (e.g., American films in Poland or Japan), although this can just as easily work against it in other countries (American films in Iran or France, perhaps).

Scale, differentiation, and anticipation are nowhere stronger in the United States than in the utopianism of its ethnic diversity—the *e pluribus unum* it boasts of on its currency. The United States is, for the most part, a nation of willing or forced immigrants, native Americans being the notable exception, and has treated some immigrant groups poorly throughout its history and even to this day (e.g., a 1996 federal law denying legal immigrants access to social services). Regardless of how the United States has treated immigrants, however, the fact remains that it is diverse. This pluralism has been seen, rhetorically at least, as a source of strength, most recently through multicultural education in the public schools. It has also been a source of conflict. What it ultimately means for the media, however, is that the American audience brings with its expectations for movies and television many different ethnic, religious, linguistic, and social backgrounds, and in many cases, no common history. If the media are to find a large audience, they must cater to as multicultural an audience as possible. Consequently, the media must pare down narratives to their essentials. This yields films and television programs that may look simple, but are, in fact, quite sophisticated: They are capable of conveying meaning to very different people. That is a significant differentiation and a powerful anticipation of international markets that are, obviously, also diverse.

Although the American home audience creates a demand that anticipates and mimics international demand, a few words about those diverse non-American audiences are needed. Generally, they prefer indigenous film and particularly television to the American variety: "Audiences in Europe—and around the world—prefer their own national entertainment in their own language" (Tunstall, 1995). Although they prefer homegrown media to U.S. media, the problem is there is not enough of that variety to satisfy demand, either in the number or order of magnitude that the American media do. So, although the American media are sometimes the first choice, they are usually the second, but—importantly—they are everyone's second choice; when the domestic first choice is either Swedish, Polish, or Nigerian, being everyone's next choice makes for a gigantic market share.

Every audience, then, is different; the American audience's difference helps confer, in part, an advantage. It is the basis of American home demand, an important consideration in explaining its home-base advantage in the moviemaking and television production, but a nature that Porter (1990) neglected to examine in such detail, for this or any other industry. The relation between the American audience and the American media text just discussed shows that their relation is symbiotic, creating a desirable differentiation and an anticipation of international demand. The mechanism that allows these texts to speak so convincingly to so many different audiences, as discussed in chapter 1, is *transparency*—a process that makes certain texts seem indigenous in many different cultural situations. Ultimately, it is in transparency that all the demand factors create a transportable media text. By virtue of its ethnic diversity, the U.S. media product is differentiated and anticipatory.

This observation yields several questions. What does such diversity look like in a text itself? What allows a text to welcome diverse readings? What, in short, is the mechanism of transparency? How does it take a product that has been differentiated to suit the U.S. audience and make it seem familiar and meaningful to audiences from very different cultures? To answer these questions requires a close examination of the American media product itself, the transparent text. Therein lies the most salient aspect of American competitive advantage in the film and television industry: how the culture factory creates international desire for a Hollywood planet.

5

The Transparent Text

In the end, it's all a bunch of stories, and you can pick the one you want.
— President of the Disney Development Company
(cited in Klein, 1993, p. 253)

The culture factory produces a transparent text. This is a product of the connection between the home-base demand of diverse American audiences and the American media texts themselves, of how attributes of those audiences lead to films and to television programs that are differentiated from other media and anticipatory of international demand. How do these same media actually connect to those international audiences who view them? The relation between text and audience is different outside the United States than within—indeed, it is different in every case. Each audience has its own reception. Looking carefully at the transparency of the differentiated text reveals how those manifold receptions are made possible.

It was established in chapter 1 that media texts perform some of the functions of myth and are often treated as myth (Barthes, 1972). Myths satisfy human needs. These needs are universal and are themselves the deep structure of all myths, forming a system of affective expectation and fulfillment called a *mythotype*. There is a special relation between myth and the process of communication; "throughout history, one chief function of writing systems has been to guard and transmit sacred knowledge" (Harris, 1995, p. 20). Sacred knowledge is now primarily written through film and television. The media currently satisfy some of the needs that myths have satisfied in the past. Some movies and television programs are particularly adept at manifesting affective mythotypes, and the manner in which they do so can be cataloged.

So, just as myths gratify human needs, so does television. Myths are not quite the same thing as television, of course, but they do perform a number of similar functions. The more elemental the need satisfied by television and movies, the more mythic they seem. Popular media satisfy needs that correspond to the needs satisfied by myth; this is what makes them popular. The most popular of these enable the satisfaction of elemental needs by allowing those needs to be satisfied in a manner that replicates and resembles the traditional path to satisfaction; that is to say, they look like indigenous myths to the indigenous population. They are transparent.

Garnham (1984) noted that "cultural [imperialism], like economic imperialism, works through the specificities of the local power structure" (p. 5). This certainly accounts for the power of the media, but does not address how they enact this amazing transformation: How is it possible for an imported media program from one culture to insinuate itself into the specific local exigencies of the many other cultures into which it goes? It is not possible for it to address each of those exigencies in particular, which would require an absurd level of research on the producer's part and would lead to an internally contradictory and incoherent text. Rather, something inherent in the nature of the textuality of these films and television programs enables them to mutate and attach themselves to local traditions and beliefs. The transparent text has characteristics that allow other cultures to project into it subjective, indigenous, mythic meaning.

The relation between human needs and mythic satisfaction has been extensively studied. Separate from this body of literature on myth, the relation between needs and the media has also been studied. There are many similarities, which is not surprising: The breadth of human psychological needs can be reduced to a short list of categories. These needs can be gratified in a number of ways, but certain modes of gratification predominate. Given the eternality of myth and the ubiquity of media, it is not surprising that these are two of the primary methods by which human needs are satisfied.

The name most associated with the study of human psychological needs is Maslow (1970). His familiar hierarchy suggests that the needs we all have come in levels and that we do not require our sophisticated needs to be fulfilled until our basic needs are met. These needs are formed in a hierarchy in such a way that as the needs of one level are satisfied, the needs of the next level—previously not recognized—manifest themselves.

Maslow's (1970) seven levels of need are as follows:

1. *Physiological needs*, such as food, water, and protection from the climate.
2. *Safety, security, and stability*—a sense that one need not be constantly fearful for one's life and livelihood.

3. *Belonging and love*, emotions that connect one to other people and make one feel a part of something bigger than oneself.

4. *Esteem*, the ability to respect and appreciate oneself.

5. *Self-actualization* or the sense and ability that one controls one's own destiny and may become what one wants to be.

6. *The need for knowledge and understanding*—a curiosity about why things are as they are and an ability to systematize what has been learned.

7. *Aesthetic needs*, the need for beauty to be realized through the appreciation of art and music.

Before one can progress to a higher order level of need, one must satisfy the needs of the lower orders: For example, one cannot need belonging and love, according to Maslow, until one feels safe, and one cannot need esteem until one feels a sense of belonging. As these needs become more sophisticated, note that they become harder to satisfy. Self-esteem, for example, can be elusive due to reasons beyond the tangible and rational.

Although it was not Maslow's (1970) intention to connect them, these needs can be linked to narrative meaning; in other words, stories and myths can, in part, satisfy human psychological needs. For example, the need for belonging can be satisfied by nationalist myths and the need for love can be satisfied by soap operas and formula romances. Myths and stories cannot usually satisfy a physical need, but they appear to satisfy psychological ones. The uses and gratifications approach to the mass media can be seen as an elaboration of Maslow's hierarchy and an examination of how these needs are satisfied by a particular form of narrative meaning the television program. Berger (1982), for example, delineated some 24 different needs that the media satisfy, including the needs for amusement, distraction, identity, and justice.

The question of whether these needs are satisfied on a culture-specific basis, or whether they have some measure of universality, is seldom addressed, as is the question of how a single media text might satisfy different needs in different cultural contexts. The difference between a single culture and the common human experience is the difference between myth and mythotype.

MYTH AND MYTHOTYPE

Myths may be useful for analyzing human interaction with narrative in a particular cultural tradition, but they are of limited use in analyzing the international success of certain media narratives because myth is culture-specific. Another concept is necessary to account for, say, the global popularity of *Jurassic Park* (1993); it is not enough to say that this film is meaningful because it displaces certain Western myths because these myths are either unknown or insignificant in many parts of the world where the film was successful.

Yet, myth has its utility in analyzing meaning in a text. Perhaps most significant in this regard is Barthes (1972), who explored the extent to which contemporary cultures mythologize media texts, superheroes, laundry detergent, and other modern archaeologies. For Barthes, *myth* is a type of speech, an utterance that exists within a language system so as to appropriate meaning from the signified and distort it so that it serves to legitimize the system of which it is a part. Consequently, myth for Barthes is not a subject matter, but a manner of speaking. This is significant for the discussion here because it disconnects myth from its traditional sense as a religious system not shared by its critical observer and replaces it with the semiotic sense that mythology continues to surround and involve modern and postmodern cultures through advertising, marketing, broadcasting, and other iconic forms. Barthes is not interested in the differences mythologies might exhibit in different cultures, however.

Fiske (1987) was more interested than was Barthes in the particular cultural and subcultural effects of the contemporary media environment. He used the methods of both Barthes (1972) and Lévi-Strauss (1964) to examine the narrative structure and ideology of American television, connecting it to the Western mythic tradition. Ultimately, this approach does not explain the more subtle yet transnational effects of the mass media. Certainly, Western narrative archetypes guide the production of scripts and program in Hollywood—how could they not, given that the producers there were raised within these narratives? Yet, why would a Western narrative necessarily speak to a non-Western member of its audience, someone who might be unfamiliar with the narratology, archetypes, and iconography a Westerner takes for granted? Aesop's fables may be unfamiliar to a Parsi. The vast popularity of American media indicates that some other, more universal factor must be operating, something not Western but human. Barthes and Fiske did not give much direction as to what that might be.

Blumenberg (1985) did, however. His work on myth provided the best window through which to see the human needs behind the Western narrative, or behind any narrative, and in doing so, established the building blocks of myth. His subject was what humans want and need from myth that makes myth so persistent, even in the face of the Enlightenment, modernity, and compulsory education. Whereas for Barthes (1972) and Fiske (1987) myth was situated in language, for Blumenberg, myth is affect.

Affect is universal, even if particular myths are not; that which humans seek from myth is similar across the human experience, but the satisfaction of their emotional quest takes different forms, all culturally coded. The needs that myths address, then, are shared by different cultures, even if the myths are culturally unique. Underneath the labels given to dramatis personae, settings, narrative structure, and voice, myths are all the same in their purpose: They manifest representations of and resolutions to the same human affective needs. They are uniquely able to do this because:

> Myths are stories that are distinguished by a high degree of constancy in their narrative core and by an equally pronounced capacity for marginal variation. These two characteristics make myths transmissible by tradition: their constancy produces the attraction of recognizing them in artistic or ritual representation as well [as in recital], and their variability produces the attraction of trying out new and personal means of presenting them. (Blumenberg, 1985, p. 34)

Within a cultural tradition, myths can have a long life because their relatively simple component of constancy lends itself to continue adoption, co-option, and variation.

These manifestations and resolutions are called *mythotypes* because they are the needs that undergird all mythology and the architecture of human longing at its most elemental. Mythotypes are not the same as Joseph Campbell's *monomyths* (Campbell, 1949; Carroll, 1993); Campbell feels there are universal mythic narratives common to all cultures, but a mythotype suggests no such universality because it is a priori myth itself. The notion that specific myths are universal is obviously contentious, but the argument presented here does not rely on any such condition.

The notion of mythotype is roughly equivalent to Swadesh's theory of universal lexical concepts (Miller, 1991). Swadesh, a linguist, argued that whatever forms language might take, certain essential concepts always need expression. As such, these concepts find their way into every human language, although the manifestation they take is of course subject to all of the factors that make languages around the world different and distinct: diffusion, linguistic and cultural evolution, assimilation, and so forth. Swadesh postulated that such concepts as *I, thou, we, this, person, big,* and others would be expressible in all human languages, and empirical research has largely confirmed his hypothesis. Mythotypes are similar to these universal lexicals: They find some mode of expression in all human cultures, but the particulars of that manifestation are culture-specific.

Mythotypes have only a few simple elements. For Blumenberg (1985), the most basic of these is what he calls:

> The absolutism of reality. What it means is that man [sic] came close to not having control of the conditions of his existence and, what is more important, believed that he simply lacked control of them. It may have been earlier or later that he interpreted this circumstance of the superior power of what is (in each case) other [i.e., not himself] by assuming the existence of superior powers. (pp. 3–4)

Humans need to resist the absolutism of reality, to deny their lack of control, and myth satisfies this need well.

The absolutism of reality is the sense in each person that he or she lacks "control of the conditions of his [or her] existence" (Blumenberg, 1985, p. 4). This is a horrifying prospect, one that needs to be resisted and negated. There are two ways to resist this horror: One is to assert personal agency and control; the other is to attribute control to a superior power that acts on behalf of human interest. Myths can accomplish both of these tasks and limit the absolutism of reality because they "convert numinous indefiniteness into nominal definiteness" (p. 25)—the randomness, the chaos, and the disinterest of the universe are given structure, coherence, predictability, and meaning.

How does myth accomplish this? Myth is affective or rather it conveys a particular set of affective responses, ones that are conducive to negating the absolutism of reality. As Wilhelm Wundt said, "Myth is affect converted into idea and action" (cited in Blumenberg, 1985, p. 20); culture results from the particular forms this conversion creates. Most aspects of mythology are culture-specific, but the affective responses myth encourages are essentially universal. These emotional states are relatively few, and include the following:

1. *Awe*, a combination of reverence, admiration, and fear: To put it colloquially, it is a belief that "there are things which are bigger than you."
2. *Wonder*, the ability to marvel at uncanny occurrences and eternal questions: "this world is amazing." As Blumenberg (1985) noted, "Myth itself is composed of wonderful things" (p. 26).

3. *Purpose*, a sense of personal significance: "Your life has meaning, and nothing happens without a reason."
4. *Joy*, a delight in goodness: "You can be jubilant and find pleasure in the beauty and virtue of this world."
5. *Participation*, the sense that one belongs to something important in which one is an active agent: "This world needs your help."

In other words, mythotype encompasses those narrative structures designed to inspire awe, wonder, purpose, joy, and participation, hence denying the absolutism of reality. Particular cultures superimpose onto these affective intentions the specific plots, characters, settings, and interpretive codes that we have come to know as myths, but beneath that veneer, these affects remain essential ingredients in so far as they seek to negate human lack of control over nature and existence. Whereas myths cannot be universal, these affective intentions inevitably are; they are not myths, but mythotypes.

MORPHOLOGY OF THE MYTHOTYPE

Within any particular culture, the mythotype manifests itself as myth because it has been given a plot, dramatis personae, a dominant decoding, and other things necessary for it to be intelligible and meaningful in a local sense. This is itself a kind of displacement, from latent emotional intention to mythic manifestation. A further displacement occurs when these myths are reconstituted as elite or popular culture: the Pyramus and Thisbe myth within Shakespeare's *Romeo and Juliet*, the Odyssey within *Ulysses* (Joyce, 1961), or the Arthurian cycle within *Star Wars* (1977).

This notion that the media convey myth has been widely asserted (Barthes, 1972; Fiske, 1987; Kaminsky, 1974). This is unsurprising: As just shown, myths exist to enable personal resistance to the absolutism of reality, and because the media similarly satisfy elemental human needs, they have a myth-like function and appearance of necessity. Frequently, movies and television programs will be direct displacements of well-known myths, but even when they do not invoke a particular myth directly, the invocation of affective mythotype (e.g., joy, awe, and wonder) is frequently present. The morphology of the folktale has been documented (Propp, 1968), as have the many ways myths have been displaced. Unfortunately, this is as far as most media criticism has gone.

Yet, this can be done for the mythotype as well: The morphology of mythic satisfaction can also be cataloged. To do so is to identify the architecture of the mythotype, the mechanism of transparency itself. Although movies and television are too diverse to replicate the sort of detailed morphology found in Propp (1968), there have been some attempts to categorize the mythic archetypes found there. Barthes (1972) laid out a rhetoric of contemporary Western bourgeois myth, which is nearly synonymous with the media. His system included *inoculation*, the prevention of subversion through acknowledgment of small institutional evils; *the privation of history*, subjugating it to mythic abstraction; *identification*, the objectification of the Other; *tautology*, the rationalization of causality; *"neither-norism"*, resisting choice by rejecting options; *the quantification of quality*, the projection of materiality and empiricism onto that which is ephemeral; and *the statement of fact*, which is the rending of all narrative into proverb and aphorism (pp. 150–154).

Genre analysis helps demonstrate the sort of morphologies found in American film and television. Pye (1986) described the morphological structure of the cinematic western. Yacowar (1986) documented the archetypal forms of the disaster genre. Kawin (1986) characterized the structural differences between science fiction and horror. In examining how these iconic genres function, it becomes clear that their work is in many ways analogous to the role of myths in traditional cultures; this is especially clear when the genre critic uses one of Lévi-Strauss's structural approaches.

The cataloging of the media's mythic archetypes is a different process than developing a morphology of transparency, however, because transparency is mythotypic, not mythic per se. Most of the structural approaches to media textuality, however, consider only the mythic dimension, which privileges certain cultural readings while denying the polysemic possibility of others. What is needed is an analysis of media textuality from a mythotypic rather than mythological standpoint.

To do so is to systematize the narratological devices and apparatuses of the media from an affective perspective, opening the texts up to diverse mythotypic readings rather than closing them off to particular mythic ones. It is possible to identify the following general attributes of movies and television that exhibit a fairly direct embodiment of mythotype: openendedness, virtuality, negentropy, circularity, ellipticality, archetypal dramatis personae, inclusion, verisimilitude, omnipresence, and production values. These are the specific devices through which mythotypes are conveyed, so each is an apparatus of transparency. Some texts use these, others do not. Those that do are transparent.

Openendedness

An openended narrative is one that has no end. Most narratives close themselves off at their conclusion, settling their characters into a resolution of the plot that needs no further embellishment. A vivid example of such a closed-narrative apparatus is " … and they lived happily ever after," which insists on no further elaboration. Openended narratives, to the contrary, insist on further iteration. Almost every narrative, however, resolves at least some of the narrative threads that run through it.

By design, serial and episodic television is openended: Each installment of a series raises its own problems, which may or may not be resolved, but the plot leaves the viewer with the explicit potential for further narrative recitation at another time in the future. This is particularly true of American network television, where a money-making series franchise stays on the air for years and years with no greater narrative closure than the weekly resolution of episodic predicaments. For example, the popular television program "Cheers" (NBC TV) produced 22 episodes a year for 11 years; at the end of each episode, the implied future narrative remained open to all the same possibilities it had possessed all along: The characters and setting remained for the most part unchanged, ready to manifest another openended narrative next week, next month, next year. Even the supposedly conclusive final episode left open the possibility for subsequent narrative development, and generally speaking, it is only the final episode of an American television series where any closure, however remote, is possible. American soap operas are probably the most like Scheherazade's example of narratives without end: Some have been on the air for 20 years, broadcasting 260 hour-long episodes each of those years, creating a single narrative that can be 5,000 hours long (and counting). Even "Dallas," whose final episode concluded with the apparent suicide of J.R., was reopened in occasional CBS TV movie specials with J.R. restored to good health.

To a lesser degree, motion pictures are also capable of openendedness. Some movie franchises are particularly well-suited to subsequent enunciation by design: James Bond, Pink Panther, and Police Academy franchises are examples. These have survived cast changes, increased competition, social transformation, and other obstacles. Because sequels are expected to generate about two thirds of the revenue of their predecessor, there is some incentive to produce movies with at least the possibility of regeneration. In some cases, reiteration can be much more lucrative: *Goldeneye* (1995) was the most financially successful of all the Bond films despite being seventeenth in the series.

Openendedness enhances the mythic qualities of the media by addressing the mythotype. The mythotype is always open itself—there is always the sense of an "ever after." This encourages the sense of participation common in mythic systems. Because the text has no end, the spectator has a continuous obligation to return to the program, either that or no closure for either text or reader is possible. Participation results because "an audience's acquired stock of knowledge gives it a competence in reading inflections and innuendoes and in particular narratives which are not specifically articulated, but rely on the 'memory' of the program" (Tulloch & Alvarado, 1983, p. 30). Because television shows and some movies rely on repetition to remain openended, the habitual audience member participates in a code unavailable to less frequent viewers. This fan audience revels in the openendedness of the text so much so that they themselves participate in elaborating on it, making use of copyrighted characters and their own imagination to create and circulate homemade scripts and stories that constitute their own episodes of the narrative (Bacon-Smith, 1992). They are able to do this because the narrative itself is openended, and so permits nearly infinite permutations.

Virtuality

Virtuality is another way that the visual media connect an audience to affective mythotypes. The term *virtual reality* is used by most writers to mean *cyberreality*: a computer-generated artificial world (Rheingold, 1991), a digital synthetic reality, or telepresence (Steuer, 1992). The capability of computers to do this is relatively new, but *virtual reality*—the creation of a psychologically convincing, electronically simulated environment—is not new. Television has been creating virtual reality for years, as radio did before it (Jones, 1993).

Evidence for the long-standing duration of virtual reality in the mass media can be easily found. The separation anxiety many felt when "M*A*S*H" (CBS TV) went off the air is just one example: This sitcomedic fictional family had become more real to many viewers than their own family. The psychological effects basis for and consequences of surrogate, personal communities created by television have been extensively examined (Kubey & Czisktemaholy, 1990; Liebert & Sprafkin, 1988; Meyrowitz, 1985).

Serials or episodic series with a continuing cast of dependable characters encourage hyperreal relations with the audience because of the intimacy they seem to offer. The line between virtual and unmediated realities is further confused by reality programs like: "Cops" (Fox TV), "Rescue 911" (NBC TV), and "The Real World" (MTV). Such programs present themselves as unmediated records of the natural environment, as antisimulations. This is deceptive: Editing, camera angle, gatekeeping, and other factors create semiotic environments with meaning as asserted as in any fiction. "The Real World" has a particularly fantastical distance from its eponymous signified: A handful of 20-something roommates are selected for their dramatic potential from hundreds of applicants, are assembled together in an urban apartment laden with video cameras and microphones, and live their lives under an electronic glare, waiting to see how well the Neilsen families like them. That several of these real people have gone on to become media celebrities themselves, mostly on MTV, belies the extent to which this reality has been contrived.

Even when the media-generated world is clearly fantastical, the line between it and the world of everyday experience is blurred or, as Gabler (1998) observed, people come to see themselves as media characters and their lives as movies. "Star Trek" is probably the best example of a synthetic reality, insinuating itself into human behavior and beliefs, its followers among the most ardent in collecting merchandise and memorabilia from the show and participating in its narrative thread through clubs and online chat rooms. Other media realities that have similarly asserted themselves on the other side of the screen include "Twin Peaks" (ABC TV; see Jenkins, 1994), "Alien Nation" (Fox TV), and numerous soap operas. In this model, the audience is seen as active (Morley, 1993), another example of poaching (de Certeau, 1984; Jenkins, 1992). By creating their own meanings for television programs and films, audience members subvert corporate advertising strategies with their own countervailing tactics. Homoerotic Kirk–Spock stories written by fans (documented by Bacon-Smith, 1992) assertively resist the official, prescribed meanings for "Star Trek" intended by Paramount Pictures, NBC Television, and Gene Roddenberry.

Clearly, then, virtual reality is not new to computers, and the distinction between real and unreal has been blurred for many decades. What is new about computer-based virtual reality is that the technology attaches itself to human hands, eyes, and ears: The user is conjoined with the machine into an ephemeral bionic cyberbeing, whereas television has traditionally stayed at arm's length, the connections purely psychic.

The virtuality of the media enhances their transparency by connecting the audience to the affective mythotypes that undergird mythic narratives. It confounds the absolutism of reality by permitting resistance to it; in contrast to the "real" environment, which is chaotic, unpredictable, and hostile, the virtual experience is orderly, dependable, and inviting. It is in fact so orderly, dependable, and inviting that many extensive users of the media find the virtual environment preferable to the physical one, experiencing separation and isolation from the latter. This separation can sometimes turn dangerous and destructive, as with the *otaku* subculture (Greenfeld, 1993), a group of solipsistic, aggressive, and hermetic young computer hackers in Tokyo. More often, however, it merely reinforces disassociative behavior. The reason for this is that media's virtuality provides a comforting cognitive opiate which Kubey and Czisktemaholy (1990) call "negentropy".

Negentropy

Kubey and Czisktemaholy (1990) proposed one of the most compelling observational and theoretical explanations of how the media can become a virtual reality for its audience. They used the term *negentropy* to describe the psychological pull that television has on particular members of its audience—"the amount of order it produces in [their] consciousness" (p. 4). Television becomes a mechanism for conveying sense and meaning in a world that otherwise appears senseless and meaningless. For heavy users, the media create a redundancy that continually reinforces for them "what is 'real,' what is worth paying attention to, working for, and living for" (p. 182). Yet, this reality is a constructed one, a replacement for a reality based on human interaction, a model rather than the thing itself, a signifier instead of what is signified.

Tichi (1991) reinforced the Kubey and Czisktemaholy (1990) thesis in her examination of the use of television as a synthetic environment. Her interest was the extent to which the whole environment—the dominant culture found in advertising, the fine arts, journalism, and other places—is influenced by television. An examination of these artifacts reveals that television has helped create an environment in which it is the dominant cultural determinant. Consequently, television has become *naturalized*—the behavior of its characters and the environment in which they live insinuate themselves into American beliefs and attitudes and come to seem normal.

Perhaps the primary reason why the visual media are so good at conferring a sense of negentropy to the viewer is that most of what is seen on television or the movie screen operates comfortably within the bounds of genre and formula fiction. Cawelti (1976) argued that formulae in fiction are something that the reader comes to expect. According to Cawelti, "the formula creates its own world with which we become familiar by repetition. We learn in this way how to experience this imaginary world without continually comparing it with our own experience" (p. 10). This reinforcement, then, functions the way myths do, which are themselves highly formulaic. The cognitive appeal of formulaic narrative for its audience is that it constructs "an ideal world without the disorder, the ambiguity, the uncertainty, and the limitations of the world of our experience" (p. 13). Formula, like myth, conveys order.

Because of its natural tendency to think in categories (Lakoff, 1987), the human mind is naturally drawn to formula fiction, genres, and myths, and all forms of generic presentation. Indeed, categories have been a preoccupation of the human mind at least since Aristotle, as has genre. Familiar story lines and archetypes in the American cinema perfectly address this preoccupation:

> The meaning of an image is not only produced on the basis of the reality (or the impression of reality) expressed in it. The meaning also emerges from the relationship between this image and others that the audience has already seen. This process of interaction and exchange constantly nourishes memory of the American image industry. (Mattelart et al., 1984, p. 95)

Mattelart et al. (1984) called this process *the syndrome of repetition.*

Because genre operates on fairly rigid and perpetually reiterated conventions, it creates a diegetic universe with its own logic, epistemology, and ontology. The state of being for a character in a genre tale is considerably less complex than the state of being for the reader because the rules of the generic universe are finite and predictable, whereas the rules of the real world are not. Of course, everyone constructs narratives about their own lives, and many of these could be characterized as following generic formulae, because that confers a level of comfort and confidence to the person creating it. A personal narrative fortress runs a risk, however, that fictional ones do not: the threat that new events inconsistent with their ontology—or worse yet, the threat of a whole new ontology—could topple its reassuring walls. Fictional genres do not intrude.

Audiences find generic intrusion more comforting when it is framed as a spoof than when it is presented as some new generic hybrid. For example, the conclusion to *Blazing Saddles* (1974), a sort of generic unraveling, finds the protagonists hurtling from genre to genre in a zany chase sequence that had the audience laughing. On the other hand, when elements of the secret agent genre (e.g., a secret island base for a megalomaniacal scientist who was threatening to freeze the world with a death ray, but who was stopped in the nick of time when Agent Scorpio and his friend Luke Spencer flung him into a cryogenic reactor) invaded the soap opera genre on "General Hospital" (ABC TV) in the 1980s, fans were disoriented and uncomfortable. It was as if "General Hospital's" formula experimentation created an ontological paradox for the fans: If this formerly predictable universe could conjure up such confusion, what does that say about the world at large?

Because media texts confer a sense of negentropy to certain audience members, they act to reduce chaos and increase order. Negentropy, then, works with the virtuality effect of the media to resist the absolutism of reality, reinforcing that mythotype and its role in narrative by reassuring the viewer that there is order in the world despite the evidence to the contrary that he or she might glean from their unmediated experience. Negentropy is helped in this project by narrative circularity.

The repetition of negentropy, that which makes it most reassuring, and the tendency of films to be presold internationally, are together what makes such films international successes: "It [is] hard to anticipate the market for an unmade film. Therefore, it [is] imperative to put together a film package that resemble[s] previous successes as much as possible" (Wasser, 1995, p. 431). The inherent negentropy of such a product comforts audiences and investors alike.

Circularity

The importance of circularity in mythic systems found throughout the world can hardly be overstated. *Circularity* refers to the tendency of the narrative to arrive where it began, to restore equilibrium and deposit its dramatis personae in a circumstance similar to the one from which they departed, what Ang (1985) called the *ad infinitum effect*. Classical and fairy tale examples include any journey home (e.g., Odysseus), the inevitable fulfillment of an oracle's prophecy (e.g., Oedipus), or the attempt to restore vitality to a land or its people through a quest (e.g., King Arthur, Jason and the Argonauts, and Jack and the Beanstalk). Circularity reinforces the mythotype of purpose because it suggests that although journeys may have frightening or dangerous passages to them, there is a reason why they occur (i.e., things do not happen by accident), and they ultimately lead the wanderer to where the cosmos expects him or her to be. This purposefulness helps elicit a further mythotype—joy—such as in the parable of the prodigal son and a thousand other tales like it.

Eliade (1954) called the circularity of myth *the eternal return*, by which he meant ongoing repetition, the abolition of time through perpetually recurring actions that are endlessly enacted. Unlike Barthes (1972), Eliade saw human events as manifestations of myths, as opposed to seeing myths as rationalizations of human events. For Eliade, even wars were the acting out of ancient mythic dramas, because "each time the conflict is repeated, there is imitation of an archetypal model" (p. 29). Eliade's circular mythos revolved around a sacred center, a mountain or temple that acts as *axis mundi*—the center of the world. The hero embarks on a dangerous journey that conveys him or her from the unholy to the holy, from illusion to reality. Rebirth follows death, final triumphant victory annuls defeat. Todorov (1990) identified these circular stages as *equilibrium, disruption, disequilibrium,* and *renewed equilibrium.*

Frye (1957) used the circularity of the four seasons as the basis for his genre-based system of literary analysis. In Frye's system, each of the four seasons corresponds to a literary genre: spring to comedy; summer to romance; fall to melodrama; and winter to irony. To understand how these genres function, one must consider the evolution of a garden or a city through the stages of its life. Spring represents new birth, the early flowering of a garden or the establishment of a new city. For Frye, this framework parallels the framework of a comedic narrative, which concerns itself with the establishment of order out of chaos, of the promise and sensibility of youth. Summer represents the full flowering of the garden or the golden age of a city, both of which are maturing but remain vital. This imagery is, for Frye, that of romance—legends, chivalry, knights, and adventure. Fall represents the decline of the garden or the city, their days of glory gone, the leaves turning brown and the walls crumbling. Melodrama, Frye argued, relies on such imagery through the episodic travails of its extravagant characters, most of whom are overwhelmed by the plot. Winter is the death of the garden or the city: The trees are barren, the city overrun and desolate. Frye compared this to irony, in which the fool is king, everything is subjected to satire, and faith and hope are impossible. For Frye, this seasonal circularity is endemic to Western literature. Frye and Eliade were not concerned with media narratives per se, but Kaminsky (1974) applied many of their concepts and approaches to films and television.

Examples of circularity in the popular media are numerous, and although they serve a mythotypic function, they result largely from an economic motivation. A vivid example from the cinema is *The Wizard of Oz* (1939), in which Dorothy Gale goes on a fantastic journey only to discover that "there's no place like home." She returns to the place and time of her initial departure, which the story argues is where she truly belonged anyway. *Babe: Pig in the City* (1998) is a more recent iteration, one where the hero of a thousand faces has a porcine snout.

Almost any episodic television series, especially a situation comedy, is circular in structure: Although every episode introduces a crisis, the ending inevitably restores equilibrium. With scarce exceptions, even those few series that came to a deliberate narrative conclusion retained their circularity: The WJM news on "The Mary Tyler Moore Show" (CBS TV) was returned to the state of disequilibrium it was in before Mary arrived; Sam Malone decided to go on running the bar "Cheers" (NBC TV); and even though his turn as a Vermont innkeeper turned out to be a dream in the final episode of "Newhart" (CBS TV), the actor Bob Newhart woke up back on the set of his prior series, "The Bob Newhart Show" (CBS TV), as if that series exerted such circular gravity that "Newhart" ultimately could not escape. At the conclusion of the final episode of "Seinfeld" (NBC TV), the characters found themselves repeating the very words of dialogue that began the first episode of the series, completing a perfect circle with only the slightest awareness of déjà vu.

The notable television exceptions to the rule of circularity are "Nichols" (NBC TV), which concluded with the titular character (James Garner) being murdered; "Hill Street Blues" (NBC TV), which concluded with the station house burning down; and, most interestingly, "St. Elsewhere" (NBC TV), where it was revealed that the entire series had been the fantasies of an autistic boy. Even "M*A*S*H" (CBS TV), which ended with the conclusion of the Korean War and the dissolution of the 4077 military medical unit, embodied a return home for its protagonists.

Ellipticality

Ellipticality refers to the narrative apparatus through which detail is left out. The most descriptive of novels inevitably leaves out a near infinity of details because words can never perfectly describe images. Movies and television programs, although conveying much more detail than the written word, are still elliptical: There will always be off-screen time and space. *Fractal theory* demonstrates that the world is full of infinite detail, so even at the level of personal experience, our eyes do not see everything, our ears do not hear everything, and so on. There is some evidence that the brain acts to suppress a preponderance of detail, that some cognitive dysfunctions—such as attention deficit disorder (ADD), result from an inability to filter out and ignore sensory stimulation, and that memory and intelligence are the results of a cognitive process to weed a modicum of meaning out of a miasma of chaotic sensory inputs (Freeman, 1991; Goleman, 1990, 1994; Young & Concar, 1992). In other words, meaning is impossible without ellipses.

The narratology of Genette (1980) is particularly useful in uncovering the elliptical apparatuses available to the media. Genette was interested in the role of time in narrative, identifying five different narratological aspects of narrative: *order, duration, frequency, mood,* and *voice.* Order, duration, and frequency are the three of these that most directly concern the use of time in narrative, and hence, are all related to the issue of ellipticality.

Order refers to the sequence in which events of the narrative are presented. Often, this sequence is chronological, but it may take other forms, including flashbacks, flashforwards, and nonchronological narrative framing devices. The manipulation of the order of events contributes to narrative ellipticality and in doing so, contributes to its transparency. For example, the complex narrative ordering of *Citizen Kane* (1941) or *Back to the Future II* (1989) actively engage the viewer, drawing him or her into the narrative, where he or she is ultimately responsible for assembling a cognitively coherent whole.

Duration is the length that a particular passage, section, shot, or scene lasts in a narrative. In the written narrative, duration has no direct correspondence to real time, but in the iconic narrative, the image can have the sense of moving at the same rate as time in the real world. This can be easily manipulated, however. The simplest examples are when time is slowed down or sped up. Editing can also be used to stretch out or compress time. Countdowns, such as when a bomb is about to go off, usually move more slowly in the cinematic world, yet the rest of the narrative tends to move much more quickly—movies whose subject matter spans years still last 1 1/2 hours, just like those that span days or hours. Certainly a great deal of material is ellipsed.

Frequency also contributes to the ellipticality of narrative. It refers to the ability of a narrative to repeat time, either to convey that a particular action occurs repeatedly or to emphasize a singular occurrence by retelling it. A narrative has four frequency apparatuses at its disposal:

1. It can portray once what happened once (e.g., "Today I went to bed early"), perhaps the most common narratological use of frequency.

2. It can convey many times what happened many times (e.g., "Monday I went to bed early. Tuesday I went to bed early. Wednesday I went to bed early"), a variation of the first, and almost as common.

3. It can convey many times what happened once (e.g., "Yesterday I went to bed early. Yesterday I went to bed early. Yesterday I went to bed early")—a rather rare usage of language, more common in poetry than prose (e.g., "and miles to go before I sleep, and miles to go before I sleep," Frost, 1979).

4. It can convey once what happened many times (e.g., the Proustian (1913) "For a long time I used to go to bed early"), a device common in the written word, but rare in iconic narratives. (Genette, 1980)

Chatman (1978, 1981) borrowed from Genette (1980) to examine the differences in ellipticality found in between the written word and the visual image. Their narratology is not the same, and for Chatman, their differences revolve around point of view and description. Both of these devices are elliptical, albeit in different ways depending on whether words or images constitute them. In the cinema, *point of view* is associated with a particular gaze, a certain site of spectatorship, but film does not really convey what the gazer is thinking—it shows but does not tell. The written word can not really show, so it only tells. Description is another difference. Film is filled with an infinity of details, although some are foregrounded through the use of lighting, camera movement, focus, and color. Written narrative presents only those details the author selected for presentation. A novel may not tell us the color of the protagonist's hair, but a film must.

Initially, Chatman's (1978, 1981) analysis of point of view and description seemed to indicate that the written word is the more elliptical, but this is not a reasonable conclusion. The iconic narrative is equally elliptical, albeit in different ways. Although the descriptive details in a visual image are theoretically infinite, they are in fact practically finite, and the duration of their presentation limits their perceivability in a way a written narrative does not: A passage in a book may be reread to further expose the nuances of a particular description, but once a shot in a movie has passed, it is gone. Similarly, although a point-of-view shot may seem comprehensive, it ellipses out information easily gleaned from a written narrative: tone, attitude, and voice, for example.

Ellipticality primarily reinforces the mythotype of participation. Participation is served because the absence of detail allows the spectator to be involved in completing the picture; missing bits of time and space then belong to the viewer. This helps to draw the viewer in, making him or her a participant in the narrative they observe. This is especially true of soap operas, which are known to attract and retain viewers who feel participation in and ownership of the narrative (see Allen, 1985; Ang, 1985); this form is particularly elliptical, because much of the action occurs off-screen, but is nonetheless talked about ad infinitum.

Archetypal Dramatis Personae

The most transparent of characters are those whose own situation and personality are closest to the mythotype: those engaged in awe, in choice, in participation. Few literary archetypes transcend culture and identifying them is problematic if one wants to avoid Jungian mysticism. It is easier to identify archetypal continuity within a culture. For example, the Empedoclean elements can be seen to have an influence on Western romantic narratives and legends. Empedocles proposed in the fifth century B.C.E. that four elements (earth, air, fire, and water) constitute all matter. As such, it is not surprising to find them mirrored in the four medieval aspects of human beings: Earth is associated with the flesh (material pleasure and consumption), air with the soul (the ethereal spirit), fire with the heart (passion), and water with the mind (more on this later). These dyads are likewise manifest in archetypes and their epitomes. The four instrumental characters in Western epics and legends are the fool, associated with earth and the flesh; the wizard or cleric, associated with spirit and air; the knight, associated with fire and the heart; and the king, associated with water and the mind. In the West, each of these archetypes is epitomized by his or her embodiment in the Arthurian cycle: the fool, Pellinore; the wizard, Merlin; the knight, Lancelot, slave to his fiery, passionate heart; and the King, Arthur, whose wisdom and authority emanate from water and its Lady of the Lake, water to which he ultimately returns.

These strictly Western archetypes are endlessly recapitulated in modern media mythic displacement. The most obvious examples are found where the displacement is slightest, so it is fairly easy, for example, to associate C3PO from the *Star Wars* trilogy (1977, 1980, 1983) with Pellinore (a wanderer), the fool (fussy comic relief), the earth (he is made of metal), and the flesh (preoccupation with his physical condition). Obiwan Kenobe can be associated with Merlin (similar physical characteristics), the wizard (his dramatic function in the epic narrative), the air (his ethereal nature, especially after death), and the soul (or "The Force" as it is called in the film). Han Solo is connected to Lancelot (who steals his King's Queen, Leia), the knight (his dramatic function is to serve the king), fire (his encasement in smoky carbonite), and the heart (his function as romantic lead). Luke Skywalker embodies young King Arthur (a squire who does not know his own royalty, and for whom a close relative is the worst enemy), the king (who must reestablish the proper order), water (Luke is a water farmer on Tattoine), and the mind (Luke's self-control is his—and the rebellion's—salvation). These parallels are hardly a surprise, however, because *Star Wars* deliberately displaces the Arthurian cycle.

These parallels are evident in other works, however, where the displacement embodies a greater disparity. *The Wizard of Oz* (1939), meant to be a uniquely American myth, nevertheless still inculcates the Empedoclean structure. The Cowardly Lion functions as the Fool and as a woodland creature who is closely associated with the earth (particularly the forest), he is preoccupied with the flesh—his aches and pains and physical safety. The Tin Woodsman is the knight, in armor and carrying a knight's weapon, with fire and steam driving his mechanism (he spouts smoke), and a heart being the object he seeks, but the thing that—as with the other characters—he already has in abundance (the Tin Woodsman is the most emotional character, who cries with enough frequency to cause him mechanical problems). The Scarecrow is the king (which he literally becomes with the departure of the Wizard), associated with water (his only defense against fire), and the mind (although he protests his lack of a brain, his plans are the ones that ultimately succeed in reviving Dorothy, saving Dorothy, etc.). This leaves the wizard who, despite initial appearances, must surely be Dorothy. It is clear that the Man Behind the Curtain/Professor Marvel is not the wizard: He has no particular mystical powers, as the narrative makes clear, so is really just a mountebank and confidence trickster on both sides of the rainbow. Dorothy, on the other hand, kills two witches, levitates houses, and—most remarkably—travels between dimensions of reality, creating for herself new ontologies. She is, consequently, associated with air (tornadoes) and the soul or spirit. She is the title character of the film: Dorothy is The Wizard of Oz.

Other examples from literature and film are possible, from The Beatles to The Fantastic Four, but these displacements of the Empedoclean structure are native only to Western narrative. Consequently, they do not contribute to the transparency of media per se. They do, however, reflect the manner in which mythotypes express themselves in archetypes. These characters all engage the essential affective components of mythotype: Their existence in the narrative is what allows transcultural connections.

Inclusion

McLuhan (1964) was one of the first to suggest that the visual media, particularly television, made the viewer feel as though he or she was participating in what they observed. Television was, by virtue of its low definition image, a highly involving medium, akin to a storyteller at a prehistoric tribal campfire. For McLuhan, television so encouraged this sense of involvement that it would create a sense of universal community he called *the global village*. Ongoing wars attest that at the end of the 20th century, this village still does not exist, but clearly television and the cinema have become shared experiences that bind groups together and encourage viewers to believe they are a part of something.

Ang (1985) concluded that the ability of the viewer to project himself or herself into a television program was essential to them finding it pleasurable, what Mattelart et al., (1984) called "the desire to rediscover known emotions" (p. 100). This suggests that the narratives that will create the greatest pleasure for the majority of the audience are those that foster a sense of *inclusion*, a sense that the spectator is somehow a participant in the spectacle. This is one of the mythotypes, a major function of myth being the encouragement of participation and acculturation within the culture.

Inclusion is itself a product of the sense of simultaneity that television in particular creates:

> Television time … is the present instantaneous—the immediate, intimate and yet mass communicated image of the world, presented "here-and-now" especially for me as viewer, and drawing for its credibility on the "truth" that "the camera doesn't lie." (Tulloch & Alvarado, 1983, p. 23)

The viewer is bound to feel as though he or she participates in the television narrative given the pace at which it unfolds. The same is true of contemporary feature films, which are designed more like amusement park rides than novels in the sense that they are organized around the delivery of a series of participatory emotions rather than a conventional plot.

Inclusion is a by-product of narrative. According to Yoshimoto (1994), "The ultimate purpose of narrativizing experience is to naturalize consumption activities" so that visitors to Disneyland and other similar media consumers "consume without being aware of it" (p. 187). Narrative helps the reader or viewer feel as though he or she is participating, but what he or she is really participating in is a consumption ritual. In short, inclusion works as a form of niche marketing, "reinforcing the target audience's image of itself" (Rafferty, 1996, p. 77).

Verisimilitude

To the believer, myth is real. In fact, naturalness is essential to myth. This is not to say, of course, that myths cannot be fantastic, which they often are. Rather, it means that they appear to the reader to convey some deeper, self-evident, and universal truth about life, something not environmentally natural but cognitively or morally natural. Barthes (1972) accurately noted that myth:

> transforms history into nature. We now understand why, in the eyes of the myth-consumer, the intention, the adhomination of the concept can remain manifest without however appearing to have an interest in the matter: what causes mythical speech to be uttered is perfectly explicit, but it is immediately frozen into something natural; it is not read as a motive, but as a reason. (p. 129)

This is no less so for the myths conveyed via television or films, which seem to successfully convey to their audiences that what they portray "is so." A television show or movie actually has a great advantage in this regard over other media of storytelling: Because they use iconic signs, their signifiers seem to have a natural association with the signified. They do, however, have the appearance of naturalness, which has subsequent narratological effects: the appearance of immediacy, of literalness, in short, of verisimilitude (see Chatman, 1978, 1981).

Of course, verisimilitude is a generic construct like any other—what passes for realism is a function of conventional rules to which artists assiduously adhere. This is especially true of the visual media, which seem to function as though they are a window to the world they depict, whereas they are as conventionalized and formulaic in their presentation of the world as any pulp romance. Bazin (1967) argued that painting frequently aspired to "the duplication of the outside world" (p. 11), but that soon after its invention, photography seized supremacy over the conventions that passed for realism, freeing painting from its own obsession with realism (p. 16). Cinema further reinforced photography's claim to presenting nature somehow untampered with, but actually created a new set of representational rules which, although conveying verisimilitude, showed the influence of formula and artist over image. Although giving the appearance of reality, film delivers something else: "through the contents of the image and the resources of montage, the cinema has at its disposal a whole arsenal of means whereby to impose its interpretation of an event on the spectator" (p. 26).

That Hollywood's style has become the *lingua veritas* for film and television export is ironic given the range of representational possibilities found in drawing, photography, and cinema. Gombrich (1969) noted that visual images create verisimilitude through the use of conventionalized rules: "Why is it that different nations have represented the visible world in such different ways? Will the paintings we accept as true to life look as unconvincing to future generations as Egyptian paintings look to us?" (p. 3). In addition, Tuchman (1978) detailed how cultures unfamiliar with the Hollywood representational mode evolve quite different cinematic languages. The iconic image, then, presents many linguistic possibilities, yet the world cinema and television market seems to have more or less coalesced around a single choice, one that claims verisimilitude but is no less representational than the other possibilities.

The apparatuses thus far described (openendedness, virtuality, negentropy, circularity, ellipticality, archetypal dramatis personae, inclusion, and verisimilitude) can be termed *internal*, in the sense that they deal with structural relations within a narrative. Two other apparatuses, however, must be termed *external* because they are more closely related to the physical attributes of the media and their relation to their environment. These external apparatuses include *omnipresence* and production values.

Omnipresence

Electronic bombardment is an external attribute of transparent media narratives (Baudrillard, 1988, p. 49). Just as a mythic system seems to permeate the environment itself, with the sky and water acting as reminders of the structuration of belief, so too do the media permeate the contemporary environment. American grocery checkout counters, restaurants, apparel shops in department stores, doctor and dentist waiting rooms, airport lounges, bars, museums, sports arenas, and schools all situate television monitors in positions of prominence, barraging the populace with a steady and uninterrupted diet of video. Even the home, once regarded as a refuge from the world, has become what Gumpert and Drucker (1998) called a communication hub, continually linked to the flow of electronic information worldwide. The overwhelming omnipresence of the film and television environment led Real (1989) to call it *super media* and led Meyrowitz (1985) from the world, has become what Gumpert and Drucker (1998) called a communication hub, continually linked to the flow of electronic information worldwide. The overwhelming omnipresence of the film and television environment led Real (1989) to call it *super media* and led Meyrowitz (1985) to speak of how Americans have become disconnected from any environment except the prevalent one of synthetic media.

Most of what is seen on these omnipresent monitors is the promotion of some commodity, frequently the consumption of other media—movies, music, books, and the like. This omnipresence serves the mythotype: It instills a sense of inclusion and participation, because the media are everywhere. The faculty of my own department felt participatory when the senior faculty member brought a television into a staff meeting so we could watch the O.J. Simpson verdict live along with untold millions of other Americans. The design of transparent programs that allow them to create this seemingly seamless web is discussed further in chapter 6.

Production Values

Not all manifestations of affective mythotypes are narratological. It is undeniable that the scale of certain productions—the budget that has been poured into a particular movie or television show—becomes itself a part of how it satisfies its audience's needs for myth, becoming what Mattelart et al., (1984) called *the law of the spectacle* (p. 97). The biggest of Hollywood feature films have budgets approaching the Gross Domestic Product (GDP) of small countries. It is estimated that *Waterworld* (1995) cost $180 million (Cox, 1995) and *Titanic* (1997) is rumored to have cost over $200 million. Few countries have the capability of producing films on such a scale.

What does that kind of money buy? Wonder and awe, perhaps the two most elemental and universal of mythotypes. No mythology lacks grandeur and spectacle, and the history of human art suggests that these are a preoccupation of all peoples in all times. The Great Pyramid, Machu Pichu, the Sistine Chapel, and the Great Wall of China all possess a majesty that inspires veneration and amazement. Although the venue may be less formal, movies and to a lesser extent television fulfill the same need: "Amazing! That's impossible! How was that done?" The fundamental difference is the raw material: pixels instead of stone and mortar.

Of course, most of the magnificence of the movies is illusion. Color, lighting, and 3-D design tricks like forced perspective, create an appearance of depth and scale to sets as they appear on television which do not appear the dinosaurs in *Jurassic Park* (1993) come close to an illusion of life. Because such tricks rely on the most powerful parallel processing computers, however, they are quite expensive. In spite of the costs, large budget American mega films are likely to become increasingly common, because analyses indicate that they are less risky financially than medium-budget films ("Entertainment has become ...," 1997).

Production values do not need to be epic, however, to be polished and effective. They also entail paying close attention to the technical aspects of production: lighting, editing, sound, and other similar matters. Media analysts such as Arijon (1976) and Zettl (1990) carefully systematized what passes for standard Hollywood style—the slick, tight, ubiquitous aesthetic system that is a synthesis of the dichotomy between Eisenstein's and Kuleshov's montage on the one hand and Welles' and Renoir's realism on the other. Extreme technical care can be lavished on the most disposable and narrowcast soap opera or weather report. Conversely, the best written script can be slapped together in a shoddy fashion, without regard for its appearance.

These 10 devices constitute the narratology and apparatus of transparent media: openendedness, virtuality, negentropy, circularity, ellipticality, archetypal dramatis personae, inclusion, verisimilitude, omnipresence, and production values. Transparency enables indigenous, polysemic readings. These devices foster transparency because they enable audiences to see the mythotype, to resist the absolutism of reality. Not all of these apparatuses are unique to Hollywood, and consequently, they do not offer an exclusive competitive advantage to American filmmakers and televisionmakers seeking to capitalize on the transparency phenomenon. Ellipticality, for example, contributes to transparency, but is an essential part of all storytelling and offers no particular advantage to any one media producer. Hollywood possesses a competitive advantage in several of these areas, however. For reasons previously discussed, production values are a particular advantage for Hollywood. Openendedness is another U.S. advantage because American television programs and films (at least the successful ones) are perpetually recycled and extended. Omnipresence is another U.S. advantage because the television screen or movie poster so dominates the whole of the cultural landscape. There are others as well.

More important than any of these singular product attributes to exportability is the general structure they compose when grouped together, a structure of flexible mythotypes. That interaction, more than anything else, makes certain films or television programs transculturally intelligible, hence allowing them to function as myths, increasing demand for them. Texts that do not use these devices are not transparent, but may still be interesting, albeit closed, entropic, linear, anti-archetypal, exclusive, and so forth. An example is the film *Ulysses* (1967), an American film based on the eponymous James Joyce novel. It would be hard to see Gbagwulu or *izzat*, Punjabi family honor, both of which are discussed in chapter 1, there. Such films have little hope of international box-office success, yet internal conditions lead many national film industries to produce films of this type.

The American industry, however, generally never strays far from the mythotypes. It is because the mythotypic sensibility that the American media evoke can be readily coopted and retooled for any purpose that they are so successful and their appeal is so nearly universal. Lincoln (1989) showed that because myths are stories with credibility, authority, and a claim to truth, they can be used forcefully for any number of reactionary or revolutionary purposes; "It is precisely through the repeated evocation of [mythic] sentiments via the invocation of select moments from the past that social identities are continually (re-)established and social formations (re-)constructed" (p. 23). Consequently, the mythic component of popular film or television tends to be a conservative force, one that reinforces the status quo, especially in genre movies and programs that are "purely mythic" (Wright, 1986).

Television and films continuously mine mythic themes, and in doing so, mine the mythotypes. Frye (1957) was the first literary critic to examine in a systematic fashion the appearance of mythic themes and archetypes in literature, a phenomenon he called *displacement*. In popular film and television, myths are sometimes displaced beyond easy recognition (e.g., the Pyramus and Thisbe tale retold in *Some Kind of Wonderful*, 1987, or "General Hospital," ABC TV) and at other times are hardly displaced at all (e.g., the Hercules character retooled for *Superman*, 1978, or "Lois and Clark," ABC TV), but in either case, a myth is not too far beneath the surface. The myths embedded in these dramatic enactments serve as cultural rituals (Schatz, 1986) in a similar sense to Lincoln's (1989) cultural establishment and construction.

Beyond the narrative attributes of media texts themselves, there are ancillary products packaged along with the texts that also contribute to their exportability: These include merchandising, licensing, intertextuality, and hyperreal environments. These traits can be grouped together under the term *synergy*, the process through which a particular iconic concept is put to maximum use in as many different forms as possible. Synergy is the topic of chapter 6.

Looking closely at media texts in the context of the system that developed them puts in sharp relief the narratological apparatuses that have conferred competitive advantage on American media exports. These devices make texts transparent because they are much closer to the mythotype we all share than to the cultural peculiarities of myth that divide us. The films and television programs that address the mythotypic needs described here have essentially become mythic themselves, and "these fables now have a world-wide resonance" (Mattelart et al., 1984, p. 100). The Hollywood planet makes local myth of America's transparent text.

6

The Extensions of Media

I am totally optimistic that one and one will add up to four here.
—Michael Eisner, CEO of Disney *(cited in Auletta, 1995a, p. 31)*

Extratextual materials act as reinforcement to the indigenous myth projected into America's transparent texts. These are the extensions of media, and only recently have scholars become interested in them. Past scholarly interest was in the flow going the other way. McLuhan's (1964) *Understanding Media* was subtitled "The Extensions of Man" [sic]. For McLuhan, media were the extensions of the human body, bonus electronic eyes, ears, and limbs. Furthermore, the media were, for him, an extension of the human mind:

> It is a principal aspect of the electric age that it establishes a global network that has much of the character of our central nervous system. Our central nervous system is not merely an electric network, but it constitutes a single unified field of experience. (p. 348)

So, bodies and minds have been extended beyond their traditional organic confines and projected onto the objective world of nature. The subjective world punctured the objective world as subject and self transcends body: The mind and its informants transcend their shell and replicate themselves outside it, making the actual an even greater extension of the internal. That model of media, one in which they are an extension of the human body and self, continue to define media theory (e.g., Brummett & Duncan, 1992).

Ironically, however, this extension has not led to greater control of the environment by the average television watcher or moviegoer. The extensions of men and women have not kept pace with the extensions of media. Even as the human body extends itself through media, the media extend themselves into human space and the human body, resulting in an environ-ment in which media simulacra are inescapable and in which transparency is reinforced by making it seem omnipresent and natural. Anthropologists have observed that *selective advantages* arise when human populations ex-ploit the expanding advantages of their interconnectivity, what Corning (1983) called the *synergism hypothesis*. The media industry also calls its own variation of this process *synergy*, a strategy through which it tries to glean as much market advantage out of characters and concepts as possible by spreading them across media platforms (e.g., movies, television, CDs, com-puter games, etc.) and by merchandising related artifacts (e.g., toys, clothes, games, etc.). As McChesney (1997) argued, "firms without this cross-selling and cross-promotional potential are simply incapable of com-peting in the global marketplace" (p. 21).

The effect of this synergy is that the glass surface of the television screen has become diaphanous: Just as characters on a movie screen step out of their fictional film world and into a fictional real one in films like *The Purple Rose of Cairo* (1984) and *Last Action Hero* (1993), so have media characters moved from artifice to mimesis. Simultaneously, media-related products and environments increasingly allow humans to walk into worlds of media fantasy. Synergy makes the distinction between the world of media and the real world increasingly ethereal and evanescent.

This is accomplished because synergy compliments the media product it-self by transforming its concept into something persistent and pervasive, even unavoidable. This serves the mythotypic device of omnipresence. In pursuit of further revenue, synergy extends movie or television characters and situations into other places: the other media, apparel, toys, games, food, and theme park rides. *The Flintstones* (1994), a comedy about a prehistoric family whose attitudes and possessions parody 20th century middle-class suburban American culture, is a good example of synergetic media in ac-tion: in addition to the theatrical feature film, there were four antecedent animated television series ("The Flintstones," ABC TV; "The Adventures of Pebbles and Bam-Bam," ABC TV; "Back to Bedrock," ABC TV; and "The Flintstone Kids," ABC TV) that were put back into extensive airplay; a pop music remake of the Flintstones theme song by the dance group the B-52s (renamed the B.C. 52s) for the radio, a CD and cassette, and a music video for MTV and VH-1; an MTV special hosted by Rosie O'Donnell; Flintstone rock candy; Flintstone T-shirts and other clothing; a bewildering variety of Flintstone toys of two types, one featuring the likenesses of the original cartoon characters, the other the likenesses of the actors in the feature film; a marketing tie-in with McDonalds, which had Flintstone Happy Meals featuring toy cars from the film, and an appearance in the movie of a fast food restaurant called *RocDonalds*; other feature film tie-ins with and visual plugs for Chevron (*Chevrock*), CNN (*Cave News Network*), Rolling Rock beer (no prehistorization needed), and the film *Jurassic Park* (1993)—another Universal Studios product; children's chewable daily vitamins; breakfast cereal (Fruity Pebbles); and an insert found in many American newspapers, labeled *The Bedrock Times*, which promoted the movie through an architectonic impression of what a prehistoric newspaper (again a parody of 20th century style) might have been like. *The Flintstones* extended itself into all media, virtually every shopping venue, and even into food products. These tangential items promoted the film even as they generated revenue independently: Consumers were purchasing what amounted to advertising. Did consumers want these Flintstone products? Frequently, invention is the mother of necessity.

A good example of this is Disney wedding planning, a newly introduced product from the Disney Company that allows brides and grooms to become characters from Disney films, acting out scenes from the film as part of their wedding ceremony and celebration. The most popular and successful of these is the Cinderella wedding package, whereby, thanks to the Disney costume department, the groom is dressed as Prince Charming, the bride as Cinderella at the ball, the bridesmaids and others in the wedding party as other characters in the film (apparently some brides choose to costume their bridesmaids as Cinderella's ugly stepsisters), and transportation to the castle is provided by a horse-drawn pumpkin coach. In other words, on what could well be the most important day of their lives, the bride and groom have chosen to play act as fictional characters.

The visual media, especially television, are regular, dependable antidotes to the insecurities the world engenders for exactly the reason that Kubey and Czisktemaholy (1990) postulated with their *negentropy theory*: elliptical dramatic television plots, with each episode in the serial returning the diegetic balance to exactly the point where it found it, create a comforting wholeness. No doubt aware that many marriages end in divorce, Disney brides opt for a "happily ever after" scenario.

Synergy is comprised of several contributing strategies, some within the media and some in related industries. Michael Eisner of Disney defined *synergy* as a "cross-promotion ... engine that helps drive our company" and articulated well the foundation for synergy within the media: "the four most important programming platforms that enable media and entertainment companies to compete successfully in overseas markets are news, sports, movies, and family entertainment" (cited in Auletta, 1996, p. 28). Disney's purchase of ABC Cap Cities, for example, was an attempt to round out their synergetic possibilities by adding news and sports to what they were already doing and also to secure a content delivery system. The primary synergetic strategies all center on the dispersal of a single narrative concept through related industries, and include merchandising and licensing, product placement, intertextuality, theming, and environmental simulacra. Each of these strategies is a different device for enhancing textual transparency, consequently bringing in additional international audiences, which brings in increasing revenues.

MERCHANDISING AND LICENSING

A tremendous amount of the cost of producing and distributing a motion picture is recouped from its merchandising and licensing, the direct manufacture of consumer products related to the narrative being synergized, or the temporary exchange of cash and revenues between the copyright holder and a manufacturer for permission to market related products. It is no wonder that merchandising and licensing are popular, because film producers get back from 6% to 10% of the retail price of each piece of related merchandise sold (Mattelart et al., 1984). This is particularly true of large-scale event pictures aimed at a crossover youth–adult market, pictures like *Jurassic Park* (1993), *The Lion King* (1994), *Independence Day* (1996), *Men in Black* (1997), *Godzilla* (1998), or *Armageddon* (1998). Yet, even lowly independent features can cash in on t-shirts, caps, and similar products. In addition, merchandising is not strictly a Hollywood phenomenon: The Brazilian celebrity Xuxa has successfully marketed 50 products related to her television series, including games, apparel, toys, music, and food, propelling her to the short list of the wealthiest entertainers in the world (Valdivia & Curry, 1996), and the Japanese video game Pokémon has been parlayed into a television series, a comic book, and toys. From a financial standpoint, the challenge is in designing a motion picture or television show that naturally lends itself to toys, apparel, food, and other products—making a movie popular enough that it generates demand for related products, which can naturally be derived from the text itself.

Merchandising and licensing are not limited to film. Clever marketing of television programs, and not just those aimed at children, has created synergy similar to that of film merchandising. The prime-time soap "Dynasty," for example, merchandised apparel, eyeglasses, furniture, jewelry, linen, and a perfume called "Forever Krystle," named after one of the main characters, and featuring the actress who played her in its advertising. Such merchandising apparently encouraged "Dynasty" fans to get dressed up in their best clothes in order to watch the program (Gripsrud, 1995). "Twin Peaks" generated similar adult feverishness through its merchandising, which included an *Access Travel Guide* to the fictional town, trading cards featuring the characters, and a cassette tape ostensibly made by Dale Cooper, the protagonist, for his secretary Diane.

Television has been known to parody merchandising, too. The comedy program "Saturday Night Live," for example, dissected the subservient relationship of the text to its merchandising possibilities in a mock advertisement for *Philadelphia* (1993), a film about AIDS discrimination in the workplace. The spoof featured a Philadelphia Action Playset, with GI-Joe-like action figurines bearing resemblances to Tom Hanks, Denzel Washington, Jason Robards, and other actors from the film. Unlike the film's protagonist, who is dying of AIDS, the Tom Hanks action figure is a Transformer, capable of morphing into weapon-laden "battle mode." The absurdity of this false marketing underscores the power and control it exerts over other, less high-minded Hollywood products.

Disney has no equal in merchandising its images and concepts. In addition to its chain of Disney Stores, which sells housewares, videos, books, collectibles, apparel, and toys, its products are found in department, toy, video, record, and book stores. It has cooperative marketing ventures with both Burger King and McDonalds restaurant chains wherein Disney toys are given away with Happy Meals for children. These inexpensive plastic figurines are available only for a limited time and serve to promote the feature film, theme park, or television program from which they are derived. Demand for *Lion-King*-related Kids Meal toys was so strong that anxious parents would consume deliveries of new toys almost as quickly as they were loaded off the truck at some Burger King restaurants.

These toys strive for a transparency of their own. One particularly telling set of Happy Meal toys was a McDonalds line of figurines promoting Disney's EPCOT theme park in Florida. The most familiar of Disney's characters were transformed for these dolls into ambassadors of selected world cultures, embodying American expectations of what those cultures are: Pluto the dog is French, with a blue beret, white shirt, and red bow tie; Donald Duck is Mexican, wearing an orange sombrero and green poncho; Minnie Mouse is Japanese, in a pale blue kimono and yellow sandals; Goofy is Scandinavian, in a Viking helmet and hair shirt; and Mickey Mouse is—what else?—an American Uncle Sam, in red, white, and blue top hat and tails. These figurines are meant to promote the World Pavilion at EPCOT, a sort of Disney United Nations simulated environment, discussed at length in the following text. They are a good example of effective merchandising because they attract customers to McDonalds, promote a family vacation in Florida, and keep related Disney products (i.e., toys, videos, movies) in the customers' minds, all while sending a message that Disney is committed to a global good neighbor policy, but remains, at heart, American. A Mexican Mickey is unthinkable for Disney. It was Donald, after all, who was deemed suitable to befriend Joe Carioca the Brazilian parrot and Poncho the Mexican rooster in *The Three Cabelleros* (1945).

Disney's synergistic strategy has paid off well: *The Lion King* (1994) has generated over $1 billion in total product profit from box-office receipts that were in the several hundred million dollar range, and even *Hunchback of Notre Dame* (1996), which earned less than $100 million at the U.S. box office, still generated $500 million in total profit (McChesney, 1997). This is like spinning golden straw into platinum.

Paramount Pictures enjoyed the benefits of merchandising and licensing primarily through its line of Star-Trek-related products. The dedication of hardcore Star Trek aficionados, and their willingness to consume a litany of Star-Trek-related merchandise, often stretches credulity. A prescient example concerns the marketing of *Klingon*, a language spoken by a race of warrior space aliens on the television show, which is apparently the fastest growing language in the world (Tu, 1996) and is now spoken by more persons than those that speak Esperanto (Dolan, 1994). Whereas Esperanto was meant to de-Babelize the world, Klingon re-Babelizes it, and turns a profit too. Language instruction books, tapes, and two CD-ROMs—*Conversational Klingon* and *Power Klingon*—sold well. A Philadelphia professor has even opened a Klingon Language Institute (KLI), which proclaims on its website that:

> The KLI has two main goals, missions which have driven us from our inception and which have expanded as our resources and membership have grown. The first of these missions is to promote, foster, and develop the Klingon language, and the second is to bring together Klingon language enthusiasts from around the world and provide them with a common forum for the discussion and the exchange of ideas … But this is only the beginning of what we do with this amazing language. As you explore this World-Wide Web site, you will have the opportunity to both hear Klingon, and to see the

writing system (which the Klingons call <pIqaD>). Further, you can learn about the KLI's ambitious projects, such as our translation efforts with the Bible and the works of Shakespeare. (Schoen, 1997)

They have already succeeded in translating *Hamlet*, for example, into Klingon. The Bible translation apparently caused some problems since Klingon has no word for *love* (Dolan, 1994). *The Klingon Dictionary* sold 250,000 copies. There are two Klingon academic publications: *HolQeD*, a peer-review refereed journal of Klingon linguistics, and *Jatmey*, a Klingon literary periodical (Tu, 1996). Weddings have been performed in Klingon. In short, and in spite of the fact that it is the trademarked, copyrighted, and profitable property of Paramount, Klingon is becoming a linguistic force.

As the Klingon case well illustrates, merchandising and licensing succeed because for many media consumers, the vicarious experience of favorite movies or television programs is insufficient. They are interested in a more direct experience, through play or roleplay, but in any case, through some further form of consumption. This clearly is served by the mythotypes of *virtuality* (it feels real), *negentropy* (it conveys order), *inclusion* (it makes one a part of something), *verisimilitude* (it looks real), and *omnipresence* (it is everywhere), as discussed in chapter 5. By rendering the physical environment an extension of the media environment, they expand the reach of transparency, expanding profits as well.

Synergized products not only penetrate our world from the media world, but in some cases, films and television programs run de facto but unlabeled advertisements for consumer products. This process is called *product placement*.

PRODUCT PLACEMENT

Product placement is the process by which movies and television contain small and subtle advertisements for particular consumer goods, such as the frequent references to the popularity of drinking Tab soda in the film *Down and Out in Beverly Hills* (1985). That soda is mentioned by name several times in the film and is portrayed as a favorite beverage of the rich and famous. Companies bid for the privilege of participating with a movie in this way, because this association can be extremely lucrative for the manufacturer. By associating products with favorite characters, audience emulation and identity become associated with their consumption.

Action films are the most common site of product placement because they tend to glorify the pleasure of consumption. James Bond films, for example, consume Marlboro cigarettes, a Wetbike, a BMW, a Phillips car stereo, and other products, usually with a close-up of the product logo for good measure. *The Saint* (1997) prominently featured actor Val Kilmer as Simon Templar using a cellular telephony/Internet/fax product called *The Communicator* a few weeks before Nokia began to market it; Nokia's television advertisement was composed solely of clips from the film and stressed that owning the device would make the consumer more like protagonist Templar. Audience members, forming their identities through emulation, project their desire onto the products that James Bond, Simon Templar, and other characters consume.

Product placement is most prominent in films aimed at children, a way of encouraging them to equate consumption with identity at an age when that identity is still forming. *George of the Jungle* (1997), a Tarzan spoof, depicted its protagonist consuming many identifiable products, with conspicuous shots of each corporate logo. In each case, that consumption was depicted as desirable, pleasurable, and necessary. These images included a spending spree at Nieman Marcus; George watching a Chock Full o' Nuts© coffee advertisement and then eating the coffee as a prelude to mating; eating Doritos©; eating a McDonalds value meal; shipping himself safely to Africa via UPS; and running through the jungle in Nike Air tennis shoes. George's best friend, a gorilla, is shown reading *The International Herald Tribune*. In each case, the use of the brand-name product was shown to be natural, just as seeing brand-name products in feature films is coming to seem natural.

The story of product placement in the film *ET: The Extraterrestrial* (1982) is a famous one, more so for what was not placed in the film than for what was. Director Stephen Spielberg invited the Mars candy company to feature its M&M candy in a portion of the film where the children leave a trail to be retraced later, akin to the one left by Hansel and Gretel in the well-known folk tale. Hollywood speculation at the time guessed that director John Carpentar's *Starman* (1984) would be a bigger hit, so Mars demurred. Spielberg then invited the participation Reese's Pieces (an M&M-like product) instead, and that candy was featured prominently in the film, which went on to become the highest grossing film in history of that time, a crown it only recently passed along. Reese's Pieces saw a concomitant increase in the sale of its candy.

George and ET are not alone in the children's market. Animated films and television also make use of product placement. The animated Disney film *Oliver and Company* (1988) featured product placement for the newspaper *USA Today*, featured as a poster on the side of a bus. A unique form of product placement has been enacted by Disney regarding the professional hockey team it owns, *The Mighty Ducks*. In spite of a patchy win–loss record, this is the most profitable franchise in the National Hockey League because the Mighty Ducks merchandise it sells as a result of the tremendous number of tie-ins associated with it, including an eponymous feature film. Since acquiring ABC, Disney has programmed a daily "Mighty Ducks" animated television series (Auletta, 1996). Placement has become so prevalent in children's entertainment that entire movies have been constructed around the placement of a product, such as *Mac and Me* (1988), an *ET*-imitator produced by McDonalds and prominently featuring its hamburgers. Similarly, the film *Space Jam* (1997) was a feature based on a Nike television commercial.

As a result of all this product placement, audiences have become increasingly aware of the practice, and this has given filmmakers license for even more overt placements. *Wayne's World* (1992), for example, places products even as it hypocritically decries the practice. Wayne (Mike Myers) and Garth (Dana Carvey) produce a low-budget cable show in Aurora, Illinois that is picked up by a major distributor and given a large budget. The new producer (Rob Lowe) informs Wayne that the advertising sponsor is allowed, by contract, to have a featured spot on the show, and Wayne resists:

Wayne: Well, that's where I see things just a little differently. Contract or no, I will not bow to any sponsor.
          (Wayne opens a pizza box prominently displaying the Pizza Hut logo and begins eating a slice.)

Producer: I'm sorry you feel that way, but basically it's the nature of the beast.
          (Wayne holds up a Doritos bag and extracts a chip.)

Wayne: Maybe I'm wrong on this one, but for me the beast doesn't include selling out.
          (Wayne eats a Doritos chip and smiles.)
          Garth, you know what I'm talking about, right?
          (Camera reveals Garth to be wearing Reebok sneakers, a Reebok warm-up suit, and a Reebok hat.)

Garth: It's, like, people only do things because they get paid, and that's just really sad.

Wayne: I can't talk about it anymore. It's giving me a headache.

Garth: Here, take two of these.

Wayne: Ah ... Nuprin!
          (Garth shakes two pills into Wayne's hand. We see the pills in an ex-

> treme close-up.)
> Little ... yellow ... different!

Producer: Look, you can stay here in the big leagues and play by the rules, or you can go back to the farm club in Aurora. It's your choice.
(Wayne holds a can of Pepsi next to his face.)

Wayne: Yes! And the choice of a new generation!

This scene relies on audience members recognizing the conventions and commerce of product placement, and even their own complicity in the process, but the scene engages in the very practice it seems to be critiquing, because products by Pizza Hut, Doritos, Reebok, Nuprin, and Pepsi are conspicuously and self-consciously placed. Other films, such as *Space Balls* (1987) and *Hercules* (1997), self-consciously place semi-imaginary products for humorous effect (as when Hercules opines "Look! I'm an action figure!"). Audiences familiar with the practice of product placement seem to find it amusing rather than annoying.

INTERTEXTUALITY

Intertextuality is the process through which texts refer to other texts. Every text is in a sense intertextual, because no text exists in a vacuum, but some texts more prominently and overtly rely on audience recognition of characters, ideas, situations, sounds, and images borrowed from other texts. To do so is to engage in the *pastiche*, or uncritical appropriation, which is itself a prominent feature of postmodernism.

In most cases, intertextuality serves to create an in-group sensibly among those who understand its reference. In advertising, this helps build a loyal customer base, one that regards itself as knowledgeable insiders. Advertisements for Absolut Vodka, for example, feature the shape of the bottle in numerous intertextual situations that test the reader's cultural awareness: "Absolut Shelley" features the parts of several bottles crudely stitched together like the Frankenstein monster; "Absolut Roswell" feature the bottle shape hovering over a New Mexico desert. These visual puns are understood by some and not others, and the some then feel an inclusive affinity for the product. This is easily done in other media. A television commercial for *Men in Black* (1997) that advocated seeing the film a second time relied on audiences having already seen the film; those not having seen it would not understand the significance of actor Tommy Lee Jones putting on his sun glasses and making a white flash of light from a pen-like object, followed by actor Will Smith saying "See it again." The advertisement creates an in-group among those who have already seen the film by delivering a joke only they can understand.

The horror comedy *Scream* (1997) similarly used intertextuality to create in-group recognition, but the film would hardly make sense to one unaware of the metafictional aspects of its narratives. The characters in the film talk endlessly about horror movies with an affective detachment toward their own lives. They are interested primarily in what would be happening to them if they were actually in a horror movie, which of course they are. Their own lives are benchmarked against the defining films of the slasher subgenre: *Psycho* (1960), *Halloween* (1978), *Friday the Thirteenth* (1980), and *A Nightmare on Elm Street* (1984). The last of these is particularly lampooned because it and *Scream* share the same director, Wes Craven. At one point, a character is heard to say, "The first *Nightmare on Elm Street* was good, but the rest sucked," a wink to audience members who knew that Craven directed that one but not the next three; later in the film, intertextually minded audience members recognize a school janitor as *A Nightmare on Elm Street's* antagonist Freddy Krueger. As *Scream* proceeds, characters accurately detail standard Hollywood horror conventions, and the film plays with our knowledge of these, with the fact that they are being articulated, and with its own willingness to violate them. For example, one of the characters asks the suspicious heroine (and the audience), "What do I have to do to prove to you that I'm not the killer?"—a question that is answered as it is always answered in such films: He is the next one murdered. *Scream 2* (1998) played even more intertextual games.

Children's programming and films have often used intertextuality as a way of keeping parents interested, letting them in on a visual joke that the youngsters would not recognize. When Ursula rushes to rescue George of the Jungle in the eponymous film (1997), she commandeers a tugboat and stands expectantly on its prow as it rushes through the harbor. Older viewers recognize the image and a few measures of music accompanying it as an homage to *Funny Girl* (1968), albeit a postmodern one without apparent motivation. The conclusion of the film features an intertextual moment that even the kids can enjoy, as George and Ursula proudly hold their baby aloft on a cliff surrounded by all the creatures of the savannah—the cliff is Pride Rock, and the image a pastiche from *The Lion King* (1994).

From the standpoint of transparency, intertextuality serves the purpose of creating a synthetic but mimetic universe, one in which artificial creatures seem to take on something approximating life. Fictional television characters appear in crossover episodes of other unrelated shows, reinforcing the appearance that they have an existence irrespective of their fictionality. Characters from the drama "E.R." (NBC TV) have turned up on the situation comedy "Friends" (NBC TV); characters from "Law and Order" appear on "Homicide" (NBC TV) and vice versa; doctors on Boston-based St. Elsewhere go out for a drink and end up in "Cheers." Such crossovers serve the mythotype of verisimilitude, making the fictional universe of television and films seem more like the universe that living beings inhabit.

Intertextuality cuts across not only different programs in a single medium, but from medium to medium as well. Sony, for example, plans to capitalize on the synergy possible in promoting intertextuality between its consumer electronics division and movie production through a 32-bit PSX CD-ROM multimedia system (Calica, 1995). Movies are made out of television shows (e.g., "The Brady Bunch" or "The Avengers") and out of comic books (e.g., *Batman* or *Blade*), and television shows are made out of movies that were made out of comic books (e.g., *Men in Black*). Music videos are made out of anything, and into anything.

Intertextuality, then, not only reinforces verisimilitude, but also reinforces omnipresence. Major media events, such as summer blockbuster movies, become unavoidable, whether one sees the film or not. A process called *theming* further reinforces this process.

THEMING

Theming is designing a building, product packaging, or an environment around a single idea or icon, such as a corporate logo ("In the mouseketeerish style," 1994). The concept drives the product, and the simpler the concept the better: The simplicity invites polysemy, whereas complexity cuts it off. Polysemy in turn enables transparency and maximum readability. In some cases, theming hinges on the most singular and simple concepts—even a single word. The film *Armageddon* (1998), for example, first had a title, then a marketing plan, and only then the beginnings of a story. Disney had to engage in extensive negotiations just to get the word *Armageddon* as a title (Orwall, 1998).

As with many aspects of synergy, Disney excels at theming. Its most common theming proceeds from the image of three circles arranged in an inverted triangle: Mickey Mouse's silhouette. This shape predominates the Disney pantheon: It is the shape of the lake at Walt Disney World, of a teapot and teacups at the Disney store, of the water tower at MGM Studios

Florida, of the Disney channel logo, of the archway at a Disney office building in Florida. The idea is visually and conceptually simple, but what it invites is complex. After all, what does Mickey Mouse mean? The answer to that question has more to do with the cultural projections of a viewer than with any inherent signification; Mickey Mouse is a semiotic black hole.

Architect Michael Graves (1994) is the preeminent themer for Disney, and his postmodern style lends itself particularly well to a corporate imprimatur. Team Disney headquarters in California, for example, looks from a distance like a classical Greek temple, but on closer inspection it can be seen that its columns are actually the Seven Dwarves. His Dolphin Hotel at Disney World features gigantic cartoon dolphins and is shaped like a dolphin's back breaking the surface of the water. Such buildings embody neither the ornateness of baroque nor the "less is more" simplicity of a Mies van der Rowe glass box. They are simultaneously simple and recognizable ("That's a dolphin") and semiotically complex ("Hey! That *building* is a *dolphin!*"). Like transparency itself, such themed buildings produce familiarity and intimacy, but in different ways for different observers.

Brand name counts for everything in theming. The success of Celebration, Florida, Disney's synthetically created yet nevertheless actually inhabited real community, attributes its attractiveness to its theme—America's past meets America's future—and the Disney brand name: "One reason people wanted the houses was that they were *Disney* houses" (Rybczynski, 1996, p. 37, emphasis original). Twenty thousand residents are expected to populate Celebration's 49,000 acres by the year 2010, and it is apparently having no trouble attracting prospective residents ("It's a small town, after all," 1995).

These residents seem eager to live in a synthetic but utopian community. Celebration is designed along the lines of a set from a 1950s Disney film: a quaint town center and classic colonial style houses with front porches, back alleys, and white picket fences. Even the elementary school was Disney-designed and influenced and will serve as a testing ground for Disney computer "edutainment" products. All this simulacra gives the impression of a set from a Disney film, and an old-fashioned one at that. Celebration's utopianism is the closest the company has come to fulfilling Walt Disney's utopian futurist dreams.

Celebration in some ways epitomizes theming, because it uses pastiche to solicit both half-remembered nostalgia and high-tech utopian futurism. Celebration itself signifies America. What looks simple on the surface, though, is deeply polysemic: What, after all, is America? Celebration exists somewhere between spontaneous and natural communities and those so synthetic as to be populated by robots, communities best called environmental simulcra. In each case, space becomes the *signifier*, a sign so superficially simple but fundamentally complex as to have a multiplicity of meanings. As mentioned in chapter 4, Baudrillard (1988) and Eco (1986) called such environments *hyperreal*; the reality they possess is more intense, excessive, heightened, and abnormal than what usually passes for real. As with Gresham's law (Boorstin, 1964) such environments seem to be pushing real environments out of the way.

Environmental Simulacra

Environmental simulacra, environments that are hyperreal, enable fantasy to adopt a physical existence that surrounds the consumer. Consequently, media fantasies have begun to insinuate themselves into nature, into the world, and into the actual in many ways: clothing or fragrances designed to emulate a media personality or character; food with some connection to a movie or television show, such as Flintstones cereal or Bubba Gump Shrimp; toys; shops, such as the Disney or Warner Brothers stores; and pseudocities dedicated to further marketing. Some (but not all) Native American casinos like Foxwoods in Ledyard, Connecticut create cinema fantasy worlds (Cinetropolis) for those tired of gambling. All of these exist in a twilight between media fantasy and everyday experience.

In appropriate postmodern fashion, however, the hyperreal environment serves deliberate, strategic, commercial corporate purposes, acting in concert with the media and their many incarnations to rend culture into a commodity. The manufacturing of culture is nothing new, nor is its exploitation for commercial purposes, or even its embodying itself into physical space; what is new in 20th century *fin de siècle* America is the relative seamlessness with which television, film, radio, the recording industry, advertising, merchandising, manufactured products, theme parks, and technology work together toward marketing synergy.

It is clear that the physical environment is saturated with media (Real, 1989). Television and film are being increasingly vivified: media characters and environments are given a tangible, physical reality beyond mere picture tube or projector bulb simulation. Media environments and inhabitants no longer remain in the parallel time and space of the screen but are replicated in human time and space. These replicated environments or hyperreal settlements include Disneyland, Walt Disney World, EPCOT, and Eurodisneyland; the Mall of America and Camp Snoopy; Universal Studios; Las Vegas; and the unrealized Disney American History. These places are good examples of the physical manifestation of hyperreality in Baudrillard's (1983) sense of signifiers distantly removed from the signification of anything found in the real world, in nature.

Because semiotic analysis is based on linguistics (e.g., de Saussure, 1960), the signifier has usually been studied as a structural element in language, such as a word, an image, a note in a song, a television sitcom, a magazine advertisement, or a frame from a movie. Architecture and city planning can also be approached semiotically, and as media signification increasingly extends itself into physical environments, it is imperative to consider the signification implicit in a building or town plan. This has been done sporadically: Goodstein (1992), for example, examined the effect of Southern physical environments on television programming, and Gumpert and Drucker (1992) examined the effect of electronic technology on physical space and shopping habits. Both of these approaches look primarily at how the media are semiotically affected by space, however; work also needs to be done on how space is semiotically affected by the media.

It is surprising that there has not been more work done on the semiotics of space, because spatial signifiers per se are nothing new. The pyramids, the Temple Mount, the Wailing Wall, Machu Pichu, and Mecca are all examples of signifying space. What is new and different about hyperreal spatial signifiers like EPCOT and Disney American History is that their primary purpose is commercial, not spiritual and communal; although environmental simulacra do serve a spiritual or communal function, it is spirit or community as commodity. Interestingly, by mimicking classical forms and structures, environmental simulacra elevate commercialism to a level of spirituality. Tourists at EPCOT or Las Vegas fulfill, in part, the traditional role of pilgrims and worshippers. Ironically, however, in a postmodern environment the moneychangers are the temple.

One reason for the success of hyperreal environments is that the phenomenon of mythotypes, mentioned in chapter 5, is not limited to electronic representations. Spatial environments that effectively evoke myth can be just as powerful because they involve a pilgrimage and the public consumption of spectacle. In a sense, a journey to the ersatz Great Pyramid called *Luxor Las Vegas* has a lot in common with a spiritual journey to an actual pyramid with one exception: Sacrificial offering at the former holds the promise of spontaneous earthly wealth.

In *environmental simulacra*, then, myths narrowly displaced into popular media are given spatial concreteness, but these myths serve the purposes of commodification and commercialization, not of value definition, assimilation, or other traditional mythic functions, although these too are clearly ancillary effects. The process of *media vivification* means that characters and places with a mythic familiarity are transplanted from their electronic reality into our reality, are given life, and empowered to extend themselves further into a seamless commodified environment.

Perhaps the simplest and least subtle example of a physical manifestation of a media fantasy environment is the Cheers bar found at many U.S. airports. These bars look a lot like the one from the television program "Cheers": the interior is decorated like the television set, in the same mix of brass and wood, with the trademarked Cheers logo prominently displayed. This, by itself, is not so different from any neighborhood bar in America, but what is remarkable about airport Cheers bars is that denizens of the electronic version have emerged from the television to inhabit it. Sitting prominently at the bar are automatons who approximate Cliff (John Ratzenberg) and Norm (George Wendt) from the television series. These robots drink their beer, look around, and carry on a pointless conversation, no differently than they did on television.

The success of this particular environmental simulacrum can be attributed to the sort of patrons who habituate it: travelers on their way to or from home, probably feeling a mix of bittersweetness, anticipation, depression, excitement, and loneliness, emotions shared with the characters on the show. The Cheers bar presents travelers with a perfectly familiar environment, even in a town they have never been before because of its similarity to the one in the television show, a place that has probably been a part of their lives for many years. As the theme song of the show intones, "Sometimes you've got to go where everybody knows your name."

Why are hyperreal settlements like the Cheers bars becoming more common? Precisely because of the artificial sense of comforting déjà vu that they provoke. In hyperreal settlements, as in most postmodernism, a familiar facade has been plastered over something frightening, mysterious, and new. If modernism was "the shock of the new" (Hughes, 1981), then postmodernism is the comfort of the alien. From both a literary and psychological perspective, it is safe to say that most people do not like surprises. Their comfort in familiar story structures has a powerful impact on the construction of popular and literary storytelling (Cawelti, 1976; Jauss, 1982) of which there is ample evidence in the preponderance of movie sequels and television spin-offs that duplicate with only the slightest changes in their veneer. Consequently, it should come as no surprise that hyperreal settlements, such as the Cheers bar, coopt familiar environments from the mass media, because many Americans probably know these spaces better than any others.

Even chain restaurants like Planet Hollywood or the Hard Rock Cafe, carefully cultivate a sense of déjà vu among their patrons through the display of familiar memorabilia and consistent design from city to city; the memory that is reclaimed is of some media experience, prompted by the display of the Terminator's motorcycle or Keith Richard's guitar. As with the airport Cheers bars, a diner at one of these restaurants can feel at home wherever they are, surrounded by comfortable cultural artifacts. Even the name *Planet Hollywood* seems to imply some sort of plan—utopian or otherwise—for global monocultural conquest, a beachhead for a Hollywood planet.

The messy real world, such as it is, has no place in environmental simulacra. The visitor or occupant is to some extent expected to become a part of the hyperreality, and the chaotic, unpredictable, organic outer world is eschewed. A simple example of this is that the Captain EO exhibit, which featured a filmed performance by Michael Jackson, was withdrawn from Disneyworld the same time that the performer developed legal and public image troubles. Boorstin (1978) described how *pseudo-events*—intentionally manufactured occurrences designed to look like and become news to accomplish particular political or commercial agendas—came to dominate the news media because they are so easily controlled, predicted, manipulated, and convenient; in his formula, real news is uncontrollable, unpredictable, impervious to manipulation, and inconvenient. Hyperreal settlements present the same advantages of pseudo-events in 3-D space.

Recent high-tech developments in Las Vegas illustrate these advantages, although one cannot escape the sense that as with *West World* (1973), promises that "nothing can possibly go *worng*" [sic] are not entirely reassuring. The Luxor hotel, the aforementioned gigantic black glass Great Pyramid, is a postmodern replica that bears an appropriately striking resemblance to the Masonic "eye in the pyramid" design on the back of U.S. one dollar bills. On the one hand, the scale of the spectacle detracts from its intended replication: The actual Egyptian Great Pyramid does not have a simulation of the Nile river circumnavigating a casino, nor does it have animated robot talking camels inside encouraging visitors to spend more money, nor inclinators that angle their way up and down the hollow inside surface, nor a lobby that could hold nine 747 airplanes. On the other hand, the spectacle at Luxor has as its singular purpose the commodification of ancient Egypt. For example, the Egyptian antiquity museum in the basement, billed as an authentic replica of the tomb of Tutankhamen, displays only plaster and plastic simulations of the treasure, but in the gift shop, where one is deposited on exiting the museum, there are actual ancient Egyptian antiquities for sale. True antiquities are a commodity, and the museum exhibits simulations. The whole experience is primarily cinematic (Taylor, 1998).

Other Las Vegas hotels are similarly hyperreal. The MGM Grand across the street from the Luxor tries to recreate the journey of Dorothy Gale from a Kansas cornfield to the Emerald City of Oz. Simulacra automatons of the characters from the MGM musical film *The Wizard of Oz* (1939) are scattered throughout the gargantuan hotel in a manner more overpowering than their cousins Cliff and Norm in the Cheers bars. That the MGM Grand uses the Wizard of Oz theme and not the potential James Bond theme (the rights to which they also own) says something about the audience to which the new Las Vegas is targeted.

Less derivative of contemporary media environments than the MGM Grand, the Treasure Island casino created its own hyperreality by airing an infomercial disguised as dramatic programming on NBC in prime time (Bird, 1994). To enhance the illusion that it was actual programming, during the infomercial, commercials for other products were aired. This program concisely illustrates the linked semiotics of hyperreality, because it acts as a signifier of the hotel–casino called Treasure Island, which is itself a signifier for Hollywood pirate movies, which are signifiers of Robert Louis Stephenson's novel, *Treasure Island*, which signifies a historical period of thievery on the high seas. It also illustrates the commodifying and commercial purposes behind hyperreality, because the infomercial tries to revive what is essentially a dead genre and fuel a hitherto unrecognized demand, particularly among kids, for pirate merchandise. As the infomercial demonstrates, this need can be no better satisfied than in the Treasure Island hotel–casino gift shop, which features a full line of eye patches, cutlasses, skull and crossbones flags, and talking robot parrots suitable for putting on one's shoulder. Interestingly, and unlike the other new hotels in Las Vegas, the Treasure Island hotel–casino makes due with actual humans instead of automatons in the full-scale pirate ship battle that takes place periodically in the synthetic lagoon in front of the hotel.

It is telling that in that life-sized battle between a British frigate and a pirate ship that takes place in the ersatz atoll in front of the casino, the pirates win. All of Las Vegas shares Treasure Island's new-age pirate mentality. For example, the *Secret of the Pyramid*, a high-tech Showscan movie–ride–experience shown inside the Luxor hotel, has as its villains the American government, the military, big business, and organized religion. This is an ironic—even cynical—narrative device: Although it seems that the entertainment being experienced is pirate anticapitalist, renegade, anticommercial, and anticonventional, the preponderance of associated gift shops and casinos belies a more traditional capitalist orientation. It suggests that if one wants to thumb one's nose at the system, one need only consume a product. This nicely serves the contradictions about Americans observed by de Tocqueville (1945a) and Baudrillard (1988), and discussed in chapter 4.

Predictably, no one is more successful at creating environmental simulacra than the Walt Disney Company. This is not surprising: Walt Disney had been a modernist, futurist, and utopian (Klein, 1993; Wilson, 1994). He conceived of EPCOT not as another theme park (as Disneyland was), but as a prototype for future human society. The name *EPCOT*, in fact, is an acronym for Experimental Prototype Community of Tomorrow. Although its eventual embodiment after Disney's death ended up looking more or less like another theme park, its origins as an engineered human habitat remain just beneath the surface. Utopian futurist dreams still guide Disney corporate-development plans so long as they hold the promise of a profit.

EPCOT is a mix of Disney sensibility, Jetson technology, and real-world simulacra, so it is not really Walt Disney's modernist vision, but rather Disney CEO Michael Eisner's postmodern vision. This is particularly attenuated at the sanitized World Cultures Pavilion, where there is a miniature Germany, a tiny Japan, a little Morocco, and other microcountries, each populated by employees in Disney versions of the national costume, serving up cuisine and souvenirs meant to represent the designated culture. At the German pavilion, for example, Disney cast members, wearing Lederhosen, yodel as they serve beer and sauerkraut. These exhibits are not so much what these cultures are as what Americans, or Disney, would like them to be. By gathering these little hyperreal enclaves in one spot, EPCOT becomes the logical antithesis of the Hard Rock Cafe: If at the Hard Rock Cafe one can go around the world and stay home, at EPCOT one can stay home and see the world. EPCOT's vision of the future is of the multinational corporate kind, because its exhibitions are sponsored by Exxon, AT&T, Kraft Foods, and others. A recent manifestation of this is an exhibit called *Innoventions*, where park guests find that the glimpse of tomorrow they receive is actually a laboratory to test the market viability of new products. The hyperreal future is never far removed from consumer product marketing.

Merchandising and licensing, product placement, intertextuality, theming, and environmental simulacra all create a synergy between different aspects of the media, between entertainment and aspects of life not previously thought of as being connected to it, and create an environment in which identity is associated with consumption. Synergy is the extension of media, an extension that renders the mythotypes underlying transparent narrative texts to be inescapable and omnipresent. This reinforces the power of those mythotypes, but also makes them more familiar, creating new opportunities for the polysemic projection that transparency encourages. In that synergy, to paraphrase Michael Eisner of Disney, one plus one equals four (cited in Auletta, 1995a). Eisner was certainly talking about magically compounding revenue and profits, because elements within any synergy serve as advertisements for the other elements. There is another place where one plus one equals four, though: As texts become transparent, and as they make increasingly more references to each other and products, one text plus another text makes at least four texts, and certainly many more—as many texts as it has readers.

7

The Transparent and the Opaque

Nobody's going to say that Huckleberry Hound is too American.
—David Levy, Senior Vice President of International Advertising
Sales, Turner Broadcasting (cited in Mifflin, 1995, p. D1)

The American prime-time soap opera "Dynasty" was phenomenally popular in Norway, but Norwegian audiences apparently were watching a different show than were American audiences. Because "Dallas" was not shown in Norway, the reception of its chief competitor was enthusiastic, but conditioned by local audience attitudes and beliefs. Gripsrud (1995) documented these alternative readings, which due to a variety of domestic reasons, did not include the predominant American reading of "Dynasty" as high camp (p. 160). At the same moment, no Norwegian television programs were being shown on U.S. television.

Looking at successful international media texts like "Dynasty" reveals how they embody transparent apparatuses. Conversely, looking at texts that have not been internationally successful reveals how they have made use of other, nontransparent devices. This latter type can be considered *opaque* media to the extent that they resist indigenous readings. A film like *The Lion King* (1994) or a television show like "Walker: Texas Ranger," "Maria la del Barrio" (Galavision TV), or "Neighbours" embody transparency created by the apparatuses of openendedness, virtuality, circularity, archetypal dramatis personae, ellipticality, negentropy, inclusion, verisimilitude, omnipresence, production values, and synergy. By contrast, the Polish television show "Polski Zoo," a huge hit in its native country, or the international coproduction *Breaking the Waves* (1997) exhibit almost none of these properties. Their textual resistance to polysemy render them opaque. The export prospects of "Polski Zoo" or *Breaking the Waves* are limited because they are not easily opened to alternative projected readings.

THE TRANSPARENT

Children's programming is one of the four most exportable types of television programming, the others being news, sports, and music. In each category, brand-name recognition has meant an ability to dominate that market segment: The international news world has CNN, the international sports world has ESPN, and the international music world has MTV, all American companies that dominate the market. They are competing for a market worth more than $100 billion (Mifflin, 1995). Meanwhile, Disney, Nickelodeon, Fox, and Turner Broadcasting (the Cartoon Network) are competing to become the preeminent children's broadcasting provider.

Children's programming is, in part, so readily exportable because so often language is not a barrier: The movement of animated characters' mouths and of puppets or actors in full-head costumes do not pose any challenges to dubbing. The animals and fantasy creatures that make up a significant portion of children's television are internationally recognizable. Betty Cohn, president of the Cartoon Network, summarized what makes her job easier in an anecdote told to the New York Times; "I have a friend who grew up in Mexico and moved to the United States as an adult, where she was stunned to learn that Fred Flintstone could speak English" (cited in Mifflin, 1995, p. D4). The transparency of "The Flintstones" is so complete that it is not only accepted as an indigenous program, but in this instance, also perceived actually to be an indigenous program.

The Lion King

Disney's *The Lion King* (1994) exemplifies better than almost any other film the exportability of programming for children. Its transparency made it Disney's biggest hit ever, and a close examination of the text reveals why. *The Lion King* is a textbook case of openendedness, virtuality, circularity, archetypal dramatis personae, ellipticality, negentropy, inclusion, verisimilitude, omnipresence, production values, and synergy. Whether or not Huckleberry Hound is American, Simba is global.

Openendedness. *The Lion King* narrative does not close itself off to further iterations, but rather opens itself up to and invites them. Simba's family and most of the other characters are intact and triumphant at the conclusion, leaving no doubt as to their subsequent narrative viability. Like a few other Disney films, such as *Aladdin* (1993) and *Pocahontas* (1995), *The Lion King* has a sucessful direct-to-video sequel called *The Lion King II: Simba's Pride* (1998). To further iterate the open text, Simba's sidekick characters Timon (a wisecracking meerkat) and Pumbaa (a slow-witted warthog) had their own spin-off television series with occasional visits from some of the other *Lion King* characters. These openended devices serve to make *The Lion King* transparent because they render it polysemic and myth-like; like most myth systems, the narrative is seen as open and ongoing.

   Virtuality. Virtuality in a film or television program is the dimension through which it feels real, as if the artificial environment it has created is whole and consistent. In a sense, virtuality is the opposite of metafictionality, the tendency of postmodernism to play language games with the audience and make it aware that it is watching something artificial. Virtuality is closely related to the Hollywood omniscient visual style that seeks to make camera work, montage, and indeed, the whole filmmaking process invisible and unobtrusive. Cartoons by nature tend to be more artificial than virtual, because the license to defy nature is one they abundantly possess. Animator Tex Avery epitomizes the artifice of the animated genre in that his characters bounce, stretch, mutate, fall apart, explode, and otherwise never let the viewer forget that he or she is watching something artificial. That school of animation is also found in Disney's own *Aladdin* (1993) and *Hercules* (1997). *The Lion King*, however, strives for extreme naturalism, almost never indulging the potential its medium allows. It goes out of its way to mimic aspects of live action photography, such as in a rack focus from a parade of ants to a herd of zebras. Such a change of focus would have been necessary had the shot been of real ants and zebras, but animation does not share those lens limitations. Still, it affects that change of image in order to seem natural, to seem unanimated. Consequently, the talking animals seem much more real than they seem in a Bugs Bunny or Mickey Mouse cartoon. This is important if audience members are ultimately to accept the narrative as something of personal significance, which, judging from the box-office figures, they did.

   Circularity. The circularity of *The Lion King* also serves its transparency. Circularity is, in fact, the major theme of the film, evidenced in part by the Elton John–Tim Rice song at its beginning and end, "The Circle of Life":

> It's the circle of life and it moves us all
> through despair and hope, through faith and love
> 'til we find our place on the path unwinding
> in the circle, the circle of life.

Characters in the film articulate a philosophy of life consistent with the song. The lion king, Mufasa, explains to his heir, Simba, that all life is a circle, a journey that ends where it begins eternally and that even includes the King of Beasts: When lions die, Mufasa says, they become the grass that feeds the antelopes that feed the lions.

The narrative structure of the film is similarly one of departure and return—the Lion King is eternal, even if particular lions are mortal. Indeed, the title refers to Mufasa, to Simba, and to Simba's nameless heir revealed at the conclusion. Like the song, the film ends where it begins, with the birth and presentation of a new lion cub and heir to the throne. These two bracketing images—the presentations of the future king—are so strikingly similar that they are the image most often associated with the film (and an easy target of parody, as in *George of the Jungle*, 1997). The visual and aural implication of this narratology is consistent with the spoken belief systems of the characters: Life is circular, things find their natural place and time, and destiny is inescapable. Aspects of these notions are found in most world religions, so their mythotypic invocation in *The Lion King* easily invites projection.

Archetypal Dramatis Personae.   Myth systems create archetypal characters. Although those archetypes are particular to a specific mythic system, and in that sense there are no universal archetypes, the tendency to create archetypes cuts across all myth systems. This should cause no surprise: It is necessary, at the heart of all narrative. Characters with no basis in the familiar are incomprehensible. Disney therefore labors to allow indigenous archetypes to be projected into its films.

One of the simplest ways this archetypal projection is allowed is through the use of anthropomorphized animal characters, a device common to all Disney animated films. Virtually every system of myth and legend possesses anthropic animals, and animals are well-suited to archetypal projection for that reason. They are further well-suited because their raison d'être is projection: Animals are not human, after all, but in narratives we attribute human traits to them for narrative convenience. At the heart of Disney's empire, after all, is an anthropomorphized mouse.

Disney films always have animals of this type. In some cases, especially the more naturalistic animated features of the 1990s, they are human-like but cannot speak, such as Meeko the raccoon and Flit the hummingbird in *Pocahontas* (1995), Djali the goat in *Hunchback of Notre Dame* (1996), and Cri-Kee the cricket or Little Brother the dog in *Mulan* (1998). Most often they are humans in animal guise. Sometimes, they share a world with humans, including Jiminy Cricket in *Pinocchio* (1940), all the elephants except the unspeaking *Dumbo* (1941), the mice Jaq and Gus in *Cinderella* (1950), the love-struck dogs *Lady and the Tramp* (1955), Archimedes the owl in *The Sword in the Stone* (1963), Mowgli's friends in *The Jungle Book* (1967), the cats and dogs of *The Aristocats* (1970), and Tod and Copper respectively as *The Fox and the Hound* (1981). Less frequently, they live in a world inhabited only by animals, such as the pantomimic *Robin Hood* (1973), in which foxes, lions, and snakes act out the human roles from the familiar legend, or the somewhat more naturalistic *Bambi* (1942; humans do affect the narrative line in *Bambi*, but remain off-screen). *The Lion King* belongs to this latter, more naturalistic but humanless category: a world where humans are unseen, one which is similar to the actual habitat of the creatures depicted, and where they retain many of the behaviors of their real-life counterparts.

Clearly, talking animals transcend cultures. After *The Lion King*, the most successful Disney film internationally is *The Jungle Book*. There are simple reasons for this: Animated films are easier to dub into a different language than live action films because the mouth movements of the characters are more simple; animated animals are even easier to dub because audience members have few preconceived notions about how a talking lion's mouth ought to move. The absence of humans in *The Lion King*, and the relative lack of them in *The Jungle Book* (which has only Mowgli and, briefly, an unnamed girl), render them more polysemic, and therefore more transparent. With few or no humans around, few readily identifiable cultural traits exist that would exclude the audience. Even though the location and creatures are exotic, the characters are utterly familiar, precisely because the audience has great license to project indigenous values and assumptions onto them. It is no wonder that these two films were so successful.

Ellipticality.   More than any other mythotypic device, ellipticality encourages polysemy. An *ellipsis* is a leaving out of narrative information, an absence that must be filled in by the viewer to make the narrative coherent. The greater the absence, the more that needs to be filled in, and the filling-in, because it is supplied by the reader or viewer, inevitably involves projection. What they put in is what they possess already. Too much ellipticality and a narrative becomes incoherent and incomprehensible; little or none diminishes polysemy, leaves less room for projection, and hence inhibits transparency. Disney is skillful at finding a middle path, one with enough detail to tell a story, but not so much as to make that story culturally specific or exclusive.

An example of ellipticality from *The Lion King* is the opening sequence in which the animals of the Sahel gather around the towering Pride Rock. Rafiki, a baboon, makes his way through the crowd and climbs to the top where he embraces Mufasa, a male lion. Behind Mufasa is a female lion, Sarabi, cuddling newborn cub Simba. Mufasa sprinkles some dirt on the cub's head, ceremonially opens a melon and spreads its juice on Simba's brow, then holds the baby aloft to the cheering animal multitude. Characters in the film refer to this scene as "The Presentation of Simba," and these events clearly signify a ritual, with Rafiki acting as shaman or priest. Audiences are apt to find that ritual somewhat unusual (because animals are performing it, and dirt and juice are its symbols), but also familiar (because babies in most cultures are initiated into religious systems, shamans or priests perform such rituals, and a community typically is invited). The lack of narrative definition—the ellipticality—of what is going on allows the audience to project easily their own ideas of infant initiation onto what they are seeing on the screen. To Christians, it looks like a baptism, in which water symbolizes a new birth in the Holy Spirit. To Jews, it looks like a bris, in which Abraham's covenant is fulfilled by circumcision. Muslims might recognize the *shahada*, which involves whispering the articles of faith and the call to prayer in the ears of a newborn, or the *aqika*, where a lock of an infant's hair is cut so as to calculate its weight in gold. The Ibo of Nigeria would be reminded of the passage to manhood, which similarly embodies ritualized food, drink, clothing, and tribal elders who manifest animistic spirits. The Shona of Zimbabwe could project their ritual shamanistic circumcision practices (Gelfand, 1973). Practitioners of Shinto might link it to a ceremony in which an infant is registered at the temple, just as some castes of the Hindu faith might see a resemblance to their ritual of initiation at the time of a boy's puberty. Through the inevitable projection of each of these separate rites onto the polysemic movie screen, this simple sequence in *The Lion King* is well understood across many cultures, although not in precisely the same way. The presentation of Simba is none of these rituals and all of them. The details it leaves out allow the viewer to relate it to his or her own understandings and experiences.

Negentropy. The psychological need to believe that the universe is fundamentally ordered and purposeful, rather than chaotic and meaningless, is called *negentropy*. Kubey and Czisktemaholy (1990) showed that many television users rely on narrative programming to overcome the sense of disorder and pointlessness that they experience in their daily lives. Teleological myths served that purpose long before television did, and continue to do so as they are projected into polysemic media. *The Lion King* is powerful negentropic salve.

Narratives typically encourage negentropy through showing a tide of mounting chaos that is stemmed by a protagonist who restores rightful verdant innocence and order. This is certainly true of most mythic narratives: In the Western tradition, for example, Moses, Jesus, and Mohammed each purge the world of mounting sinfulness, chaos, and godlessness, themselves acting as the passageway to a world of sanctity, piety, and purpose. Film and television narratives are just as likely to adopt this negentropic strategy.

The Lion King fashions Simba as a hero analogous to others in the negentropic tradition. A monarch chosen by the gods brings vitality. Mufasa, the rightful king, is murdered by his avaricious brother Scar, causing a young and guilt-prone Simba to abdicate his inheritance. The rightful king signifies, embodies, and bestows order, so his death signifies, embodies, and bestows chaos in the form of Scar and his minions. Soon, the once verdant and bountiful pride land becomes an uninhabitable desert of bare trees and dry bones. Scar's hyena henchmen complain of the lack of food. There are dark hints of cannibalism. Nala, Simba's childhood sweetheart, is sent to look for food, but finds a fully grown Simba instead. She and the shaman Rafiki persuade Simba to return to Pride Rock, where—after a storm of purging fire followed by a shower of cleansing rain—Scar is defeated and eaten by his own lackeys. The next scene shows the pride lands restored to green, lush, and bountiful health. The parallels to Arthurian legend, in which a robust Arthur means a robust England, are unmistakable. Proper order vanquishes chaos.

Simba's journey parallels a cyclic and negentropic passage through Frye's (1957) four mythos genres. *The Lion King* begins in the mythos of spring, *comedy*, a time of birth, hope, and young love. Indeed, during this part of the film, Simba is born and betrothed to Nala, and all seems well in the kingdom. The song for this section, "The Circle of Life," promises that no matter what happens, things will work out in the end. The second section, the mythos of summer, or *romance*, begins as Simba reveals his fatal flaw: hubris.

He sings about the power he expects to inherit without much regard for how one should wield it:

> I'm going to be the main event like no king was before.
> I'm brushing up on looking down and working on my roar ...
> Everybody look left!
> Everybody look right!
> Everywhere you look I'm standing in the spotlight ...
> Oh, I just can't wait to be king!

Romance is epic adventure, and this song leads Simba and Nala into an adventure in an elephant graveyard where hyenas pursue them but from which, through a deus ex machina, they manage to escape.

This heralds the third major section of the film, the mythos of fall, *melodrama*. *Melodrama* is a literary form dominated by ongoing interpersonal conflicts between characters that embody simple emotions or dispositions; here, that conflict is between Mufasa, Scar, and Simba. Scar issues his warning in the song "Be Prepared":

> It's clear from your vacant expressions
> the lights are not all on upstairs,
> but we're talking kings and successions.
> Even YOU can't be caught unawares!
> So prepare for the chance of a lifetime.
> Be prepared for sensational news.
> A shining new era is tiptoeing nearer ...
> I know it sounds sordid but you'll be rewarded
> when at last I am given my due
> and injustice deliciously squared.
> Be prepared!

Scar, enacting typical behavior for a melodramatic antagonist, conspires with the hyenas and implements a plan that allows him—in melodramatic fashion—to murder his brother while shouting, "Long live the King!" He then manages to convince Simba that the young cub is responsible for his father's death, and Simba, ashamed, flees the pride land.

Here, the film enters its fourth and darkest phase, the mythos of winter, *irony*. With Scar in power, the proper order of things is utterly reversed, the barbaric hyenas given the run of the kingdom, and the pride land decimated. Simba's fortune has also undergone peripeteia: he is consigned to live with the lowliest of creatures (a meerkat, Timon, and warthog,

Pumbaa), eat the lowliest of foods (insects), but in exchange, gets to live a life free of royal worries and responsibilities. Timon and Pumbaa express the appeal of this reversal of fortune in the song "Hakuna Matata," a Swahili phrase that means "no worries, no responsibilities":

> Hakuna Matata, what a wonderful phrase.
> Hakuna Matata, ain't no passing craze.
> It means no worries for the rest of your days.
> It's our problem-free philosophy: Hakuna Matata!

The narrative eventually makes clear that this is not the life for Simba, though. The pride land has become so desolate that cannibalism seems to be contemplated, and Simba himself senses that his life is mystically connected to the other animals and that collectively they are unfulfilled. His father, Mufasa, returns to him in an apparition to say, "Simba, you are more than what you have become. You must take your place on Pride Rock." There is a second peripeteia.

Having been brought low, the king can now ascend the better for having lived as one of his humblest subjects. Scar is defeated, and a reprise of the song "Circle of Life" heralds the fifth and final phase of the film, a coda in which spring blooms again, winter is forgotten, and the mythos of comedy and the land itself are restored, this time with a new king, a new queen, and a new heir. Though new, all three of them are perfect stand-ins for the kings and queens and princes who have come before, a point the film's replicated mise-en-scène tries to underscore. Scar's entropy is vanquished, just as such chaos will always be vanquished, and in that vanquishing we get a stronger, wiser, empathetic king. In the world of mythic narrative, the Second Law of Thermodynamics does not hold. The audience is encouraged to see the ascension of kingly order as natural and proper, a dose of negentropy to help them cope with another day's worth of chaos in their real lives.

Inclusion.　　The mythotype of inclusion is the strategy of myth systems to encourage the reader–listener to sense that he or she is being addressed directly by the narrative and consequently, that he or she is participating in something, rather than merely observing it. Obviously, the text can go only so far to nurture this sensation, because it is actually the audience members' active projection into the text that creates it. Certain narratological devices are better than others, though, in coaxing out that projection.

The Lion King encourages audience identification and inclusion in numerous ways, urging audience members to think to themselves, "This is about me." Indeed, it tells a story of great simplicity but also of familiarity, a retelling of *Hamlet* in which it is easier to identify with the melancholic prince because of the preferable end to which he comes: Hamlet joins his father in death, but Simba joins his father in life, a comforting and wistful Hollywood platitude also on display in *Field of Dreams* (1990), *The Return of the Jedi* (1986), and hundreds of other movies.

Simba regains what we all hope to regain, so we are included in his triumph. Likewise, Mufasa is talking to all of us when he says, "You are more than what you have become." This inclusiveness is further reinforced in the Broadway stage version in a new song, "They Live in You," sung by Mufasa and reprised by Rafiki, an assurance that if any of us look hard enough into ourselves, we will see those who have gone before us, and they will live again:

> They live in you, they live in me.
> They're watching over everything we see.
> In every creature, in every star,
> in your reflection: They live in you.

Of course, Mufasa, and by rights, Simba are kings, and therefore are somewhat removed from our experience. *The Lion King* is merely one expression in a long tradition of king worship narratives. These narratives are either national or religious or, in some cases, both. Religious king narratives include the Judeo-Christian story of King David found in the Pentateuch, the Christian narrative explaining how the man Jesus became the earthly messiah and heavenly king Christ (or, more accurately, how the king became a man), the transformation of the earthly prince Siddhartha into the divinely inspired Buddha, and many others. Such narratives are not in and of themselves inclusive, but their ubiquity, and their invocation in contemporary media narratives, enables a viewer to feel that he or she is included in something familiar. Furthermore, the narratives cited evoke religious kings with a human nature, aspects of God or the gods to which the rest of us can relate.

All of these narratives have to do with the notion of election. Specifically, they present election by divine providence, an act that creates a thereby rightful monarch. Although on one level this is certainly exclusive rather than inclusive, in romance narratives, kings are embodiments of a people and a land by virtue of their ordinance. Thus, when King Arthur is ill, England has a famine, and vice versa. Likewise, when one-true-king-elect Simba abdicates, the land goes barren, the river dries up, and the circle of life is broken. Audiences are included in the worship of the king, and in a narrative sense, are embodied in the king. The king includes us.

Election engenders worship. Cults of personality currently propagated by the media are one manifestation of the inclusion phenomenon similar to the religious or secular king tradition. In the cases of Madonna, Leonardo diCaprio, or others like them, the media are manipulated to foster a sense of personal inclusion among fans of the artist, who feel as though they know him or her personally. This is particularly evident when the object of such dedication dies, as with Diana Princess of Wales, Haile Selasie, Tupac Shakur, Andy Kauffman, or Elvis Presley. Devotees not only grieve as though their late hero were a close friend or family member, but in some cases they even deny their death. Tupac Shakur, Andy Kauffman, and Elvis are purported to have staged their own deaths to find another private life, and Haile Selasie has been essentially deified by the Rastafarian religion. It would be reasonable to anticipate a similar response to the death of Princess Diana over the long term.

Verisimilitude.   Whereas virtuality makes a media text feel real, verisimilitude makes it look and sound real. One often, but not necessarily, leads to another. Virtuality is propagated through the Hollywood omniscient style, a set of conventions that have come to stand in for naturalism when it comes to visual narratives. That style entails motivated cuts, invisible montage, master shots, cut aways, shot–reverse shot, the 180° rule, eyeline match, point of view, and narrative closure. The elements of Hollywood omniscient style are described in minute professional detail in Arijon's (1976) *Grammar of the Film Language* and in more cultural terms by Fiske (1987). The point that both Arijon and Fiske made is that naturalism and verisimilitude are more a function of the form of a visual narrative than of its subject matter: A bizarre fantasy story shot in the Hollywood omniscient style could have a greater sense of verisimilitude than a documentary shot more experimentally.

Although it is an animated film, *The Lion King* plays it safe, adhering closely to the Hollywood omniscient style, which in this case, must be drawn as much as shot. No medium more than animation allows more radical divergence from the omniscient style as the films of Norman McLaren or even early Walt Disney demonstrate. Most Disney feature films cleave closely to formulaic convention. One exception is *Aladdin's* (1993) protean Genie, who defies the normal rules of the omniscient style, and even those of animated filmmaking: For example, in the final scene, he rips the cliché "into the sunset" shot off the screen and shouts, "Made you look!" Such Tex Averyish experimentation is rare in Hollywood films.

There are two attempts in *The Lion King* at breaking from the Hollywood naturalistic mold, the darkly expressionistic and Riefenstahl-inspired "Be Prepared" sequence and the wildly colorful pop imagery of "I Just Can't Wait to Be King." The rest of the film goes out of its way to emulate the omniscient style as a way of naturalizing what is portrayed. This includes changes in focus when no such camera is being used; long dolly shots, such as the one that follows Zazu the bird in the opening sequence; master shots that cut away to shot–reverse shot dialogue, as when Mufasa explains to Simba what happens to kings when they die; point-of-view shots, such as when Simba, Timon, and Pumbaa speculate on the nature of stars; eyeline match, regardless of whether those eyes happen to be at the level of a tiny meerkat or a tall giraffe; and careful maintenance of the 180° rule, such as how Pride Rock only shows its left side. These devices, used consistently throughout the film, suppress its plasticity as animation, enhance its realism, and convey verisimilitude.

Omnipresence and Synergy.   For huge international hits like *The Lion King*, omnipresence and synergy are nearly synonymous. While it was in theaters, and later when it was released on video, *The Lion King* was almost inescapable, regardless of the medium. This omnipresence was a by-product of carefully planned and implemented synergy strategy. Products and ideas related to *The Lion King* saturated the media: In addition to the film, there was a soundtrack album with music by Elton John and Tim Rice, which itself generated several top-40 hit songs, one of which won an Academy Award; there were several specials on The Disney Channel and other television media; several different book versions of the story were published, ranging in target audience from infants to adults; there was another high-quality, expensive book targeted at the art-book market, called, *The Art of the Lion King* (Finch & Jones, 1994); two children's CD-ROMs based on the film were sold, one an animated storybook and the other a series of games; these were assorted games for Nintendo and Sega video game systems; an official internet website and numerous unofficial but admiring sites sprung up; there were movie reviews, billboards, newspaper and magazine advertisements, and commercials. When the film was finally pulled from theatrical release, there were VHS videos in regular and deluxe packaging; a high-quality laserdisc edition; a television series based on two of the film's characters, "Timon and Pumbaa"; and an acclaimed Broadway musical version in the restored and Disney-owned New Amsterdam theater. The musical generated a new CD music release, new apparel featuring the play's logo, a new website, a book, a Tony Awards appearance, numerous Tony awards (including Best Musical), television specials, and other media, just as *Beauty and the Beast* did when it opened on Broadway.

The Broadway *Lion King* was itself a marvel of awe, wonder, purpose, joy, and participation: awe in the sheer scale of the spectacle and the amazing restoration of the New Amsterdam theater; wonder at how its many and various tricks and illusions are performed; purpose in its reassurances that a stage version of this tale would not repeat but enhance its telling; joy in the exuberant firsthand witnessing of the restoration of the circle of life; and participation through the theatrical devices that brought the audience into the narrative, particularly at moments such as "The Circle of Life," during which the audience participates in the presentation and adoration of Simba.

Outside the media, *The Lion King* was similarly extended through licensing and merchandising. Burger King gave Lion King toys away with children's hamburgers and sold Lion King cups. Uncountable merchandise could also be purchased: apparel of every type—T-shirts, sweatshirts, hats, pajamas, jackets, and tennis shoes, among others; beach towels; backpacks; plates and cutlery; keychains; pencils; clocks; watches; crayons; coloring books; sticker books; soaps; tooth brushes; and board games. Then, of course, there were the toys: stuffed plush versions of the characters in large and small sizes; small plastic figurines sold singly or in play sets; large articulated plastic character figures; plastic child-safe versions of the characters for toddlers; Halloween costumes; non-Ty Beanie Babies; and too many others to cataloge.

In short, *The Lion King* found its way into every medium, every room in the home, every aspect of contemporary consumer life. Each of these served as an advertisement for the others, magnifying the effect of the synergy. *The Lion King* achieved the kind of omnipresence reserved for a very short list of media events, rivaled only by the *Batman* films, *Jurassic Park*, and *Titanic*. That omnipresence granted the narrative an ethereal, myth-like quality, enabling further transparent projection.

Production Values.   Hollywood is known for lavishing large budgets on its feature films, and *The Lion King* is no exception. The typical 35mm film used in filmmaking and television making flashes 24 frames, individual images, on the screen every second. The illusion of motion results because these frames pass by so quickly that they are not perceived as a series of images, but as a single moving image. In the case of animated film or television production, that translates into a lot of drawings. To save money, television cartoons and many animated features use only one drawing for every two frames, or 12 drawings a second. This results in significantly lower production costs, and a shorter production cycle, because only half as many drawings are generated, but it comes at the price of a noticeable diminution of picture quality. The movement of characters in such productions is more jerky than in full animation productions. *The Lion King* made use of full animation, or about 130,000 sets of animated cels, that were actually shown on the screen. Many more drawings were generated, because each set of cels breaks down into several individual drawings, many cels were edited out, and many sketches rejected in preproduction.

There are other ways that low-budget animation saves money that producers of *The Lion King* were content to spend. Television series, and some low-budget animated features, reuse cycles of cels when a movement is repeated. For example, when characters on "The Flintstones" or "The Simpsons" go for a walk, the same few cels are shot repeatedly, because the motion is essentially repetitive. One second's worth of cels could thus be reused for the entire sequence, saving both time and money. Similarly, backgrounds can be repeated as characters pass them, resulting in the oddly configured Flintstone living room: chair, lamp, window, chair, lamp, window, chair, lamp, window. *The Lion King*, by contrast, used an animation technique called *character animation*, which requires that character movement not be repeated and that each character move in a distinctive way, a very expensive proposition that results in teams of animators working only on one or two characters in the film. Furthermore, *The Lion King* and other Disney features make use of detailed, handpainted or computer-rendered backgrounds that again put the price up.

Disney also uses familiar Hollywood talent as the voices of its characters, further increasing the costs. This would be almost unheard of on television, and other animated feature films tend to use only B-list talent, but Disney is strictly A-list. *The Lion King* featured the voices of Jeremy Irons, Whoopie Goldberg, Matthew Broderick, and James Earl Jones; other recent Disney features used the voices of Demi Moore, Danny DeVito, Kevin Kline, Robin Williams, James Woods, Mel Gibson, and Eddie Murphy.

Interestingly, of all Hollywood studios, Disney has a reputation of being the most cost-conscious of the Hollywood studios. A notorious memo from

Jeffrey Katzenberg, when he was in charge of feature production, urged cutting salaries for the talent and using more unknowns. Although the memo contributed to Katzenberg's dismissal from Disney a few years later, the philosophy remains in place. Disney tends to put the plurality of resources into animated feature production, simultaneously producing more and smaller features with few or no name stars on lower budgets, such as *George of the Jungle* (1997), *AirBud* (1997), and *The Parent Trap* (1998).

Production values are a modern equivalent to the Taj Mahal or St. Peter's Basilica: an opportunity to marshal extensive human and capital resources toward an object with mythic significance. The result in the spectator is awe, one of the fundamental mythotypes. Many of the specific scenes within *The Lion King* are designed to be awe-inspiring in and of themselves, particularly the aforementioned opening and closing sequences that feature representatives of every manner of sub-Saharan African animals worshipping a newborn king. Another epic scene is the stampede in the gorge, which features hundreds and thousands of rampaging antelopes. Clearly, *The Lion King* is transparent enough to encourage indigenous projection. There are many other films and television programs similarly adept.

"Walker: Texas Ranger"

Transparency is not limited to films like *The Lion King*. Television programs can also be transparent. "Walker: Texas Ranger" is an internationally successful television program whose success can be accounted for by the mythotypes. Like *The Lion King*, and indeed like all transparent media, the program is flexibly familiar. Publicity materials for the program describe its protagonist Cordell Walker as "one of the last old-fashioned heroes in the West" (CBS website marketing.cbs.com), situating the program in the Western genre, even though its setting is contemporary. In actuality, the program is a postmodern recombination of a Western, a martial arts film, and a cop buddy drama.

"Walker: Texas Ranger" is clearly an international success, although perhaps not of the magnitude of *The Lion King* or even "Dallas." Still, it has consistently been among the highest rated American shows domestically and is seen by roughly one billion persons internationally every week (Minkoff, 1998), entering its seventh season in 1998. In Germany, for example, "Walker: Texas Ranger" is shown successfully on RTL2 television. The program began airing in 1995 on Sundays at 9:00 p.m., and in 1997, it was moved to Mondays at 8:15 p.m., its time on air expanding to two episodes shown back to back. These double showings were at first repeats, then the new season was shown, followed again by repeats, even though repeating episodes in primetime is quite rare in Germany. Given its steady time on air, "Walker: Texas Ranger" is extremely successful.

According to Stephan Lerchegger, organizer of the German "Walker: Texas Ranger" website, "The [general] 'feeling' (in both countries) about the show is pretty the same as in the US—violent, 'dumb' and other attributes like that (well, except for die-hard fans)" (email, June 22, 1998)—those fans are having a more mythotypic and projective experience. "Walker: Texas Ranger" has also been shown in Slovenia (SLO2), Belgium (Club RTL), Great Britain, and France, and is broadcast or received by satellite in many other countries.

Although "Walker: Texas Ranger" needs to be considered as a melding of the Western, martial arts, and cop buddy genres, the Western influence is arguably the strongest. *Walker* demonstrates most of the mythotypic properties of that genre. It is open-ended to the extent that within the Western genre, and within the basic structure of the show, endless recombination and retelling are possible. Every Western is in some ways a recapitulation of a single American mythic narrative, Frederick Jackson Turner's (1962) "Frontier Thesis." The Texas Ranger of history, legend, film, and literature is one identifiable embodiment of this myth, finding expression in as recent a cycle as McMurtry's "Lonesome Dove" series (the novels and television miniseries *Lonesome Dove, Streets of Laredo, Dead Man's Walk,* and *Comanche Moon*). "Walker: Texas Ranger" reiterates this narrative in a contemporary setting.

In terms of circularity, the essentially conservative nature of the three genres represented in "Walker: Texas Ranger" assures an eternal return to order. Classic Westerns, cop buddy films and television, and martial arts movies typically follow a conventional structure of equilibrium, disruption, disequilibrium, conflict, restoration, equilibrium; any given episode of Walker hews closely to this pattern. The program is a little more unconventional in terms of its appearance because the genres that constitute it have distinctive associated iconography. In the case of "Walker: Texas Ranger," this leads to a higher degree of virtuality and verisimilitude. The cowboy hats, boots, six-guns, bolo ties, sagebrush, horses, saddles, and badges of the Western are juxtaposed with the contemporary iconography of the cop genre: flashy cars, semiautomatic assault rifles, shopping malls, and contemporary dress.

The action also exhibits a juxtaposition of elements. The conclusion of the episode "Deadly Reunion" (also titled "The Reunion") contains elements of all three genres: martial arts, Westerns, and cops. Walker has tracked down an assassin who plans to shoot a U.S. Senator. After taking away his rifle, the two men begin a martial arts battle. This ends with the two squaring off, face-to-face, without speaking, as if in a classic Western shoot out—each one serendipitously equipped with a sidearm. As in any Western, the villain draws and fires first, but misses. Walker shoots and hits. Unlike a Western, the setting is not the main street of a frontier town, but a competition firing range where the National Law Enforcement Pistol Competition is undergoing its final round. Also unlike a Western, the villain, only wounded, is dragged away by police officers. Such juxtapository recombinance invites polysemy.

Such recombinance is found throughout the program. The archetypal dramatic personae found in "Walker: Texas Ranger" are a postmodern hodgepodge consistent with the premise of the show. The character of Uncle Ray is a Native American shaman and C.D. Parker is a Texas Ranger-cum-barkeeper in the familiar Western generic idiom. Two other characters are straight out of the cinematic cop buddy genre embodied by films like *Lethal Weapon*: one is Jimmy Trivette, described by the website as Walker's "slick and hip" African American partner who rose up out of the slums by playing professional football before becoming a Ranger; the other is the exasperated but sincere assistant district attorney, Alex Cahill, Walker's sometime romantic interest. Cordell Walker himself combines elements of both the Western and the Cop genres, but the casting of Chuck Norris adds the additional dimension of the martial arts genre because Walker prefers kickboxing to gunplay. The result is a polysemic and disorienting generic melange.

Ellipticality, the leaving out of some information and the condensation of others into easy-to-read packets, is evident in the dialogue of "Walker: Texas Ranger." The following interaction occurs during the pilot episode, "One Riot, One Ranger," between Cordell Walker and district attorney Alex Cahill, after one of Walker's Ranger friends has been murdered:

Alex:	Walker, I'm sorry. I don't mean to be insensitive at a time like this, but I need to talk to you about something very urgent.
Walker:	Alex, I've a lot on my mind right now.
Alex:	Will you just hear me out? I'm sure you know we've had a circus in town all week.
Walker:	Yes, I know.

Alex:	Well, a young performer, a trapeze artist, was raped and beaten by three local men. They were arrested, but they're already out on bail! Since then, they have threatened the girl and the only witnesses who saw it happen, two other people from the circus. All three of them are absolutely terrified.
Walker:	Why are you telling me this?
Alex:	Because, they're planning to leave town tomorrow when the circus goes. That's what they've been told to do by those three animals, which means I have no case, and those rapists go scot-free.
Walker:	You still haven't answered my question. Why are you telling me this?
Alex:	Well, I thought if the circus people had a place to say, where they would feel safe ...
Walker:	If you're going to say what I think you're going to say, forget it.
Alex:	Walker, I need your help. She needs your help. Her name is Lisa Edwards. She's only sixteen years old. (Shows photo) This is what she looked like after those men got through with her. This poor little girl is destroyed. If we don't help her, this case is going to slip through the seams of the criminal justice system, and that would be a tragedy.
Walker:	Okay ... um ... take 'em to my ranch. I'll call Uncle Ray, and he'll take care of 'em until I get there.
Alex:	Walker, there is a special place in heaven for people like you.
Walker:	Yeah, and I can't wait to get there.

This scene takes place about 15 minutes into the episode. None of the action up to that point has concerned Lisa Edwards, the circus, or the rapists, so the audience is being introduced to this information for the first time. The narrative, rather than showing its audience these events, tells the audience about them—a significant narratological difference, one that saves time. To further economize, Alex characterizes Walker as heavenly, the rapists as animals, and the 16-year-old woman as a "poor little girl." To further simplify and characterize the nature of the situation, Alex gives her opinion of the legal system (of which she is a part) in a nutshell by saying that Walker must help or "this case is going to slip through the seams of the criminal justice system." As if to further punctuate the significance of that, Alex adds "and that would be a tragedy." All this information is conveyed in less than 2 minutes in a single, continuous take.

In terms of negentropy, Westerns—including "Walker: Texas Ranger"—reinforce a reassuring certitude that evil will be vanquished, that justice will prevail, and that the Ranger will get his (or her) man (or woman). Good and evil are drawn in sharp relief and embodied in the characters. For the most part, good people are attractive, clean, polite, and familiar, whereas bad people are unattractive, dirty, crude, and strange. The lyrics to the theme song, written by Chuck Norris, exemplify the extent to which evil is equated with strangeness:

> In the eyes of a Ranger
> the unsuspected stranger
> had better know right from wrong,
> 'cause the eyes of a Ranger are upon you.
> Anything you do, he's gonna see.
> When you're in Texas, look behind you,
> 'cause that's where the Ranger's gonna be.

This further reinforces negentropy by underscoring the vigilance and omnipresence of law enforcement. Order will be asserted when strangeness, just a temporary interruption, is purged. It is interesting to note that "Walker: Texas Ranger" airs on Saturday nights, a night that, for demographic reasons, is known for airing negentropic programming, including in the past shows like "Love Boat" (ABC) and "Fantasy Island" (ABC). As with "Love Boat," the negentropy leads to inclusion, and the large number of fan websites dedicated to "Walker: Texas Ranger" indicate a high degree of audience projection and participation.

Although not omnipresent, "Walker: Texas Ranger" has a strong presence in numerous media. In addition to the television program, there are several videotapes and assorted apparel. Chuck Norris has started a cigar manufacturing company called Lone Wolf that feeds off interest in the star and the show; his cigar smoking on the show is a kind of synergy. Websites have sprung up around the world. One German website, for example, provides an episode guide that gives correspondent transatlantic titles, such as the interesting German titles for the episodes "An Innocent Man" ("Psycho-Killer") and "Collision Course" ("Bonnie und Clyde"). The website also provides European fans with information about the status of the show in its home base, the United States. This is important because the show only becomes available to them at a later time.

The postmodernity of "Walker: Texas Ranger" contributes to its polysemy, which accounts for its transparency, which has helped to make it an international hit. The American origins of "Walker: Texas Ranger" probably help with its appeal, but international success is by no means limited to

American films and television. Any media artifact that exploits the narratological apparatuses of transparency has the possibility of global popularity. The soap opera is one genre with international appeal that is not controlled by Hollywood.

Soap Operas

Given the budgets with which American companies are able to work, it is small wonder that the films and television they produce have such high production values. Coping without such lavish budgets, and outside of Hollywood, the international television soap-opera market has come to be dominated by *telenovelas*, Spanish- and Portuguese-language exports from Latin America. Mexico produces between 30 and 40 telenovelas every year, over 4,500 hours worth, and generates roughly $500 million in revenue from them. Venezuela exports telenovelas to 30 countries, including southeast Asian and central and eastern European markets; these international sales are worth about $20 million annually. Brazil's TV Globo, one of its five networks, produces eight telenovelas a year; these bring in $31 million through exports to 70 countries (Margolis, 1997). In short, telenovelas are big international business.

The factors that account for this ubiquity are analogous to those for the American media. According to Arquimedes Rivero, head writer for telenovela producer Venevision, these programs are internationally successful because they stick to "themes that have been the same since the beginning of humanity": self-reliance, good defeating evil, romantic love (cited in Margolis, 1997, p. 50). These are embodied in shows like "Maria la Del Barrio" (Galavision TV), a huge international success about a poor young woman who moves into the house of a rich family that hates her and falls in love with one of the sons living there. Interestingly, several of these soap operas are filmed in Miami, and the Mexican producer Televisa plans to begin English-language versions of its most popular shows. The American influence is therefore felt even in the world of the telenovela. Rather than signify an end to cultural imperialism, telenovelas signify a shift of strategy—a dramatization of capitalism suited to broader tastes than American soap operas are (Oliveira, 1995).

According to Wasser (1995), however, telenovelas, such as those produced in Brazil, embody almost nothing of the originating culture: They are truly transparent. Brazilian cultural values are scarcely being exported; rather, they "undermine the autonomy of their own national culture" (p.

425). It is Wasser's sense that this is true of all successful international media and that American media can not be considered truly American any longer: International capital and international audiences have transformed Hollywood into a purveyor of transnational media for global tastes.

One example of an international soap attracting a projective audience is "Neighbours," which as Gillespie (1995b) showed became phenomenally popular among Sikh and Hindu families in suburban London. She found that particularly among young people, this show accurately replicated their life in Southall, even though "Neighbours" features an all-white Australian cast and setting. Gillespie found that gossip, as depicted in the program and as experienced in life, served as the primary polysemic link between "Neighbours" and Southall. The Punjabi youth in Southall saw gossip functioning in the soap opera in the same way that *izzat*, or family honor, functions in Sikh and Hindu families. This results in an extremely complicated and protean notion of national identity among young British Pakistanis and other groups (Jacobson, 1997).

Like all soap operas, "Neighbours" exhibits most of the 10 transparency-generating elements that render it polysemic and allow this projection. It is openended, capable of inexhaustible reiteration through the ability of characters to come and go, die and be reborn, generate previously unknown siblings, and reappear as played by other actors. This relates to its circularity, because disequilibrium will inevitably be restored, albeit in serial format this occurs over a large number of episodes, not the one-episode or two-episode equilibrium found in television sitcoms and drama programs. Gillespie (1995b) made clear the virtuality and verisimilitude of "Neighbours" in the high degree of projection it elicited from the Southall youngsters, the extent to which they felt it was descriptive of their lives. Furthermore, the soap opera was so real to these young people that they came to imitate it, to form social relationships with other young people in emulation of how characters on the show do. This was especially true of dating, which was essentially unknown to their more traditional-minded Sikh and Hindu parents, who considered it improper.

Archetypal dramatis personae are also evident in "Neighbours," as in any soap opera, which makes it easier for regular viewers to relate to the goings on. One example of such an archetype for the Southall teenagers was the town gossip, a role typically played by aunts in their culture, but fulfilled by Mrs. Mangel or Hillary on the show. In terms of ellipticality, soap operas typically tell the narrative rather than show it, perhaps more as a traditional defense against limited budgets than as a matter of aesthetic choice. Soap operas are among the most reiterative of narrative forms, leading to an elliptic shorthand through which past events are swiftly recapitulated.

Like all soap operas, "Neighbours" strikes a perpetual balance between the forces of order and chaos, so in that sense is not as *negentropic* as other genres. Their balance is predictable, however, and therefore likely to generate a reassuring level of comfort in viewers. Soap operas certainly understand the "horizon of expectations" that viewers bring to them, and how to frustrate and then satisfy those expectations (see Jauss, 1982). The *inclusion* aspect of "Neighbours," is self-evident, because personal participation is its primary attraction to Southall Punjabi families; viewers feel like participants and often watch in small interpretive viewing communities that shape and personalize the meaning. The official "Neighbours" worldwide website, for example, provides ample opportunity for fans of the show to debate which character is meanest, funniest, sexiest, or has the cutest pet, not to mention the chance to articulate what plotlines should develop on Ramsay Street, the focal point of the action. For example, one viewer expressed at that internet site the sentiment that:

> Caitlin should not die, nor leave. She should infact [sic] take a trip to England. She comes across me and we wed. I move over to Oz [Australia] and become [a] Ramsay Street trainspotter. Then, I also become Neighbours' youngest adulterer, when I have an affair with Amy Greenwood, [sic] she serves as my mistress for about three years until we part company and I move back to the UK. ("Fan Forum," 1998)

An argument could be made that part of "Neighbours'" success is its middle- and working-class setting, unusual in American television soap opera. As opposed to the urban industrial bleakness of indigenous British soaps like "Eastenders" (BBC TV) or "Coronation Street" (ITV), "Neighbours" depicts a breezier sun-and-surf life, leading to an element of wish fulfillment in its viewers. This led to a sort of omnipresence for "Neighbours" in Southall at the time; as Gillespie (1995b) described it, kids there could talk of little else.

Few other international image products rival the Hollywood monopoly, though. Australia and Latin American countries are successfully exporting soap operas. The British successfully export pop music, and India produces more films annually than the United States ("A World View," 1997), but no national entertainment industry is anywhere near as successful in terms of profit as the United States. It specializes in the transparent, whereas most cultures specialize in the opaque.

THE OPAQUE

The Lion King, "Walker: Texas Ranger," telenovelas, and "Neighbours" all exhibit the transparency necessary to become international phenomena. Not all transparent media become international hits, but films and television shows that are *opaque*—through their textual apparatuses close off meaning rather than open it up, ones that are closely grounded in or associated with particular interpretive communities—almost certainly fail to glean an international audience. Two examples of opaque media are "Polski Zoo," a popular Polish television program, and *Breaking the Waves* (1997), an international film that won the Gold Palm at the Cannes Film Festival.

Polski Zoo

The television program "Polski Zoo" is an excellent example of the democratization of transmission and reception in Poland, but also of the opaqueness of regionalized media. The program was on once a week, for 10 minutes, with a subsequent rebroadcast. It spoofed contemporary Polish parliamentary politics in classic (and complex) metered verse. Polish and international politicians appeared on the program to debate the pressing political matters of the day as animal puppets in a Polish zoo, speaking in humorous rhymed couplets. These animal caricatures function as a metaphor for the political philosophy, physical appearance, and communication style of the politician they parody. Some faces are fairly familiar to an outsider: Former prime minister Suhocka is portrayed as a llama, former president and intellectual Masowiecki is a turtle, U.S. President Clinton is a ram, and former Polish President Walensa is a lion. Representatives from scores of Polish political parties are similarly embodied. Olesky, a former communist, is a dinosaur; Pawlak of the Peasant Party, elected Prime Minister in 1993, is an ox; Michnik, a journalist, is a fox. Representatives of 16 different political parties are represented as goats, moose, ducks, gadflies, Koalas, birds, boars, mice, rats, devils, crows, bees, beavers, and other animals. Amidst the manifold political parties and democratic anarchy that make up contemporary Polish parliamentary politics, there has even been a beer drinker's party. The head of that party is portrayed on "Polski Zoo" as a gorilla in a beer logo T-shirt.

One interesting episode was "Program 89," broadcast the week after President Walensa dissolved Suhocka's parliament in June of 1993. It was an interesting moment in Polish history and for the show because the anarchy of Polish politics went from potential to kinetic. The episode began with an empty parliament as politicians scrambled to keep power and privilege.

Guard:	It sure is creepy in the high chamber today. Only the moose has something to do.
Chrzanowski:	(*Moose, National Christian Union, Speaker of the Parliament*) Yeah, someone has to close everything down.
Guard:	Hey, you, what are you doing here?
Cleaning Lady:	I'm only cleaning up.
Geremek:	(*Goat, Democratic Union*) There's no more applause in the high chamber.
Tusk:	(*Donald Duck, Liberal Democrat*) Where are the fights?
Hall:	(*Conservative Party*) Where are the debates?
Olesky:	(*Dinosaur, Social Democrat, Former Communist*) Our salary has been taken away!
Korwin-Mikke:	(*Gadfly, Union of Realistic Politics*) So were our fax machines!
Cleaning Lady:	Uh-oh ... here are some members of parliament at the door ...
Maciarewicz:	(*Movement for the Republic*) Dear lady, please let me in for a second.
Cleaning Lady:	(*seeing several animals at the door*) Who are you? What do you want?
Maciarewicz:	I left my notes in there.
Olszowski:	(*Koala, Movement for the Republic*) And I left my voting card.
Cimoszewicz:	(*Social Democrat*) I left my Parliamentary Privilege of Immunity!
Kaczynski Twins:	(*Centrum Agreement and Supreme Chamber of Control*) And we left our heads!
Bielecki:	(*Liberal Democratic Congress*) I left some bills to be passed.
Olszowski:	And as for me—I left behind complete and detailed plans for decommunization.

In this scene, a guard and a cleaning person were left in control of the parliament building as dismissed politicians plot and scurry to get inside and protect lost perks. Centrist politicians complain that they had completed perfect plans for reform that were on the verge of passage, only to have them locked away in the empty chambers. It proved easy for these animals to agree now that they had been locked out, even though the zoo was closed (that is, the parliament was dissolved) because it had reached an impassable stalemate.

A bit later in the episode, the animals comment on having been forced out of the zoo by the king of the animals, the Lion (President Walensa).

Moczulski/ Kwasniewski:	(*Bird, Confederation for Independent Poland/Boar, Social Democrats*) We wanted to give that Llama (Suhocka) a lesson.
Suhocka:	(*Llama, Democratic Union, Prime Minister*) I had some doubts myself. I saw the Lion's tricks coming.
Pawlak:	That may be, but he gave us the lesson instead.

This scene showed a fascination not just with political personalities, but also with the parliamentary strategies and tactics they use. In a corollary fashion, the scene identified the political process as the source of the chaos. It also showed that no one, not even Walensa, was above criticism on "Polski Zoo," a different lion indeed than the one in *The Lion King*, one without a divine right, and destined for defeat in the next election. Real life is not always circular.

When it was broadcast, the program was phenomenally popular in Poland and was the centerpiece of many Polish family evenings. If one considers the fact that many Americans do not even know the name of their own vice president, it is surprising that a show using sophisticated political parody could be so popular anywhere. American attempts at animated, animalized, television political humor, such as Stephen Spielberg's "Capitol Critters," have been short-lived. The ratings of such programs have been insufficient to warrant more than a few weeks' run.

In spite of its many appeals, "Polski Zoo" can scarcely be considered transparent: Indeed, its inherent Polishness makes it opaque to non-Poles. It inspires none of Blumenberg's (1985) mythic engagements, nor does it even try: Rather than inspire awe, it prompts contempt; rather than wonder, certitude; rather than purpose, a sense of aimlessness; rather than joy, cynicism; rather than participation, disengagement. In addition, it does not engage the mythotypes. Following as it does the vicissitudes of the Sejm, it lacks openendedness. Polish politics are real enough, so "Polski Zoo" needs no virtuality and in fact, pushes in the opposite direction. As this episode shows, it lacks circularity: Politicians come and go for good. Because it parodies real people, its animals are not embodiments of dramatis personae. Details are spelled out, not ellipsed. Entropy, not its opposite, is the state of affairs and its affective response. Non-Poles are excluded from recognition and participation. The program is time- and place-specific and its production values charmingly low. In short, there is nothing openly polysemic about "Polski Zoo." Alternative readings are, essentially, misreadings. It neither wants nor embraces outsiders in its opacity and will not get them. Eventually, the show became opaque even for the Poles, foundered in the ratings, and was cancelled. The giddiness of early democracy gave way to Western pragmatism, and the people lost interest.

Breaking the Waves

Another example of textual opacity is *Breaking the Waves* (1997), a disturbing variation on the Gift of the Magi tale and an international coproduction. By all critical accounts, it is a superb and landmark film. It features an international cast and crew: a Danish director, a Scottish and a Swedish star, and pan-European (i.e., Dutch, Danish, Swedish, Norwegian, French, Finnish, and European Union) financial sponsorship. The story of *Breaking the Waves* is about the scarcely comprehensible lengths to which the protagonist, Bess, is willing to go for love. Its inversion of the Gift of the Magi entails Bess's quadriplegic husband Jan, who wants her to go on with her life, so encourages her to have affairs with other men. Although she finds these affairs repulsive, she believes God has told her that they will have a mystical ability to heal her beloved. Her final act of self-sacrifice, resulting in her death, indeed seems to cure Jan of his spinal injury and Bess seems to earn God's favor. The film got extremely enthusiastic reviews in the United States and won the Grand Jury Prize at the Cannes Film Festival, but did poor box-office business due to limited distribution and obvious art-house appeal. *Breaking the Waves* was a film for cinema enthusiasts and few others.

There is no circularity to it. At the end of the film, nothing is as it was; equilibrium is reached after severe disruption, but one radically different than the equilibrium before. The protagonist is dead and her love evolved to a transcendental state from which it cannot return. In terms of virtuality and verisimilitude, *Breaking the Waves* looks and feels strange and makes little effort to hide its artifice as a film. It displays a jarring contrast in visual styles, with section titles portrayed in richly colored pastoral postcards, shot in opposition to the narrative sections (called *chapters*), which are shot in a washed-out, jump-cut, hand-held, jarring cinema verité style that evokes documentary. The contrast between the sections and section titles disrupts and subverts the audience's ability to get and stay inside the narrative, to lose oneself to the story, as does the choppiness of the storytelling itself. Furthermore, the characters act in strange ways that push the audience back, displaying emotional responses and strategies that are difficult to understand or empathize.

The film presents few familiar archetypes. It is difficult, especially, to relate to the protagonist Bess, to her ideas, faith, choices, and fate. She is enigmatic. The film is less elliptical than most, giving rather more explicit detail than an audience member is apt to want, need, or feel comfortable with. This leads to considerable audience discomfort, particularly during the scene in which Bess prostitutes herself to several psychotic merchant marines who essentially beat her to death. The film did little to create a traditional sense of order through textual negentropy, although it depends on what one means by order as to whether or not *Breaking the Waves* restores it, nor does it encourage its audiences to feel order in their lives. The negentropy of *Breaking the Waves* is of a strictly mystical and spiritual nature. On a material and physical level, the narrative is a long steady march into chaos. On a spiritual plane, however, Bess is given her desired heavenly reward—the ringing of church bells where there are none.

It is hard to feel included in *Breaking the Waves*, given the extremity and remoteness of its location and emotions. Openendedness scarcely applies to it because its narrative has nowhere else to go at the conclusion. Bess is dead and a sequel is inconceivable. Despite the many sources of international funding, the production values remained low: consistent with most international productions, but far short of a Hollywood blockbuster. In terms of omnipresence, *Breaking the Waves* was almost invisible, well-known only to art cinema interpretive communities. The film played only in foreign film cinemas in major U.S. cities and even an Oscar nomination for Emily Watson as Best Actress and a Golden Globe nomination for Best Picture failed to spark box-office revenue for the film or get it any media attention. It fostered no apparel, no novelization, no television spin-off, no video game, no amusement park thrill ride, nor could it, although the screenplay by Lars Von Trier was published.

Breaking the Waves belongs to cinéastes. "Polski Zoo" is Poland's. Yet, "Neighbours" is Australia's, Britain's, and even Southall's. *The Lion King* and "Walker: Texas Ranger" are everyone's. One is unlikely to see "Polski Zoo" on American, British, Japanese, or Nigerian television, but the tiny Baltyk Cinema in Sopot, Poland was, in June 1998, showing only five films, all from Hollywood: *Full Impact* (1998), *Flubber* (1997), *Wag the Dog* (1998), *Primary Colors* (1998), and *Blues Brothers 2000* (1998). One of the most popular television programs in Poland at that time was "Maria la Del Barrio," the aforementioned telenovela. None of these are Polish, but they feature a transparency that "Polski Zoo" lacked. Although these films and television programs are not Polish, the Polish audience sees itself. Transparency moves, but opacity stays put.

8

Cultures and Anarchy

The global audience is too infinite to be knowable.
—*Wasser (1995, pp. 434–435)*

Reading, like remembering, is dynamic. It builds on prior readings and memories. Although initial readings invite the projection of preexisting cultural conceptions, particularly when the text is transparent, subsequent readings necessarily become dynamic hybrids of projection and reception, become protean syntheses. Although they reinforce the 10 mythotypes, these syntheses couple them with new images and sounds. This, in turn, creates a new mythology in the sense of Barthes (1972) and Lincoln (1989), a *metalanguage* or "second language, in which one speaks about the first" (Barthes, 1972, p. 115), but dangerously so because "myth is always a language-robbery ... Is there no meaning which can resist this capture with which form threatens it?" (p. 131). This is not a global monoculture, but quite its opposite: thousands of Creoles, well documented by Allen (1995) and Liebes and Katz (1993) among others. The result is not a coming together in one monoculture but a coming apart. With what does that Babelization leave us—with cultures or with anarchy?

Arnold (1932) defined *culture* as "the best that has been thought and said," and saw in it the antidote to the social anarchy he felt was threatening Edwardian England. Late 20th century criticism uses culture in a different sense, equating nations with cultures: A people—a nation in the ethnic and linguistic sense—have a culture. There are, consequently, many cultures, a cacophony of cultures. In the face of this din, several questions emerge: How do we define what a culture is? How do we know one culture from another? Most importantly, in a world tightly interconnected via global media, where does one culture leave off and another begin? Transparency is likely to make issues of identity and culture murkier than they have been; its polysemy, itself a kind of anarchy, will doubtless create more cultural confusion and fragmentation.

Fear of that fragmentation has led national leaders and concerned scholars to decry imported American media. Much of that rhetoric invokes essentialist arguments about culture: a sort of updated Arnold (1932) is used by elites who argue that the best that has been thought or said in their language by indigenous authors needs to be preserved against the unwanted onslaught of inferior foreign media. Such has, for example, been the French approach (Pells, 1997) and the approach recommended by numerous international commissions (Hamelink, 1997; Vincent, 1997). Thomas (1997), likewise, adopted this construction in theorizing the role of the mass media in formulating national identity, describing "hitherto … stable understandings of national identity" (p. 4) as if Frenchness and other identities were immutable and eternal and only now under threat from global media. This is a naive approach to culture. Such a conceptualization seeks, misguidedly, to preserve a confinable, generating, and idealized wholeness to be found in a nation's past, what Prakash (1997) called "the cultural representation of the modern nation as the return of ancient solidarity" (p. 538). Prakash regarded such homogeneity as purely mythic, however, because the modern nation remains "haunted by alienating otherness" (p. 539); in short, national culture is defined by its relation to the Other and not strictly by internal properties. National identity had blurry edges to begin with; by virtue of its cultural stealth, transparency can only blur the distinctions further. The young British Pakistani fans of "Neighbours" mentioned in chapter 7, a group whose national identity has only fluid content (Jacobson, 1997), is only one example of this. Culture consequently may not be as vulnerable to homogenization as previously assumed, that process being "ineffective" and "incomplete" (Waisbord, 1998, p. 381).

Yet, the Other is seen by many nationalists as an infection, in spite of the fact that the self cannot be truly separated from the Other. Cultural preservationists see the threat to indigenous culture posed by the Other as portrayed in the transnational movement of media as one of contamination. It is true: Imported media are indeed a kind of contamination, but not in the sense that cultural conservatives mean. Rather, it is a contamination closer to the way Fisher (1995) used the term: all culture is a contamination, and all culture is already contaminated. Papastergiadis (1995) was more precise: Cultural Studies discovered that all culture is a hybrid and hybridization universal, a discovery that he follows with the exclamation, "What a relief!" (p. 9).

The problem is one of definition. What exactly is *Frenchness* or any other identity? Is it intact, self-contained, and immutable, as cultural preservationists would have us believe, or is it permeable, fluid, and mutating? Modernism postulated that identity is a "coherent cultural whole that endures through time" (Waisbord, 1998, p. 385), but that is not borne out by postmodern era evidence. To transgress the boundary of the French and non-French is to recognize that the Other is hybridized with the Self, and there are many political, economic, and cultural reasons why such osmosis may not be tolerated by those who make laws. In such a context, though, the attempt to save French culture by staving off Hollywood seems like trying to save Holland with a finger in a crumbling dike: a stop-gap measure at best, because eventually the collapse of the dike will create a Holland–sea hybrid. Like that salty mud, culture is melange. As Gillespie (1995b) put it, "All cultures are hybrid, syncretic, creolised, or impure" (p. 4).

The mass media play the primary contemporary role in blending that Creole. Thomas (1997) was right when he said:

> The media and other dominant cultural institutions play a crucial role in linking subjects to a common history of origins, continuities and futures. The mass media, in addition to educational and religious institutions, and the family, play a central role in defining national identity, charting its boundaries and maintaining its presence in the popular imagination. (p. 3)

Postcolonial theory (e.g., Bhabha, 1997; Prakash, 1997; Said, 1993; Spivak, 1995) suggests, however, that texts are not quite so mechanistic and programmable as Thomas believed and that identity is protean and therefore slippery. The media shape cultural identity, but not in the simple this–that or us–them manner that traditional cultural theorists endorse. Media tend to take an interstitial path.

The reason for this interstitiality is the contact between cultures and that is nothing new. As Bhabha (1994) and others demonstrated, cultures are not defined primarily through internal and inherent attributes, but through their constant contact with other cultures, with the Other; as Lotman (1991) put it, *culture* is how agents interpret and process the signs that surround them and form relationships with them. Often, that contact has been through colonialism. As Papastergiadis (1995) said:

> Under colonialism both the ruler and the ruled produced new self-images which were selectively drawn from earlier forms of social consciousness. Colonialism found legitimacy because it established a set of codes that were

common to both cultures, and because it was thereby able to manipulate the importance of components that were previously subordinate or recessive in these cultures. The seeds for the founding colonialism were already contained in the consciousness of both parties, and central to its legitimacy was the valorization of the pure and the denigration of the hybrid. (p. 12)

Transparent media are neither purely foreign nor purely indigenous, neither colonial nor subaltern: they are in between, interstitial, with elements of both, and with the seeds of something else. Papastergiadis called this the *hybrid text*, and like any true hybrid, it contains both this and that. Just as non-American media show traces of Hollywood, so do Hollywood media exhibit traces of the non-American: Indian director Shekhar Kapur, for example, has seen traces of Hindu film devices in Hollywood films like *True Lies* (Wasser, 1995).

What is created by films and television like *True Lies* is:

> Both a proliferation and a polarization of identities, both a strengthening of existing local identities and a formation of new identities … Thus globalization may mean neither universal assimilation into one homogeneous culture, nor a universal search for roots and revival of singular identities, but a complex, highly uneven process of many-sided translation. (Gillespie, 1995b, pp. 18–19)

Certainly, it is true that the American mass media, hegemonic as they are within the United States, have hardly created a single American culture—the melting pot is the stuff of fable, but not fact. If they could not provoke monoculture in the United States, their home base, then how likely is it that the media will produce monoculture in other countries, or indeed globally? As Wheeler (1998) noted, media researchers alarmed by the alleged encroachment of homogeneous monoculture tend to "underestimate the resiliency of local identity and cultural difference in the developing world" (p. 359). Interpretive communities are using the media to generate new, protean identities, linked in part to the official indigenous cultural identity, in part to the images found in the media, in part to international and regional cultural movements. In short, identity is adrift, navigating waters that are both familiar and strange, and using cultural traditions as its chart and the global media as its sextant.

This floating exchange between cultures slips inside the existing dialogic codes of each and causes them to mutate, changing not only perception of the Other, but of the Self. Lotman (1991) called this process of hybrid text creation *infection*. For Lotman, when a text first arrives in a new context it is alien, odd, Other, and consequently seen as a curiosity, but nothing dangerous. Soon, however, the text and the culture undergo a change: Each begins to alter the other. As this process proceeds, the text is often seen to reveal its true nature only in its new cultural context; the original source no longer speaks for or through the text in the new context. This permits the text to be assimilated into its new home, after which it has shaped the nonnative culture in its own images. After that, the text has become so much part of its host that new texts created by that host will thereafter be responsive to it, much as Bloom (1994) argued that Western literature after Shakespeare is a response to Shakespeare.

New cultures are, therefore, not synthetic, but emergent from preexisting attributes coaxed out through contact with foreignness and alterity. As Papastergiadis (1995) put it:

> Hybridity is both the process by which the discourse of colonial authority attempts to translate the identity of the other within a singular context, but then fails and produces something else. The interaction between the two cultures proceeds with the illusion of transferable forms and transparent knowledge but leads increasingly to resistant, opaque and dissonant exchanges. (p. 18)

Thus, although transparency initially eases the entry of nonindigenous texts into new contexts, it ultimately engenders a resistance to and misunderstanding of its origins.

Those most worried about the loss of their own culture under the pressures of another, then, may be looking at the problem in the wrong way. Bhabha (1997) tried to reframe such thinking, "shifting the question of identity from the ontological and epistemological imperative—*What is identity?*—to face the ethical and political prerogative—*What are identities for?*—or even to present the pragmatist alternative—*What can identities do?*" (p. 434). This refocusing entails forgetting essential definitions of culture and looking instead at functional definitions. Identities, particularly ethnic identities, shift up and down a continuum of domination, enclosure, and competition in ongoing adaptation to changing needs (Pieterse, 1997). Transparent media parallel nation-states and native language in identity construction.

The inherent hybridity of culture is perhaps more plainly apparent to Americans, whose national mythology embraces it, even if Americans do not always put it into practice. The American media industry has a fairly clear notion of what identities can do: Identities enable identification, which as Jauss (1988) showed includes admiration, sympathy, catharsis, and association. Admiration, sympathy, catharsis, and association easily turn into emulation, and emulation has consumer potential. The audience member who sees his or her identity reflected in a particular movie or television program is the one most likely to buy another ticket, buy the sound-track album, wear the T-shirt, or read the novelization. Without identification, and consequently emulation, how could *Titanic* (1997) have led to the consumption it did? Bhabha (1997) asked, "What can identities do?" The cynical answer is simple: Through the skillful deployment of transparent apparatuses, identities can promote consumption, build markets, and make the identity exploiter rich. Yet, that is not all identities can do. They can build social and political movements and momentum, rewrite history, start revolutions, topple governments, and change the world.

American media producers prefer the former role for identities, the profitable one. For cultural, political, and economic reasons, they dominate the international media marketplace and are likely to continue to do so given their preeminence in emerging technology. American political insiders see this as the primary route to sustained American prosperity. Indeed for some, it is more than that: It is a strategic way to Americanize the world, to use identity to make money and make more Americans. For example, Joseph Nye, Jr., former Assistant Secretary of Defense, and William Owens (1996), former vice chairman of the Joint Chiefs of Staff, argued:

> This new political and technological landscape is ready-made for the United States to capitalize on its formidable tools of soft power, to project the appeal of its ideals, ideology, culture, economic model, and social and political institutions, and to take advantage of its international business and telecommunications networks. American popular culture, with its libertarian and egalitarian currents, dominates film, television, and electronic communications … American leadership in the information revolution has generally increased global awareness of and openness to American ideals and values. (p. 29)

These Washington insiders, close associates of the Clinton administration, saw the media as a means not only of American profit, or even of American cultural propagation, but also of strategic political advantage. American opponents throughout the world see it exactly the same way. They share an antiquated hypodermic-needle belief in how the media work, but right or wrong this perspective is shaping foreign and domestic policy. Such policies are having a transformative effect (Buruma, 1997). Identity is power.

Consequently, deployment of these policies are only likely to intensify. As changes in work patterns increase the amount of leisure time available to workers worldwide, and the number of television sets and VCRs is likely to increase. Given that 75% of Hollywood revenues come from video and television, half of which is earned abroad, and that Hollywood currently satisfies 70% of world television narrative demand and 80% of world feature-film demand, its strength in the industry is assured for the foreseeable future ("Star Wars," 1997). This assures ongoing Hollywood dominance of the identity-plus-emulation-equals-consumption recipe.

Indeed, the sole contemporary strength of any European broadcasting company emanates from its ability to acquire the distribution rights to Hollywood films and television programs ("Television: Let a hundred," 1995); to stand any chance of international success, a feature film must either be American or an American coproduction (Pells, 1997). As digital television becomes a means of distributing media directly to consumers, the role of the European distributor is greatly diminished and may evaporate altogether. If that comes to pass, then American companies will be selling American products via American satellites to media users around the world. This means that for most of the world, identity formation is shaped in large measure by American images. That is where resistance to those images comes from. Yet, it seems that although those images are American, they are not shaping recipients into Americans. They are merely the icons of more complex hybridization.

Ultimately, as Wasser (1995) argued, the most likely outcome of international transparent media is that "fewer and fewer films will address a specific community" (p. 435). That, in a nutshell, is transparency. Films and television will be increasingly accessible to international audiences, seeming indigenous and found everywhere, but always functioning at a superficial and universal level, more about material wants than actual conditions. Identity, however, is particular. How decreasing specificity might affect identity has hardly been studied but is of growing concern. Transparency is the essential catalyst in the identification-plus-emulation-equals-consumption reaction because it is able to turn particular, local identities into identification with open, projection-friendly characters and situations. Millions of selves see themselves in a single transparent other, desiring and consuming it.

The process of *generalization*, of reaching everywhere and everyone but in superficial terms, creates ample opportunity for transparent media to accelerate and even mutate the evolution of world cultures, a kind of anarchy because the stronger solvent of transparency projection unsticks the glue of indigenous identity. If one's own story is told in *Titanic* (1997), if it fills one with awe and wonder and participation, why should one bother to support an expensive indigenous film industry? Yet, if an indigenous cultural industry is not supported, where does my culture go? Where do I see it? I see it in *Titanic*, in Hollywood, and therein lies the propensity to mutate. This transubstantiation is having numerous effects, including strong effects on sovereignty, democracy, subalterneity, and national identity. Each is worth examining in detail.

Effects on sovereignty

Nationalism occurs because, as Barthes (1972) accurately noted, myths "transform history into nature" (p. 129); in other words, history is coopted by myth to tell the narratives of the nation, its values, structures, and beliefs, as though they are natural. Transparency is a second-level cooption: Through its ellipticality, it allows the viewer, reader, or consumer to fill in narrative details with personal agency (Giddens, 1989). Such indigenous projection makes the text familiar and comprehensible. Thus, the transparent narrative seems to be about something personal, local, or domestic (indeed, it seems natural), whereas it is in fact alien. This poses a powerful threat to state sovereignty, as many states seem to recognize, hence the French resistance to GATT, or indeed the New World Information Order (NWIO, sometimes called NWICO, the *c* for communication) debates in the United Nations.

The *New World Information Order* was a movement during the 1970s and early 1980s within the United Nations and elsewhere to promote international economic development through focussing on communication development. The fundamental idea behind the NWIO movement was that because information flow was controlled and directed through one of four powerful countries (i.e., the United States, England, France, and the Soviet Union), the developing world needed to redirect that flow for self-empowerment. This was to be accomplished through numerous means, including the establishment of Third World news agencies that could serve as alternatives to the Associated Press, United Press International (UPI), Reuters, Agents France Press, and Tass. Indigenous movements were to be encouraged to develop their own media systems. The process of *devolution*, whereby political power is decentralized to smaller units and local levels (Olson, 1985), further democratized global communication.

From the perspective of the late 1990s, the NWIO seems all but dead. Globally, media power has not devolved, but has instead concentrated into even fewer hands; Time-Warner, which owns Turner's CNN, and Rupert Murdoch's News Corporation control most of the global market in television news, for example. The traditional model of national press agencies, government ministries of culture, and national control of the media—once the predominant system of media organization—has been largely replaced in much of the world with an advertising model more or less similar to the one in the United States. In this way, governments cede power to media giants and their corporate sponsors.

The position of multinational media conglomerates regarding the NWIO has favored the free flow of information, a perspective that advocates the opening of international markets to imported information so as to facilitate the international flow of capital. What stands in the corporation's way in realizing this free flow are sovereign nations and because they resist it, from the corporate perspective, "national sovereignty must be abandoned" (Schiller, 1989, p. 120). Global media successfully skirt government control.

The causes are not merely political and economic. Transparent media are in part responsible for this diminution of national sovereignty because they undermine and replace local media. As McChesney (1997) showed, although indigenous markets still exist, they are decreasingly desirable to international media producers and distributors: Unit costs are far lower and profits are higher when a single program can be distributed internationally rather than producing hundreds of unique programs locally. Bull's (1995) word for this decreasing power of sovereign nations, *anarchy*, is reminiscent of Arnold.

Effects on Democracy

Diminished sovereignty is not the only potential effect of transparency; democracy may also be at stake. McChesney (1997) argued that three factors are necessary for the healthy maintenance of democracy: the absence of gross imbalances in the ownership of capital and property; the willingness of individuals to tie their own success to that of the community; and a well-functioning political communication system. He feared that, given the increasing concentration of ownership of media companies, a diminishing sense of community, and unsophisticated political journalism, the United States is growing less democratic and that this tendency is affecting other democracies worldwide.

Five large multinational media companies have had annual sales of greater than $10 billion since 1992: Disney, News Corporation, Time-Warner, Tele-Communications, Inc. (TCI), and Viacom. All five of these have extensive vertical integration, and all but News Corporation, which is nominally Australian, have the United States as their home base. Such concentration can hardly foster diversity, at least when it comes to programming; the media products that these companies develop need to be as polysemic as possible so as to win international markets. That means television programs, movies, and even news are made transparent.

Democracy is generally considered to be the participation of constituents in the process of selecting their own leaders. It is predicated not only on access to information about prospective political candidates, but also on access to competing information, to different perspectives that allow readers to assess relative merit. As the control of distribution of that information falls into relatively few hands, the possibilities for advocacy and assessment are diminished and their potential contribution to democracy inhibited.

If politics is always local, the ubiquity of transparent media serves to create an apolitical world. Transparency, definitionally, can not encourage participation in local, national, or even global politics, unless a local politician is astute at fostering particular readings of transparent texts to serve indigenous political issues. A skillful politician can often do this with amazing aplomb: for example, Ronald Reagan used his campaign speeches to offer a patriotic, flag-waving reading of the polysemic 1984 Bruce Springsteen song, "Born in the U.S.A." The lyrics to the song might suggest a less nationalistic reading:

> Born down in a dead man's town,
> the first kick I took was when I hit the ground.
> You end up like a dog that's been beat too much
> so you spend half your life just covering up,
> Born in the U.S.A.

As with most transparent texts, the alternative reading can be substantiated. In counterpoint to the downbeat lyrics, the music itself was driving, rhythmic, and hypnotic, not unlike a military march. It sounded inclusive and negentropic and was certainly omnipresent at the time, rendering it polysemic. Furthermore, the song was associated by listeners with Springsteen's image against a huge American flag in the music video and on the album jacket, an image often used by politicians as a visual shorthand for patriotism. Part of Springsteen's appeal lies in the way he mumbles and croaks his lyrics, which in this case, meant that the only clearly intelligible line of the song was its ironic refrain, "Born in the U.S.A., I was born in the U.S.A.", but without the other lyrics, this chorus is drained of its irony. Being such a miasma of signifiers, the song attracted diverse and contradictory readings, including Reagan's gung-ho misprision, which otherwise seems to go against the written text. It never the less became, for a time, the dominant reading. Other pop songs have also found an oppositional reading become the dominant one, such as "Every Breath You Take" by the Police and R.E.M.'s "One I Love," both of which were frequently read as sweet love songs. They are evidence that Klapper's (1960) reinforcement theory of media effects retains its explanatory power.

Using polysemy to exploit demagogic local political positions can hardly be called democratic, though—it limits interpretation and explanation rather than expanding them. On the whole, transparency must be seen as potentially damaging to political interest and involvement; perhaps not coincidentally, the home base of transparency, the United States, has a low and declining rate of democratic participation.

Effects on Subalterneity

Subalterneity is also mutated by transparent media. The primary question is one of how the subaltern are to respond to an inundation of foreign media: As Hall (1992) noted, it will either erode the subaltern cultural identity, strengthen it, or create a new ethnicity. They can either submit to its presence, a response that this text considers unlikely, or find some means of resisting it, of gaining power over its meanings, or of prohibiting it and its meanings. In the face of the overwhelming contemporary volume of imported media, what options does an indigenous culture have? Interestingly, the very transparency of international media enables resistance to it, because it permits—even insists on—projection. What, ultimately, will be projected is a matter of contestation, a question of who rightfully owns what the media mean.

So, it comes down to submission or resistance. The Orang Asli indigenous minority in peninsular Malaysia, for example, apparently surrendered their traditional word-of-mouth style of communication, were coopted by broadcasting from the majority culture, and lost their oral traditions (Nicholas, 1997). What has actually been surrendered, though, and to whom? *Submission* can be said to involve one of three interactions: absorption, paternalism/maternalism, and assimilation. When the subaltern are willingly merged into the dominant culture, the process is called *absorption* (Schmookler, 1984). Presumably, the values and practices of the dominant culture are affected and recreated by this absorption in proportion to the strength of the subaltern culture; that is to say, a trace of the subaltern remains in the dominant culture even though they have disappeared into it (Bhabha, 1994; Spivak, 1995). To the extent that American media exporters have inculcated communication patterns and other norms of the cultures to which their media are exported, this trace remains, detectable by the subaltern and maybe by the dominant culture as well. The contamination is mutual and its result is hybrid (Fisher, 1995). Subtle but recognizable references to folkways in Hollywood movies might act in this way. One example of absorption used effectively is the growing success of the Brazilian and Mexican soap-opera industries. As Allen (1995) and Mattelart et al. (1984) showed, Brazilian and Mexican television producers have successfully coopted the style and structure of American soap opera, gaining significant market share in the process.

When the dominant culture gives a voice to the subaltern out of a sense (possibly misplaced) of superior moral responsibility, even pity, the situation can be described as *paternalism/maternalism*. My own research on the relation between Sweden and the Samifolken ("Lapps") regarding broadcasting power revealed a paternalist/maternalist pattern, one that, although ostensibly well-intentioned, effectively hobbled indigenous attempts at cultural and linguistic preservation (Olson, 1985). To continue the metaphor, the Samifolken were smothered by parental good intention. The Inuits of Canada were more successful at using government money to create an Inuit Broadcasting Corporation that has 5 hours of indigenous programming weekly and includes a native version of "Sesame Street" (PBS TV) called "Takuginai" (IBC TV). These Inuit programs have not, however, wholly escaped the trappings of Western media (Palatella, 1998). That, of course, is a gateway to assimilation.

Assimilation describes the situation in which the subaltern are swallowed up by the dominant culture. Almost always, the situation is absorption rather than true assimilation because a trace of the subaltern culture remains to shape the dominant culture in some way. The assimilation of the subaltern assumes that the subordinate culture surrenders itself to the dominant one, losing all distinctiveness; in terms of the media, this would mean that all meanings become the dominant meanings. As Hall (1980) showed, this virtually cannot occur. There will almost always be resistant readings and opposition. Trace elements prevent complete assimilation, however absorbed a culture may be. Transnational media will never have universal meanings. Were the Orang Asli absorbed, paternalized, or assimilated? More research needs to be done on their fate.

Resistance is almost certainly more preferable to the subaltern than submission. Mattelart et al. (1984) suggested that there are four possible resistant responses to imported media: the implementation of protectionism, such as a quota that limits the volume of imports; the promotion of cultural identity as a means to national economic development for a nation's elites; indigenous production of media programs that for all intents and purposes are copies of American media, but produced locally and slapped with a national label; and fighting fire with fire, namely through homegrown cultural imperialism. This hardly seems a comprehensive list of available responses, however; there are many other ways for subaltern cultures to respond.

Within certain cultural parameters, audiences can do what they want with media meaning. Naficy (1996) described this interaction as a media *hail* and an audience *haggle*: the media issue a call or command with which the audience negotiates. For Naficy, the media *hail* by asking audience members to enlist as subjects within a particular ideology. Audiences do not necessarily consent, however; they negotiate (*haggle*) with what they see, leading to a "counterinterpellation" in which "the audience is no longer a *consumer* of the movie; rather, it becomes the *producer* of the meaning of the movie" (p. 10). Naficy felt that this was literally true when American films were shown in his native Iran: dubbers were hired by theaters to provide live simultaneous translation, indigenizing and hybridizing the films in the process by giving characters an explicitly Iranian voice, one largely unrelated to the original film.

How can an audience haggle with the dominant media? When confronted with imported media, the subaltern have a choice between what de Certeau (1984) called *strategies* and *tactics*. *Strategies* are deliberate, coordinated, official policies. *Tactics* are coincidental, spontaneous, grassroots responses. Responses to transnational media can be strategic or tactical, aggressive or disinterested, proactive or passive. For example, advertising on billboards is strategic, but defacing billboards is tactical. Responses can be massive and well coordinated or personal and coincidental. In haggling with media imports, the subaltern invoke both strategies and tactics, but tactics are the more available of the two because they are spontaneous and at hand.

Tactics are reactions to someone else's strategy and make up the lion's share of the tool kit subordinate cultures have in dealing with media imports. Spontaneous, even unconscious haggling responses of the kind Naficy (1996) described are tactics of this sort, running up as they do against official hailing strategies of media producers. Sholle (1988) elaborated the strategies used to muffle or silence other voices. They include:

1. *Sedimentation*: the process by which only certain types of discourse are allowed to exist by the dominant culture, restricting the social options available to a few.
2. *Reification*: the process through which the existing social order is made to seem not manufactured but natural.
3. *Adaptation*: when media images are slowly manipulated by the dominant culture so as to engineer conformity.
4. *Mollification*: the process through which participants in a culture are made to feel more like observers and audiences than agents and actors.
5. *Legitimation*: when certain genres of discourse and certain types of messages are rendered official by the dominant culture.
6. *Depolitization*: creating the illusion of democracy without allowing for truly democratic practices.

Sholle did not consider that subaltern tactics might be used in resistance to these strategies. The subaltern can resist strategies of the dominant culture through countervailing tactics: *eruption, deconstruction, mutation, intensification, illegitimation,* and *politicization.*

It has been suggested elsewhere (Olson, 1994) that sedimentation is resisted by *eruption,* a subaltern strategy that expands discourse into new formats, forces unasked questions, and puts the discourse onto new ground. In America and elsewhere, the subaltern have resisted dominant media messages in this way by making use of new media (the world wide web and other internet possibilities), public access television, or sabotage techniques. In a fascinating example of eruptive transparency in action, the unfamiliar formats of the U.S. media are attributed by some Quebecois writers with unleashing new secular forces in Quebec, creating a secular Francophone society there (Collins, 1988, p. 92).

In reification, the media are used by the dominant culture to present images: ideas of what is, rather than what could be. The reinforcement aspect of the media was clearly established by Klapper (1960), so it is easy to see the potential power of reification. Yet, such images in the media can and are resisted and denaturalized. The subaltern do this with *deconstruction,* a process of textual analysis that reveals how images are produced within linguistic, conventional, and ideological codes. Courses in media literacy are efforts in this direction because they create a space in which audiences may contextualize and dissect what they see. That capability requires a fairly high level of literacy, however, a level at which the relation between signs and meanings is understood semiotically. Media literacy programs are increasingly common throughout the world (Buckingham, 1998), but as might be expected, they are rare in the media's American home base (Kubey, 1998).

Adaptation can be countered by the strategy of *mutation*, any attack on predominant sentimentalization and convention through stereotype bashing and nonlinear representations of time designed to disorient the viewer. Such disorientation widens the cognitive possibilities of the audience through art (Fleming & Wilson, 1987) or "trash" (Vale & Juno, 1987; Weldon, 1983). The Shona in Zimbabwe, for example, have been able to infuse their communication traditions into the mass media in a form of mutation (Hove, 1997), and the Inuit program "Super Shamou" (IBC TV) mutates a conventional television superhero into a native shaman (Palatella, 1998).

Discussions of how the media desensitize viewers to any number of social ills are too common to cite. It is possible for the subaltern to use the process of intensification, however, to act as antidote to mollification. *Intensification* is any process that compels viewers to adopt active agency. Propagating images that make the viewer feel empowered, angry, capable, and active would be one approach. For example, gory videos and postcards have been sent to random recipients by both animal rights activists and anti-abortion activists, encouraging intensification. In its aesthetic mirroring of a traditional ceremony, videos made by the Kayapo of Brazil encourage an affective response comparable to actual participation, intensifying the experience; the Hollywood aesthetic has been utterly avoided by the Kayapo, the technology exploited to serve their purpose (Palattella, 1998).

Legitimation takes a number of forms depending on the level of control over and involvement in the media that the government may have, so it can range from the direct and authoritarian to the indirect and subtle. *Illegitimation* is the logical approach of those seeking to counteract legitimation, and it is best accomplished through public demonstrations that legitimacy is conferred, not inherent. This is not easy to do, especially in those instances when alternative access to the media is unavailable.

True democracy is so subject to subjective interpretation that it cannot really be considered a viable goal, however desirable it might be, but it certainly is possible to observe relative degrees of democracy, for example, in an election where there is only one candidate or where the two candidates offer no real differences. *Politicization* is obviously the alternative, a process that forces discourse into a public and political forum. The videotape, *Counterterror*, an examination of what the words *terrorist* and *discourse of terrorism* mean in the broad context of war, is one example of politicization. It uses actual American news broadcasts, but inverts them to examine how *terror* is defined differently in different contexts (Goldson & Bratton, 1988).

These tactics—eruption, deconstruction, mutation, intensification, illegitimation, and politicization—act as resistance to the implicit commercial strategies of global media. They haggle with the hail. They function in a guerilla manner and seek to coopt and define the meaning of the media in a way more suitable to the subaltern culture, in a sense, exploiting the media's polysemy and transparency for indigenous purposes. Lincoln (1989) described such resistant cooption.

Reactive tactics are not the only tools available to the subaltern, however. Strategies are different from tactics in that they proact rather than react. They initiate, firing the first shot. Strategic initiatives are less likely than tactical defenses for a subaltern culture (if only because there is so much to react to), but are nonetheless possible. Elsewhere (Olson, 1994), a systematization of communication empowerment strategies was developed. These include *dialogue, mutual interest, rule changing, revolution, hostage taking, secession, sabotage,* and *solipsism.* Although intended as broad generalizations, these can be readily adapted to the particular interaction of two cultures and the media messages sent between them.

Dialogue describes the discussion between the dominant and subaltern cultures about the appropriateness of media imports. In dialogue, the parties agree to recognize that there is an unequal distribution of power in the global media marketplace and begin discussions as a means to bring about better balance. *Negotiation* is the most common form of communication dialogue; this is the process through which communication rights are bargained. It may be that the subordinate culture has something it is willing and able to trade for some change in international media creation, marketing, and distribution. The World Association of Christian Communication, publisher of the *Media Development* journal, has been a leader in promoting this strategy.

Another kind of dialogue is *mutual interest,* a process that occurs when a cooperative communication venture is of clear benefit to both the subaltern and the dominant culture. A clear example is the use of sovereign Native American land in some manner that is beneficial both to the native inhabitants and to the surrounding Anglo culture, such as gambling casinos, which provide the Native Americans with revenue and the Anglo culture with entertainment. The Pequot Indians of Connecticut, for example, have used their casino revenues to embark on an extensive and expensive campaign to increase Anglo awareness of Native American culture. Joint media ventures are often borne out of mutual interest; a large multinational media conglomerate might enter an agreement with the government of another culture in order to produce locally oriented programming. In doing so, the multinational insinuates itself into the local market (which is in its interest), providing a type of media programming that might not otherwise exist for the subaltern (which is in their interest). Still, most non-American international film successes are actually financed and distributed by Hollywood, such as *Four Weddings and a Funeral* (Pells, 1997).

Rule changing occurs when the subaltern culture refuses to accept the rules of engagement as presented by the dominant force in the interaction, and somehow engineers new rules that alter the discourse and change the balance of power. Cushman (1977), following Wittgenstein, was perhaps most closely associated with the rules approach to communication and is known for arguing that every human interaction is a type of game dictated by rules of interaction. This approach can become a subaltern strategy when the subordinate culture creates laws or rules that render it superordinate. The Television Without Borders program, for example, requires every EU member to mandate that at least 50% of its television programming be domestically produced. This is an attempt to bolster domestic production and minimize North and South American imports, in short, to change the rules. Another example is the radio network created by indigenous aboriginals and Torres Strait islanders as a way of providing alternatives to Australian broadcasting (Bayles, 1997).

Revolution is the empowerment strategy in which one culture, the subaltern, throws off its subalterneity through direct conflict with the dominant culture. Hegelians regard this process as an inevitable synthesis of conflicting forces (e.g., Grachev & Yermoshkin, 1984; Mattelart & Siegelaub, 1979). The media play an important role in revolution, serving to rally and inspire or, more likely, to disgust and repulse (such as the way that the dominant media are used by revolutionaries as something to be decoded oppositionally; Hall, 1980). It is no wonder that the capture of radio and television stations is often the first prize revolutionaries seek (e.g., Ignatius, 1993). Control of radio and television is equated with control of the culture and with good reason. Considering that media can be decoded oppositionally, although international media can be intended to homogenize and hegemonize, it may have an effect quite to the contrary. Islamic revolutionaries in Egypt, for example, have made it a goal to rid that secular state of decadent foreign media. The bombing of a Planet Hollywood restaurant in South Africa is another example (Harris, 1998).

In *hostage taking*, a subaltern cultural group has access to or controls something that the superordinate culture seeks, values, and prizes; in the case of the international media, that would be either a media resource or cultural resource. The subaltern can use force or circumstance to gain control of a desired cultural product. Elsewhere (Olson, 1994) it has been described how the Inupiat used indigenous land rights as a hostage to gain control of local media. The Inupiat did not take this land by force, but such can also be the case. Terrorists have often forcefully grabbed hostages as a way of gaining media power: A videotaped message of a political prisoner usually generates attention in the Western press to causes and ideologies that would never receive any attention otherwise. Such tactics are potentially effective, despite the obvious ethical considerations; terrorism can cause extensive destabilization by dividing popular opinion, creating fear in the mass audience, and finding new converts to the movement (Schmid & de Graaf, 1982).

If the subaltern attempt to disconnect themselves from the dominant culture, *secession* occurs, or what Schmookler (1984) called *withdrawal*. From a communication perspective, subcultures would ordinarily be the source of this withdrawal. Many such subcultures have been extensively studied by Cultural Studies scholars, including punk, gay, and lesbian subcultures; because the media rarely, even never, depict these cultures from the culture's own point of view, these tend to be secessors from the dominant culture. A particularly poignant example is the gay, African American, poor, drag, Manhattan subculture portrayed in the film *Paris is Burning* (1991); the persons depicted in this film have essentially seceded from the dominant American culture. The process of *outing* is essentially a secessionist strategy; it is the name used by some in the gay community for the radical practice of making public the names of homosexuals who might otherwise want to keep their gay identity secret (Gross, 1991).

Subaltern attempts to set traps for and play tricks on the media subvert the dominant media environment and are a kind of *sabotage*, but often go by other names. *Culture jamming* is the phrase used by Dery (1993) to describe a variety of these monkeywrenching techniques. *Pirate radio*—clandestine commercial or political radio stations that operate without the permission of the state to which they broadcast—is clearly a kind of intellectual sabotage. Depending on the intention of the pirate broadcasters, these stations are either a pesky nuisance (Radio Caroline commercial broadcasts of rock-and-roll music to England in the 1960s) or revolution itself (Basque separatist radio in the 1980s).

Media hoaxes as practiced by Alan Abel and Joey Skaggs (Vale and Juno, 1987) are another form of sabotage and use the media's own laziness and sensationalism to trick them into reporting false and absurd stories, such as a house of prostitution for dogs, as a means of exposing the deficiencies of media hegemony. Another type of sabotage is *billboard banditry*, which involves defacing and manipulating billboards into new messages that contradict the original one; one particularly prolific such artist is Mark Pauline (Vale and Juno, 1987). All of these saboteur pranks are an irritation to the dominant political and commercial structure and expand and elaborate the number of messages communicated in the culture.

Hyperreality, a sort of self-enclosure described by Baudrillard (1987) and de Certeau (1984) and observed by Meyrowitz (1985), creates a more fatalistic situation as the subalterns—and everyone else—create for themselves a pseudo-environment, which is often called *solipsism*. From a purely cognitive perspective, *solipsism* is the purest variety of self-empowerment, because power is actually created, rather than shifted from one point to another. The power created is evanescent, however. It may be, at heart, the essence of transparency, and an element of it is always there regardless of the other tactics described here. Ang's (1985) "Dallas" project and the poaching theory (de Certeau, 1984; Jenkins, 1992) seem to describe such solipsism in the face of transnational media.

Such created, nondisplaced power changes minds but not systems, however, because solipsism remains a purely personal response to saturation by the media. One example is the *Otaku*, young Japanese men who live in a self-contained virtual reality that they created (Greenfeld, 1993). This computer subculture has essentially disassociated itself from any direct contact with actual human beings, all interactions are confined to the electronic media. This group and others like it have coopted the dominant media's hardware and software for their own self-enclosed, antisocial, reality-generating purposes, gaining power by imposing subjective meanings and structures over hegemonic meanings, erasing them in the process at the cognitive level.

The media hail and audiences haggle. Haggling can be done strategically through planned and deliberate acts of resistance or, more likely, can be done tactically through spontaneous reactions and counterinterpellations. Either way, haggling is inevitable, because the polysemic nature of transparent media necessitate active readings, particularly when the text crosses cultures. The fundamental question for the subaltern, of course, is how to direct those haggled readings in a way that abets the culture, directing identity into useful mutations, answering Bhabha's (1997) question about what identities can do. Given the diversity of possible readings, direction is the real trick.

Effects on National Identity

Nationalism, like subalterneity, is undergoing changes, but it seems to be waning rather than waxing. What is replacing it? In some cases, one sees integration into pan-national movements, such as pan-Islam, The North Atlantic Treaty Organization (NATO), the EU and Eurodollar, NAFTA, or the United Nations Security Force. In other cases, there is disintegration into regionalism or tribalism, such as the breakup of the former Soviet Union and of Yugoslavia, ethnic cleansing, Native American sovereignty, Quebec separatism, Eritrea, the Basque movement, or Indonesia after Suharto. Nationalism is also superceded by employee loyalty to multinational corporations that negotiate like states, by refugee movements, by diasporic identities, by the global teenager and the global business elite, by the reemergence of city-states like Singapore, by Ted Turner's donation of $1 billion U.S. to the United Nations. Indeed, the nation-state, itself is no older than the Treaty of Westphalia, did not assert itself on the international stage until Bismarck and now—350 years on—seems likely to be just another form of political organization, not its dominant form. Transparent international media are certainly not the only trigger of this (d)evolution, but are among the most significant sociological and psychological ammunition. It is clear, though, that "the U.S. media [do] ... not necessarily seem to engender uniform conceptions of nationhood" (Waisbord, 1998, p. 382).

That ammunition has punch. Schiller (1989) quoted Ngugi wa Thiong'o, a Kenyan writer, as describing the export and import of media as a "cultural bomb," whose effect is "to annihilate a people's belief in their names, in their languages, in their environment, in their heritage of struggle, in their unity, in their capacities and ultimately in themselves" (p. 134). Bombs can be diffused, of course, but only if one can see them in time. The primary danger of the transparency bomb is that it is invisible: it does not look like a bomb at all, but like part of the natural indigenous landscape. In addition, it does not explode—it is like nuclear fallout without a mushroom cloud: all mutation, no obliteration.

A Hollywood Planet can have profound effects on the notion of what culture is and how identity relates to it. For Smith (1995), this is no simple matter:

> In any individual the sense of identity is in practice underpinned by a series of unargued and unspoken beliefs, which all appear at this moment to be collapsing at the approach of the phenomenon of the information revolution. What is a nation and who really belongs to one? Are any two of them nations in the same way? ... Who is us? And what is them? (p. 2)

Smith foresaw a global Creole with fluid identities. Interestingly, such a Creole would be a projection of the hodgepodge *e pluribus unum* cultural identity of the United States onto the world stage.

Yet, to change the world is to change oneself, and the United States has been hybridized in the process. Hybrid plants grow both ways: Transparency grows on home base U.S. soil as well as the international, mutating American identity in the process. This mutation is particularly clear in the case of Disney American History. Disney's "The American Experience" at EPCOT, cosponsored by American Express, only hints at the possibilities: an America inhabited by nostalgic, cooperative robots, clean and glossed. Disney American History would have been that and more. This controversial theme park—temporary victim of academic protesters but still on the Disney drawing boards—intended to turn important events in American history into thrill rides, hoping to lure tourists away from the real sights in Washington, DC. The appropriateness of a thrill ride as an apt metaphor for American history notwithstanding, considerable pressure from academics persuaded Disney to abandon its location of first choice (Whartob, 1994; "Disney abandons ... ", 1994), and it is not clear now precisely when, where, and if the park will be built. The EPCOT version remains an unrealized prototype.

Identities are forged, not found, and Disney protestors seem to have ignored the extent to which history is also something forged (see discussion in Appleby, Hunt, & Jacob, 1994; Beardsley, Gombrich, Harries, Hirsch, & Wellek, 1978; Blumenthal, 1994; Fischer, 1970; Handlin, 1979; Samuels, 1995). Indeed, history seems now to be another consumer product manufactured by a "corporate-sponsored, mass-media history machine. It churns out products that are processed and calibrated to corporate specifications. It provides national audiences with a historical view as seen from the top of the social pyramid" (Schiller, 1989, p. 7). Disney did not create the notion of projecting identity onto found history: History always serves contemporary culture, often for purposes of commercial exploitation, such as tourism (Leong, 1989) or worship (Pelikan, 1985). The traditionalist, preservationist reverence for battlefields is itself a modern cooption of space, one that probably has little to do with the way that space was conceptualized during the war and afterward (see Wills, 1993). Like any other text, history awaits reader reception and projection; packaged properly, American history becomes as transparent and polysemic as any other Disney product. At the American Experience, history becomes openended, virtual, circular, archetypal, elliptical, negentropic, inclusive, verisimilitudinous, omnipresent, and high in production values. As a synergetic bonus, one can envision Disney's American History merchandise: "My parents experienced American history and all I got was this lousy T-shirt."

Consequently, it is not hard to imagine that, like The American Experience at EPCOT, the sort of history that would have been found at Disney's American History would have more in common with other hyperreal environments than with a conference of the American Historical Society. It is easy to foresee a Disney American History that is itself a Creole melange of historical legend and myth, professing formative moral and cultural narratives like George Washington cutting down a cherry tree, Betsy Ross sewing a flag, and Abraham Lincoln walking 20 miles to school—stories already undergoing a revival thanks to conservative pundit Bill Bennett's "Book of Virtues" cottage industry. This sort of narrative is the stuff Disney does well, because it lays claim to the same credibility, authority, and mythic truth (see Lincoln, 1989) that Disney films like The Lion King (1994) do. Leong (1989) showed how Singapore did precisely this in crafting its official history to suit a nascent tourism industry. The very flexibility of the transparent mythotypes enable their exploitation: Because it is suited to many different mythological systems, American history may be just as transparent as The Lion King, with different lessons for Nigerians, Trinidadians, Koreans, and Americans (see Shekwo, 1984).

This has profound implications for cultures and identities, because in a postmodern economy, the symbolic meanings whose production and circulation constitute culture (Garnham, 1987), are controlled by a few producers or distributors of entertainment media programming. Colonies were military and commercial outposts some distance away from their sponsoring country, designed to channel physical resources back to the sponsor as they changed the lives of the indigenous peoples. Part of the colonizing process was laying claim to historical authority so as to inhibit resistance and silence alternative histories (Said, 1993). Transparency is a postmodern update of colonial settlements, with the same commercial intent, but a more conceptual landscape on which to build. What are settlements on a frontier, even a cognitive or linguistic frontier, if not colonies? In laying claim to American history, near Civil War battlefields or elsewhere, Disney is in a sense colonizing America, just as its films and theme parks have symbolically colonized the rest of the world. Colonizing nature is also on the agenda through Disney's Animal Kingdom, already open for business in Orlando.

The potential effect of hyperreal autocolonization is the creation of a nation slowly drained of collective, shared readings, one whose guiding philosophy is exclusively consumerism, brought about by dimming memory of the culture originally projected. Media companies have created a seamless web of product placement in movies and television programs, merchandising of movie and television products, selling the soundtrack on radio and MTV (see Aufderheide, 1986), advertising on television presented as curriculum to children in 40% of the public schools via Whittle's Channel One (Stewart, 1994) with the effect that students see the advertisements as endorsed by the schools (Greenberg & Brand, 1993). Such synergy threatens that soon all American culture will be a form of shopping. The synthetic environment that transparency manufactures bestows identity only through consumption.

This raises some troubling questions about the ongoing viability of public culture and discourse in a postmodern paradigm: What happens to a culture when commodification is equated with ritual and elevated to myth by relentless repetition in the media and in 3-D space? As programming producers, distribution companies, and technology manufacturers consolidate into megacorporations (see, e.g., Andrews, 1994; Weinraub, 1994), a series of consolidations that occur simultaneous to the relative decline in authority and power of nation-states (Ohmae, 1991; Schiller, 1989; Stavrianos, 1976) and the redesign of the human–media interface (Biocca, 1993), are there any viable alternatives to media culture? The problem is epitomized by Celebration, the Florida Disney project already discussed. It seems that in Celebration, democracy and nationality are willingly ceded to the corporation, or as Pollan (1997) put it:

> It may be Disney's boldest innovation at Celebration to have established a rather novel form of democracy, one that is based on consumerist, rather than republican, principles ... [Citizens of Celebration are] prepared to surrender power over their lives to a corporation as long as that corporation re-

mains sensitive to their needs .... Of course, the consumerist democracy holds only as long as the interests of the corporation and the consumer are one. (p. 80)

Transparency has a way of aligning those interests at least temporarily, turning identification to consumption.

Eliade's (1954) analysis of the function of myth indicates that transparency functions the way myths do: It makes things real.

> An object or act becomes real only insofar as it imitates or repeats an archetype. Thus, reality is acquired solely through repetition or participation; everything which lacks an exemplary model is "meaningless," i.e., it lacks reality. (p. 34)

Like the implanted memories of False Memory syndrome, the hybrid cultures that transparent media produce seem natural and real because they have replaced the original with an identical twin changeling. For this reason, indigenous projection only works for a few generations; then, the original is replaced in memory by imported simulations whose verisimilitude renders them to be authentic. What is left is a hybrid, a synthesis of the self and the Other, the old and the new, the native and the foreign. Disney's Celebration remembers a better time in American history, or does it? Who can remember? The same is happening everywhere else. What, then, is left of the original identity? It cannot be projected again, because it is no longer there. Its replacement is a doppelganger masquerading as the original. In this way, the original is eroded even as it is projected: Its assertion is its undoing. There is no other way, of course. Texts are always haggled, and the haggler cannot stay unchanged in the process.

There is time for one last haggle. Here is the argument of this volume in a nutshell: Transparency accounts for the phenomenal international success of American media. The evidence is clear that the United States has an overwhelming, though neither exclusive nor impenetrable, competitive advantage in producing transparent media. Economic and cultural conditions within the United States account for this preeminence in the manufacture of transparent texts. Such textual explanations are as important as political and economic ones because only they account for audience reception. The textual apparatuses of transparency are mythotypes, human needs that precede myth and are found in myth systems everywhere, such as awe, wonder, purpose, and participation. These needs are tapped through narrative devices that include openendedness, virtuality, circularity, archetypal dramatis personae, ellipticality, negentropy, inclusion, verisimilitude, omnipresence, production values, and synergy. They are identifiable in American media products and explain their success. Although subaltern cultures have some strategies and tactics to resist transparency, the onslaught of such media is daunting. It changes indigenous cultures in subtle but lasting ways, creating new hybrid cultures that progressively particularize so that they can hardly be called national cultures at all. This poses a serious threat to national sovereignty, democracy, and identity. Transparency heralds nothing short of the utter fragmentation of culture and consequently, culture's end. With its end, identity becomes unmoored, free to float from text to text.

This repudiates the commonly held belief that exposure to transnational media homogenizes culture. Exposure is not identity, though, because exposure is unidirectional. Audiences do not interact with texts that way. As Waisbord (1998) put it in a study of Latin American resistance to monoculture, "It is more fruitful to conceptualize identity formation involving a series of communication practices that construct imaginary spaces and delineate senses of belonging and difference" (p. 387). That revelation has opened up a whole new avenue of media research.

The reason more research is needed is simple: The relation among culture, identity, and media is far more complex than originally assumed. That leads to even more uncertainty in the tension between culture and anarchy. Culture is order, assurance, and shared understanding. Anarchy is chaos, disorder, and confusion—apt adjectives for a postmodern world. The choice between culture and anarchy is made not selectively, but necessarily: When the transparency of polysemous texts allows unmoored readings, culture is no longer an option, and anarchy is all that remains.

So, to return to the original question: Where are we going, to culture, to cultures, or to anarchy? The answer is not a movement toward monoculture, a simplistic explanation that simply does not reflect how audiences read texts. The answer is not Matthew Arnold's (1932) culture—such consensus is impossible. The answer is not even cultures. Cultures are mutating, dissolving, and hybridizing so fast that it becomes difficult to pin any one of them down, as fragmented, multiplied, and indeterminate as they are (Gillespie, 1995b).

What's left? Declining sovereignty, disappearing democracy, reasserting subalterneity, and the end of nationalism.

The Hollywood planet has chosen anarchy.

References

Allen, R. (1985). Introduction. In R. Allen, (Ed.), *Speaking of soap operas* ... (pp. 1–26). New York: Routledge & Kegan Paul.

Allen, R (Ed.). (1995). *To be continued* ...: *Soap operas around the world.* New York: Routledge & Kegan Paul.

Andrews, E. (1994, October 26). Sweeping revision in communication is on the horizon. *The New York Times,* pp. A1, D7.

Ang, I. (1985). *Watching Dallas.* London, England: Methuen.

Ang, I. (1988). (Not) coming to terms with *Dallas.* In C. Schneider & B. Wallis (Eds.), *Global television* (pp. 69–77). New York: Wedge Press.

Appiah, K., & Gates, H. (1997). *The dictionary of global culture.* New York: Knopf.

Appleby, J., Hunt, L., & Jacob, M. (1994). *Telling the truth about history.* New York: Norton.

Arijon, D. (1976). *Grammar of the film language.* Los Angeles, CA: Silman-James Press.

Arnold, M. (1932). *Culture and anarchy.* Cambridge, England: Cambridge University Press.

Aufderheide, P. (1986). Music videos: The look of the sound. *Journal of Communication, 36,* 57–78.

Auletta, K. (1995). Annals of communication: Awesome. *The New Yorker, 71* (24), 28–32.

Auletta, K. (1996). Marriage, no honeymoon: How troubled is the Disney-ABC union? *The New Yorker, 71* (21), 26–31.

Bacon-Smith, C. (1992). *Enterprising women: Television fandom and the creation of popular myth.* Philadelphia: University of Pennsylvania Press.

Baker, W. (1989, Winter). The global teenager. *Whole Earth Review,* pp. 2–35.

Barthes, R. (1972). *Mythologies.* (A. Lavers, Trans.) New York: Hill & Wang.

Barthes, R. (1977). From work to text. In R. Barthes, (Ed.), *Image, music, text* (pp. 155–164). New York: Hill & Wang.

Baudrillard, J. (1981). *For a critique of the political economy of the sign* (C. Levin, Trans.). St. Louis, MO: Telos Press.

Baudrillard, J. (1983). *Simulations.* New York: Semiotext(e).

Baudrillard, J. (1987). *The evil demon of images.* Sydney, Australia: Power Institute of Fines Arts.

Baudrillard, J. (1988). *America* (C. Turner, Trans.). New York: Verso.

Baudrillard, J. (1993). *The transparency of evil: Essays on extreme phenomena* (J. Benedict, Trans.). New York: Verso.

Bayles, T. (1997). Indigenous broadcasting in Australia. *Media Development, 44* (3), 18–21.

Bazin, A. (1967). *What is cinema?* (H. Gray, Trans.). Berkeley: University of California Press.

Beardsley, M., Gombrich, E. H., Harries, K., Hirsch, E., & Wellek, R. (1978). *History as a tool in critical interpretation.* Provo, UT: Brigham Young University Press.

Berger, A. (1982). *Media analysis techniques.* Newbury Park, CA: Sage.

Bettelheim, B. (1977). *The uses of enchantment: The meaning and importance of fairy tales.* New York: Vintage Books.

Bhabha, H. (Ed.). (1990). *Nation and narration.* New York: Routledge & Kegan Paul.

Bhabha, H. (1994). *The location of culture.* New York: Routledge & Kegan Paul.

Bhabha, H.. (1997). Editor's introduction: Minority maneuvers and unsettled negotiations. *Critical Inquiry, 23*(3), 431–459.

Biocca, F. (1993). Communication research in the design of communication interfaces and systems. *Journal of Communication, 43*(4), 59–68.

Bird, L. (1994, January 21). NBC special is one long prime-time ad. *Wall Street Journal,* pp. B1, B8.

Bloom, H. (1975). *A map of misreading.* New York: Oxford University Press.

Bloom, H. (1994). *The Western canon: The books and schools of the ages.* New York: Harcourt Brace.

Blumenberg, H. (1985). *Work on myth.* (R. Wallace, Trans.). Cambridge, MA: MIT Press.

Blumenthal, S. (1994). Reinventing Lincoln. *The New Yorker, 70*(37), 106.

Bohlen, C. (1998, April 26). Why *Titanic* conquered the world: Moscow. *The New York Times,* p. AR 28.

Boorstin, D. (1978). *The image: A guide to pseudo-events in America.* New York: Harper & Row.

Bourdieu, P. (1993). *The field of cultural production* (R. Johnson, Ed.). New York: Columbia University Press.

Brummett, B., & Duncan, M. (1992). Toward a discursive ontology of media. *Critical Studies in Mass Communication, 9*(3), 229–249.

Buckingham, D. (1998). Media education in the U.K.: Moving beyond protectionism. *Journal of Communication, 48*(1), 33–43.

Bull, H. (1995). *The anarchical society: A study of order in world politics* (2nd ed.). New York: Columbia University Press.

Burton-Carvajal, J. (1994). "Surprise package": Looking southward with Disney. In E. Smoodin (Ed.), *Disney discourse: Producing the Magic Kingdom (pp. 131–147).* New York: Routledge & Kegan Paul.

Buruma, I. (1997). God bless America. *Index on Censorship, 26*(3), 156–161.

Calica, B. (1995). Game players in transition. *Newmedia, 5*(1), 55–58.

Campbell, J. (1949). *Hero with a thousand faces.* New York: Bollingen.

Carroll, M. (1993). Agent Cooper's errand in the wilderness: *Twin Peaks* and American mythology. *Film Literature Quarterly, 21*(4), 287–295.

Cartwright, L., & Goldfarb, B. (1994). Cultural contagion: On Disney's health education films for Latin America. In E. Smoodin (Ed.), *Disney discourse: Producing the Magic Kingdom* (pp. 169–180). New York: Routledge & Kegan Paul.

Caughie, J. (1981). *Theories of authorship.* New York: Routledge & Kegan Paul.

Cawelti, J. (1976). *Adventure, mystery, and romance: Formula stories as art and popular culture.* Chicago: University of Chicago Press.

Chatman, S. (1978). *Story and discourse: Narrative structure in fiction and film.* Ithaca, NY: Cornell University Press.

Chatman, S. (1981). What novels can do that films can't (and vice versa). In W. J. T. Mitchell (Ed.), *On narrative* (pp. 117–136). Chicago: University of Chicago Press.

Cohen, R. (1993, December 8). U.S.–French cultural trade rift now snags a world agreement: Paris talks of film onslaught from Hollywood. *The New York Times,* pp. A1, D2.

Cohen-Solal, A. (1995). Coal miners and dinosaurs. *Media Studies Journal, 9*(4), 125–136.

Collins, R. (1988). Wall-to-wall *Dallas*: The U.S.–U.K. trade in television. In C. Schneider & B. Wallis (Eds.), *Global television* (pp. 79–93). New York: Wedge Press.

Coste, D. (1989). *Narrative as communication.* Minneapolis: University of Minnesota Press.

Cox, D. (1995, June 26). Sony pitches "net" against "Waterworld." *Variety,* p. 6.

Crofts, S. (1995). Global *Neighbours?* In R. Allen, Ed. *Speaking of soap operas* ... (pp. 98–121). New York: Routledge & Kegan Paul.

Cushman, D. (1977). The rules perspective as a theoretical basis for the study of human communication. *Communication Quarterly, 25,* 30–45.

da Cunha, U. (1994, December 12). It's the real thing for MTV India. *Variety,* p. 51.

Dannen, F. (1995). Hong Kong Babylon. *The New Yorker, 71*(23), 30–38.

Darnton, R. (1994). Sex for thought. *New York Review of Books, 41*(21), 65–74.

de Certeau, M. (1984). *The practice of everyday life* (S. Rendell, Trans.). Berkeley: University of California Press.

Le Défi Américain, Again. (1996, July 13). *The Economist, pp.* 21–23.

Dennis, E., & Snyder, R. (1995). Global views on U.S. media. *Media Studies Journal, 9*(4), xi–xv.

Derrida, J. (1977). *Of grammatology* (G. Spivak, Trans.). Baltimore: Johns Hopkins University Press.

Dery, M. (1993). *Culture jamming: Hacking, slashing, and sniping in the empire of signs.* Westfield, NJ: Open Magazine Press.

Descartes, R. (1641). Meditations de prima philosophia, in quibus Dei existentia, et animae humanse a corpore distincto, demonstrantum. Paris: Michael Soly.

de Sola Pool, I. (1977). Technology and policy in the information age. In D. Lerner & L. Nelson (Eds.), *Communication research: A half-century appraisal* (pp. 261–279). Honolulu: University Press of Hawaii.

de Tocqueville, A. (1945a). *Democracy in America.* (Vol. 1.) New York: Vintage.

de Tocqueville, A. (1945b). *Democracy in America.* (Vol. 2.) New York: Vintage.

Disney abandons plans for park near battlefields. (1994, September 29). *Hartford Courant, p.* A1.

Dolan, C. (1994, June 13). Translating the Bible into suitable Klingon stirs cosmic debate. *Wall Street Journal,* pp. A1, A8.

During, S. (1993). The culture industry: Enlightenment as mass deception: Editor's introduction. In S. During (Ed.), *The cultural studies reader* (pp. 29–30). New York: Routledge & Kegan Paul.

Eckholm, E. (1998, April 26). Why *Titanic* conquered the world: Beijing. *The New York Times,* p. AR 28.

Eco, U. (1986). *Travels in hyperreality.* San Diego, CA: Harcourt Brace.

Eliade, M. (1954). *The myth of the eternal return or, cosmos and history.* Princeton, NJ: Princeton University Press.

Ellis, J. (1992). *Visible fictions: Cinema, television, video* (2nd ed.). New York: Routledge & Kegan Paul.

Entertainment has become the United States' second-largest export. (1997). *Screen Actor, 38*(6), 4.

The entertainment industry. (1989, December 23). *The Economist,* pp. 3–4.

European films: Gumped. (1995, January 6). *The Economist,* p. 84.

Fan Forum. (June 18, 1998). [on-line]. Available: www.users.globalnet.co.uk/~dave24/fanforum.html

Faulkner, W. (1977). *The days when the animals talked: Black American folktales and how they came to be.* Chicago: Follett.

Featherstone, M. (Ed.). (1990). *Global culture: Nationalism, globalization, modernity.* Newbury Park, CA: Sage.

Finch, C., & Jones, J. (1994). *The art of The Lion King.* New York: Hyperion.

Fischer, D. (1970). *Historian's fallacies: Toward a logic of historical thought*. New York: HarperCollins.

Fish, S. (1980). *Is there a text in this class? The authority of interpretive communities*. Cambridge, MA: Harvard University Press.

Fisher, J. (1995, Autumn). Editorial: Some thoughts on "contaminations." *Third Text: Third World Perspectives on Contemporary Art and Culture, 32*, 3–8.

Fiske, J. (1986). Television: Polysemy and popularity. *Critical Studies in Mass Communication, 3*(4), 391–408.

Fiske, J. (1987). *Television culture*. New York: Routledge & Kegan Paul.

Fiske, J. (1996). *Media matters: Everyday culture and political change*. Minneapolis: University of Minnesota Press.

Fleming, J., & Wilson, P. (1987). *Semiotext(e) U.S.A*. New York: Columbia University Press.

Forbes, J. (1988). The internationalization of French television. In C. Schneider & B. Wallis (Eds.), *Global television* (pp. 59–67). New York: Wedge Press.

Foucault, M. (1965). *Madness and civilization: A history of insanity in the age of reason* (R. Howard, Trans.). New York: Random House.

Foucault, M. (1982). *This is not a pipe: Illustrations and letters by Rene Magritte* (J. Harkness, Trans.). Berkeley: University of California Press.

Freeman, W. (1991). The physiology of perception. *Scientific American, 264*(2), 78–87.

Frost, R. (1979). *Life the movie: How entertainment conquered reality*. New York: Knopf.

Frye, N. (1957). *Anatomy of criticism: Four essays*. Princeton, NJ: Princeton University Press.

Gadamer, H. (1986). *Truth and method*. New York: Crossroad.

Garnham, N. (1984). Introduction. In A. Mattelart, D. Delcourt, & Mattelart (Eds.), *International image markets: In search of an alternative perspective* (pp. 1–6). London, England: Comedia.

Garnham, N. (1987). Concepts of culture: Public policy and the cultural industries. *Cultural Studies, 1*(1), 23–38.

Garnham, N. (1995). Political economy and cultural studies: Reconciliation or divorce? *Critical Studies in Mass Communication, 12*(1), 62–71.

Gates, H. L. (1995). Thirteen ways of looking at a Black man. *The New Yorker, 71*(33), 56–65.

Gelfand, M. (1973). *The genuine Shona: Survival values of an African culture*. Gweru, Zimbabwe: Mambo Press.

Genette, G. (1980). *Narrative discourse: An essay in method* (J. Lewin, Trans). Ithaca, NY: Cornell University Press.

Geraghty, C. (1995). Social issues and realist soaps: A study of British soaps in the 1980s/1990s. In R. Allen (Ed.), *Speaking of soap operas ...* (pp. 66–80). New York: Routledge & Kegan Paul.

Gerbner, G. (Ed.). (1993). *The global media debate: Its rise, fall and renewal*. Norwood, NJ: Ablex.

Gillespie, M. (1995a). Sacred serials, devotional viewing, and domestic worship: A case-study in the interpretation of two TV versions of *The Mahabharata* in a Hindu family in West London. In R. Allen (Ed.), *Speaking of soap operas ...* (pp. 354–380). New York: Routledge & Kegan Paul.

Gillespie, M. (1995b). *Television, ethnicity, and cultural change*. New York: Routledge & Kegan Paul.

Goldson, A., & Bratton, C. (1988). Counterterror. In C. Schneider & B. Wallis (Eds.), *Global television* (pp. 147–159). New York: Wedge Press.

Goleman, D. (1990, August 14). Research probes what the mind sense unaware. *The New York Times*, p. C1.

Goleman, D. (1994, May 31). Miscoding is seen as the root of false memories. *The New York Times*, pp. C1, C8.

Gombrich, E. (1969). *Art and illusion: A study in the psychology of pictorial representation.* Princeton, NJ: Princeton University Press.

Goodstein, E. (1992). Southern belles and southern buildings: The built environment as text and context in *Designing Women. Critical Studies in Mass Communication, 9*(2), 170–185.

Grachev, A., & Yermoshkin, N. (1984). *A new information order or psychological warfare?* Moscow, USSR: Progress Publishers.

Graves, M. (1994). *Michael Graves Architecture.* San Francisco: Pomegranate Artbooks.

Greenberg, B. & Brand, J. (1993). Television news and advertising in schools: The "Channel One" controversy. *Journal of Communication, 43*(1), 143–151.

Greenfeld, K. (1993). The incredibly strange mutant creatures who rule the universe of alienated Japanese zombie computer nerds. *Wired, 1.1,* 66–69.

Griffiths, A. (1995). National and cultural identity in a Welsh-language soap opera. In R. Allen (Ed.), *Speaking of soap operas ...* (pp. 81–97). New York: Routledge & Kegan Paul.

Gripsrud, J. (1995). *The Dynasty years: Hollywood television and critical media studies.* New York: Routledge & Kegan Paul.

Groen, R. (1995). Southern exposure. *Media Studies Journal, 9*(4), 139–144.

Gross, L. (1991). The contested closet: The ethics and politics of outing. *Critical Studies in Mass Communication, 8*(3), 352–388.

Grossberg, L. (1995). Cultural studies vs. political economy: Is anyone else bored with this debate? *Critical Studies in Mass Communication, 12*(1), 72–81.

Groves, D. (1993, December 27). O'seas B.O. adds up to jolly season. *Variety,* p. 26.

Groves, D. (1994, November 14). Lion King conquers French B.O. *Variety,* p. 14.

Groves, D. (1995, September 25). *Waterworld* swims to top o'seas. *Variety,* p. 16.

Gumpert, G., & Drucker, S. (1992). From the agora to the electronic shopping mall. *Critical Studies in Mass Communication, 9*(2), 186–200.

Gumpert, G., & Drucker, S. (1998). The mediated home in the global village. *Communication Research, 25*(4), 422–438.

György, P. (1995). Seeing through the media. *Media Studies Journal, 9*(4), 109–117.

Hagedorn, R. (1995). Doubtless to be continued: A brief history of serial narrative. In R. Allen (Ed.), *Speaking of soap operas ...* (pp. 27–48). New York: Routledge & Kegan Paul.

Hall, S. (1980). Encoding/decoding. In S. Hall, D. Hobson, A. Lowe, & P. Willis (Eds.), *Culture, media, language* (pp. 128–138). London, England: Hutchinson.

Hall, S. (1992). The question of cultural identity. In S. Hall, D. Held, & T. McGrew (Eds.), *Modernity and its futures* (pp. 273–326). Cambridge, England: Polity Press.

Hamelink, C. (1997). MacBride with hindsight. In P. Golding & P. Harris (Eds.), *Beyond cultural imperialism: Globalization, communication, and the new international order* (pp. 69–93). Thousand Oaks, CA: Sage.

Handlin, O. (1979). *Truth in history.* Cambridge, MA: Belknap Press.

Harms, J., & Dickens, D. (1996). Postmodern media studies: Analysis or symptom? *Critical Studies in Mass Communication, 13*(3), 210–227.

Harris, P. (1998, August 27). S. Africa expects arrests soon in bombing. *The Indianapolis Star,* p. A13.

Harris, T. (1995). The word made flesh. *Parabola, 20*(3), 16–20.

Heisenberg, W. (1958). *Physics and philosophy.* New York: Harper Collins.

Himmelstein, H. (1984). *Television myth and the American mind.* New York: Praeger.

Hirsch, E. (1988). *Cultural literacy: What every American needs to know.* New York: Vintage Books.

Hodge, R., & Tripp, D. (1986). *Children and television.* Cambridge, MA: Polity Press.

Hollywood conquers Europe. (1996). *The Futurist, 30*(4) 5.

Home alone in Europe. (1997, March 22). *The Economist*, p. 74.

Hove, C. (1997). Oral traditions claim a place in modern mass media. *Media Development, 44*(3), 13–14.

Hughes, R. (1981). *The shock of the new.* New York: Knopf.

Ignatius, A. (1993, October 4). Russian roulette: Hard-liner challenge to Yeltsin is growing ever more menacing. *Wall Street Journal*, p. A1.

International box office. (1993, December 13 through 1995, July 17). *Variety*, pp. 11, 14, 18, 20.

International box office. (1994a, June 13). *Variety*, p. 18.

International box office. (1994b, November 21). *Variety*, p. 14.

International box office. (1995a, January 9). *Variety*, p. 18.

International box office. (1995b, June 26). *Variety*, p. 11.

International box office. (1995c, July 10). *Variety*, p. 20.

International box office. (1995, July 24 through 1996, April 1). *Variety*, pp. 11, 14, 18, 20.

Iser, W. (1980). *The act of reading: A theory of aesthetic response.* Baltimore: Johns Hopkins University Press.

Jacobson, J. (1997). Perceptions of Britishness. *Nations and Nationalism, 3*(2), 181–199.

Jameson, F. (1986, Fall). The Third World novel as national allegory. *Social Text, 15*, 65–68.

Jameson, F. (1991). *Postmodernism or, the cultural logic of late capitalism.* Durham, NC: Duke University Press.

Jauss, H. (1982). *Toward an aesthetic of reception* (T. Bahti, Trans.). Minneapolis: University of Minnesota Press.

Jehl, D. (1998, April 26). Why *Titanic* conquered the world: Cairo. *The New York Times*, p. AR 29.

Jenkins, D. (1992). *Textual poachers: Television fan and participatory culture.* New York: Routledge & Kegan Paul.

Jenkins, D. (1994). Do you enjoy making the rest of us feel stupid? Alt.tv.twinpeaks, the trickster author, and viewer mastery. In D. Lavery (Ed.), *Full of secrets: Critical approaches to Twin Peaks* (pp. 51–69). Detroit, MI: Wayne State University Press.

Jenkyns, R. (1998). Cards of identity. *The New York Review of Books, 45*(7), 49–52.

Johnson, R. (1993). Editor's introduction: Pierre Bourdieu on art, literature, and culture. In P. Bourdieu, (Ed.), *The field of cultural production* (pp. 1–25). New York: Columbia University Press.

Jones, S. (1993). A sense of space: Virtual reality, authenticity and the aural. *Critical Studies in Mass Communication, 10*, 238–252.

Joyce, J. (1961). *Ulysses.* New York: Vintage Books.

Joyce, J. (1982). *Finnegan's wake.* New York: Viking.

Kaminsky, S. (1974). *American film genres: Approaches to a critical theory of popular film.* New York: Dell.

Kang, J., & Wu, Y. (1995, May). *Culture diffusion: The role of U.S. television programs in Taiwan.* Paper presented at the International Communication Association National Conference, Albuquerque, NM.

Kapoor, S., & Kang, J. (1995, May). *Use of American media and adoption of Western cultural values in India.* Paper presented at the International Communication Association National Conference, Albuquerque, NM.

Kawin, B. (1986). Children of the light. In B. Grant (Ed.), *Film genre reade* (pp. 236–257). Austin, TX: University of Texas Press.

Kelly, M. (1996). Breaking convention. *The New Yorker, 72*(23), 21–22.

King, S. (1978). *The shining.* New York: Dutton.

King, S. (1987). *Misery.* New York: Viking.

Kinzer, S. (1998, April 26). Why *Titanic* conquered the world: Istanbul. *The New York Times*, p. AR 29.

Kivikuru, U. (1995). Peripheral mass communication: Rich in contradictions. In K. Nordenstreng & H. Schiller (Eds.), *Beyond national sovereignty: International communication in the 1990s* (pp. 148–174). Norwood, NJ: Ablex.

Klapper, J. (1960). *The effects of mass communication*. Glencoe, IL: The Free Press.

Klein, N. (1993). *7 minutes: The life and death of the American animated cartoon*. New York: Verso.

Kozminski, A., & Cushman, D. (Eds.), (1993). *Organizational communication and management*. Albany: State University of New York Press.

Kubey, R. (1998). Obstacles to the development of media education in the U.S. *Journal of Communication, 48*(1), 58–69.

Kubey, R., & Czisktemaholy, M. (1990). *Television and the quality of life: How viewing shapes everyday experience*. Hillsdale, NJ: Lawrence Erlbaum Associates.

Kuhn, T. (1970). *The structure of scientific revolutions*. Chicago: University of Chicago Press.

Lakoff, G. (1987). *Women, fire, and dangerous things: What categories reveal about the human mind*. Chicago: University of Chicago Press.

Lasswell, H. (1927). *Propaganda technique in the world war*. New York: Knopf.

Lau, J. (1998). Besides fists and blood: Hong Kong comedy and its master of the eighties. *Cinema Journal, 37*(2), 18–34.

Leong, W. (1989). Culture and the state: Manufacturing traditions for tourism. *Critical Studies in Mass Communication, 6*, 355–375.

Lerner, D. (1977). Communication and development. In D. Lerner & L. Nelson (Eds.), *Communication research: A half-century appraisal* (pp. 148–166). Honolulu: University Press of Hawaii.

Lerner, D., & Schramm, W. (1969). *Communication and change in the developing countries*. Honolulu: East West Center Press.

Leuthold, S. (1998). *Indigenous aesthetics: Native art, media, and identity*. Austin: University of Austin Press.

Lévi-Strauss, C. (1964). *Le cru et le cuit*. Paris: Librairie Plon.

Levy, J. (1936). *Surrealism*. New York: Black Sun Press.

Levy, S. (1995). Confessions of a British sofa spud. *Media Studies Journal, 9*(4), 119–123.

Lexington (1996, August 3). A cheer for Olympo-Americans. *The Economist*, p. 30.

Liebert, R., & Sprafkin, J. (1988). *The early window: Effects of television on children and youth* (3rd ed.). New York: Pergamon.

Liebes, T. (1988). Cultural differences in the retelling of television fiction. *Critical Studies in Mass Communication, 5*(4), 277–292.

Liebes, T., & Katz, E. (1993). *The export of meaning: Cross cultural readings of Dallas*. Cambridge, MA: Polity Press.

Lincoln, B. (1989). *Discourse and the construction of society: Comparative studies of myth, ritual, and classification*. New York: Oxford University Press.

Lotman, Y. (1991). *The universe of the mind*. (A. Shukman, Trans.). London, England: Taurus Press.

Lutgendorf, P. (1995). All in the (Raghu) family: A video epic in cultural context. In R. Allen (Ed.), *Speaking of soap operas …* (pp. 321–353). New York: Routledge & Kegan Paul.

Lyotard, J. (1984). *The postmodernism condition: A report on knowledge* (G. Bennington & B. Massumi, Trans.). Minneapolis: University of Minnesota.

Margolis, M. (1997). Special reportùLatin TV: Soaps clean up. *Latin Trade, 5*(4), 46–52.

Maslow, A. (1970). *Motivation and personality*. New York: Harper & Row.

Mattelart, A., Delcourt, D., & Mattelart, M. (1984). *International image markets: In search of an alternative perspective*. (D. Buxton, Trans.). London, England: Comedia.

Mattelart, A., & Siegelaub, S. (1979). *Communication and class struggle: Capitalism, imperialism.* New York: International General.

McChesney, R. (1997). *Corporate media and the threat to democracy.* New York: Seven Stories Press.

McChesney, R. (1998).The political economy of global media. *Media Development, 65*(4), 3–8.

McLuhan, M. (1964). *Understanding media: The extensions of man.* New York: McGraw Hill.

Meyrowitz, J. (1985). *No sense of place.* New York: Oxford University Press.

Michalek, B., & Turaj, T. (1988). *The modern cinema of Poland.* Bloomington: Indiana University Press.

Mickey Mao (1996, August 3). *The Economist,* p. 32.

Mifflin, L. (1995, November 27). Can the *Flintstones* fly in Fiji? Children's programming as a major U.S. export. *The New York Times,* pp. D1, D4.

Miller, D. (1995). The consumption of soap opera: *The Young and the Restless* and mass consumption in Trinidad. In R. Allen (Ed.), *Speaking of soap operas* ... (pp. 213–233). New York: Routledge & Kegan Paul.

Miller, G. (1991). *The science of words.* New York: Scientific American.

Minkoff, A. (1998). Good guys smoke cigars. *Cigar aficionado, 6*(5), 110–127.

Moerk, C., & Williams, M. (1993, December 20). Moguls swat GATT–flies: Recession and Eurocrats can't nix global ties. *Variety,* p. A1.

Mokone-Matabane, S. (1995). Opening South African airwaves: What lessons from the United States? *Media Studies Journal, 9*(4), 153–158.

Morgan, M. (1990). International cultivation analysis. In N. Signorelli, & M. Morgan (Eds.), *Cultivation analysis: New directions in media effects research* (pp. 225–247). Newbury Park, CA: Sage.

Morgan, M., & Signorelli, N. (1990). Cultivation analysis: Conceptualization and methodology. In Signorelli, N. and Morgan, M., Eds. *Cultivation analysis: New directions in media effects research* (pp. 13–34). Newbury Park, CA: Sage.

Morley, D. (1993). Active audience theory: Pendulums and pitfalls. *Journal of Communication, 43*(4), 13–19.

In the mouseketeerish style. (1994, December 3). *The Economist,* p. 103.

Na ekranach. [on screen.] (1994). *Wik: Warszawski Informator Kulturalny, 21*(485), 65–72.

Naficy, H. (1996). Theorizing "Third-World" film spectatorship. *Wide Angle, 18*(4), 3–26.

Nicholas, C. (1997). Stealing stories: Communication and indigenous autonomy. *Media Development, 44*(3), 10–11.

Nye, J., & Owens, W. (1996). America's information edge. *Foreign Affairs, 75* (2): 20–36.

O'Brien, G. (1997). Sein of the times. *The New York Review of Books, 44*(13), 12–14.

Ohmae, K. (1991). *The borderless world: Power and strategy in the interlinked economy.* New York: HarperCollins.

Oliveira, O. (1995). Brazilian soaps outshine Hollywood: Is cultural imperialism fading out? In K. Nordenstreng & H. Schiller (Eds.), *Beyond national sovereignty: International communication in the 1990s* (pp. 116–131). Norwood, NJ: Ablex.

Olson, S. (1985). Devolution and indigenous mass media: The role of media in Inupiat and Sami nation–state building. Unpublished doctoral dissertation. Northwestern University. Evanston, IL.

Olson, S. (1987). Metatelevision: Popular postmodernism. *Critical Studies in Mass Communication, 4*(3), 284–300.

Olson, S. (1993). The United States and Canada as a core market: Culture, manufacturing, and industrial strategy. In A. Kozminski & D. Cushman (Eds.), *Organizational communication and management* (pp. 9–21). Albany: State University of New York Press.

Olson, S. (1994). Strategies and tactics of communication empowerment: Toward a descriptive dictonomy. In A, Malkiewicz, J. Waskiewicz, & J. Parrish-Sprowl (Eds.), *Komunikacja spoleczna w procesach transformacyjnych: Social communication in the transformation process* (pp 31–38). Wroclaw, Poland: Ekonomiczno-spolecznych Politechniki Wroclawskiej.

Olson, S. (1995). New democratic vistas: Demassification and the Polish media. In F. Casmir (Ed.), *Communication in Eastern Europe: The role of history, culture, and media in contemporary conflicts* (pp. 167–196). Hillsdale, NJ: Lawrence Erlbaum Associates.

Olson, S. (1996). *Komunikacja w organizacji i zarzadzaniu.* [communication in organizations and business.] Wroclaw, Poland: Wroclaw Polytechica Press.

Orwall, B. (1998, June 30). Here is how Disney tries to put the event into the event film. *Wall Street Journal*, pp. A1, A6.

Palatella, J. (1998). Pictures of us: Are native videomakers putting anthropologists out of business? *Lingua Franca, 8*(5), 50–57.

Papastergiadis, N. (1995, Autumn). Restless hybrids. *Third Text: Third World Perspectives on Contemporary Art and Culture, 32,* 9–18.

Parr, M. (1961). *James Joyce: The poetry of conscience.* Milwaukee, WI: Island Press.

Pelikan, J. (1985). *Jesus through the centuries: His place in the history of culture.* New Haven, CT: Yale University Press.

Pells, R. (1997). *Not like us: How Europeans have loved, hated, and transformed American culture since World War II.* New York: Basic Books.

Pollan, M. (1997, December 14). Town-building is no Mickey Mouse operation. *The New York Times Magazine*, pp. 56–63, 76–81, 88.

Porter, M. (1990). *The competitive advantage of nations.* New York: The Free Press.

Porter, M. (1998). Clusters and the new economy of competition. *Harvard Business Review, 76*(6), 77–90.

Prakash, G. (1997). The modern nation's return in the archaic. *Critical Inquiry, 23*(3), 536–556.

Pretense, J. (1997). Deconstruction/reconstructing ethnicity. *Nations and Nationalism, 3*(3), 365–395.

Propp, V. (1968). *Morphology of the folktale* (2nd ed., rev., L. Wagner, Ed.; L. Scott, Trans.). Austin: University of Texas Press.

Proust, M. (1913). *Du côté de chez Swann.* Paris: Grasset.

Pye, D. (1986). The Western (genre and movies). In B. Grant (Ed.), *Film genre reader* (pp. 143–158). Austin: University of Texas Press.

Rafferty, T. (1996). Long, hot summer. *The New Yorker, 72*(21), 74–77.

Raghavan, C. (1995). The new world order: A view from the south. In K. Nordenstreng & H. Schiller (Eds.), *Beyond national sovereignty: International communication in the 1990s* (pp. 64–81). Norwood, NJ: Ablex.

Real, M. (1989). *Super media: A cultural studies approach.* Newbury Park, CA: Sage.

Reich, R. (1990, January–February). Who is us? *Harvard Business Review, 90,* 53–64.

Rheingold, H. (1991). *Virtual reality.* New York: Summit Books.

Riding, A. (1998, April 26). Why *Titanic* conquered the world. *The New York Times*, pp. AR 1, 28–29.

Rybczynski, W. (1996). Tomorrowland. *The New Yorker, 72*(20), 36–39.

Said, E. (1993). *Culture and imperialism.* New York: Knopf.

Samuels, D. (1995, May–June). The call of stories. *Lingua Franca*, 35–43.

Saussure, F. de (1960). *Course in general linguistics.* London, England: Peter Owen.

Schatz, T. (1986). The structural influence: New directions in film genre study. In B. Grant (Ed.), *Film genre reader* (pp. 91–101). Austin: University of Texas Press.

Schiff, S. (1985). What Dynasty says about America. *Vanity Fair, 47*(12), 64–67.

Schiller, H. (1969). *Mass communication and American empire*. Boston, MA: Beacon Press.

Schiller, H. (1989). *Culture, Inc.: The corporate takeover of public expression*. New York: Oxford University Press.

Schiller, H. (1995). The context of our work. In K. Nordenstreng & H. Schiller (Eds.), *Beyond national sovereignty: International communication in the 1990s* (pp. 464–470). Norwood, NJ: Ablex.

Schmid, A., & de Graaf, J. (1982). *Violence as communication: Insurgent terrorism and the Western news media*. London, England: Sage.

Schmookler, A. (1984). *The parable of the tribes: The problem of power in social evolution*. Boston: Houghton Mifflin.

Schoen, L. (1997, August). The Klingon Language Institute. *Klingon Language Institute*. Available: <http://www.kli.org>

Schramm, W. (1949). *Mass communications*. Urbana: University of Illinois.

Schramm, W. (1964). *Mass media and national development*. Stanford, CA: Stanford University Press.

Shekwo, J. (1984). *Understanding Gbagyi folktales: Premises for targeting salient electronic mass media programs*. Unpublished doctoral dissertation, Northwestern University, Evanston, IL.

Shenon, P. (1995, October 22). Australia's serious side fades from the screen. *The New York Times*, pp. H13, H22.

Shohat, E., & Stam, R. (1994). *Unthinking Eurocentrism: Multiculturalism and the media*. New York: Routledge & Kegan Paul.

Sholle, D. (1988). Critical studies: From the theory of ideology to power/knowledge. *Critical Studies in Mass Communication, 5*, 16–41.

Shottenkirk, D. (1994). The birth of metatheory. *M/E/A/N/I/N/G, 15*, 27–42.

The silver scream: Japan's entertainment business. (1997, August 23). *The Economist*, p. 52.

Sims, C. (1998, April 26). Why *Titanic* conquered the world: Buenos Aires. *The New York Times*, p. AR 29.

Skovmand, M., & Schrøder, K. (Eds.). (1992). *Media cultures: Reappraising transnational media*. New York: Routledge & Kegan Paul.

Slotkin, R. (1992). *Gunfighter nation: The myth of the frontier in twentieth-century America*. New York: Atheneum.

Smith, A. (1995). The natives are restless. *Media Studies Journal, 9*(4), 1–6.

Smoodin, E. (1994). Introduction: How to read Walt Disney. In E. Smoodin (Ed.), *Disney discourse: Producing the Magic Kingdom* (pp. 1–20). New York: Routledge & Kegan Paul.

Spivak, G. (1995). Can the subaltern speak? In B. Ashcroft, G. Griffiths, & H. Tiffin (Eds.), *The postcolonial studies reader* (pp. 24–28). New York: Routledge & Kegan Paul.

Star wars. (1997, March 22). *The Economist*, pp. 15–16.

Stavrianos, L. (1976). *The promise of the coming dark age*. San Francisco, CA: Freeman.

Steer, J. (1992). Defining virtual reality: Dimensions determining telepresence. *Journal of Communication, 42*(4), 73–93.

Stewart, J. (1994). Grand illusion. *The New Yorker, 70*(35), 64–81.

Strom, S. (1998, April 26). Why *Titanic* conquered the world: Tokyo. *The New York Times*, p. AR 28.

Taylor, M., (1998). *Hiding*. Chicago: University of Chicago Press.

Television: Let a hundred channels bloom, but mind the thorns. (1995, November 25). *The Economist*, pp. 63–64.

Thomas, P. (1997). Communication and national identity: Towards an inclusive vision. *Media Development, 44*(2), 3–6.

Thorne, J. (1994). Full of *Twin Peaks* secrets. *Wrapped in Plastic, 13*, 5–8.

Tichi, C. (1991). *Electronic hearth: Creating an American television culture.* New York: Oxford University Press.

Tobin, J. (Ed.). (1992). *Remade in Japan: Everyday life and consumer taste in a changing society.* New Haven, CT: Yale University Press.

Todorov, T. (1990). *Genres in discourse.* Cambridge, England: Cambridge University Press.

Tompkins, J. (Ed.). (1980). *Reader-response criticism: From formalism to post-structuralism.* Baltimore: Johns Hopkins University Press.

Trueheart, C. (1996). Welcome to the next church. *The Atlantic Monthly, 278*(2), 37–58.

Tu, J. (1996, September 11). You thought French was tough? Try speaking Klingon. *The Hartford Courant,* p. E2.

Tuchman, G. (1978). *Making news: A study in the construction of reality.* New York: The Free Press.

Tulloch, J. & Alvarado, M. (1983). *Doctor who: The unfolding text.* New York: St. Martin's Press.

Tunstall, J. (1977). *The media are American: Anglo-American media in the world.* New York: Columbia University Press.

Tunstall, J. (1994). *The media are American: Anglo-American media in the world.* (2nd ed.). London, England: Constable.

Tunstall, J. (1995). Are the media still American? *Media studies Journal, 9*(4), 7–16.

Turner, F. (1962). *The frontier in American history.* New York: Holt, Rinehart, & Winston.

Valdivia, A., & Curry, R. (1996). Xuxa at the borders of global TV: The institutionalization and marginalization of Brazil's blonde ambition. *Camera Obscura, 38,* 31–60.

Vale, V., & Juno, A. (1987). Incredibly strange films. *Re/search, 1*(10), 4–218.

Vernon, R. (1966). International investment and international trade in the product cycle. *Quarterly Journal of Economics, 80*(2), 190–207.

Vincent, R. (1997). The future of the debate: Setting an agenda for a New World Information and Communication Order, ten proposals. In P. Golding & P. Harris (Eds.), *Beyond cultural imperialism: Globalization, communication, and the new international order* (pp. 175–20). Thousand Oaks, CA: Sage.

Virilio, P. (1991). *The aesthetics of disappearance.* (P. Beitchman, Trans.). New York: Semiotext(e).

Waisbord, S. (1998). When the cart of media is before the horse of identity: A critique of technology-centered views of globalization. *Communication Research, 25*(4), 377–398.

Wasser, F. (1995). Is Hollywood America? The trans-nationalization of the American film industry. *Critical Studies in Mass Communication, 12*(4), 423–437.

Weinraub, B. (1994, October 26). Ovitz + baby bells = that's entertainment. *The New York Times,* pp. D1, D6.

Weldon, M. (1983). *The psychotronic guide to film.* New York: Ballantine.

Whartob, D. (1994, June 20–26). Disney park battle heats up in Virginia. *Variety,* p. 16.

Wheeler, D. (1998). Global culture or culture clash: New information technologies in the Islamic world—a view from Kuwait. *Communication Research, 25*(4), 359–376.

Williams, M. (1994, December 12). Gaumont 100th anniversary: The future speaks English. *Variety,* p. 57.

Williamson, J. (1994). *Decoding advertisements: Ideology and meaning in advertising* (rev. ed.). London, England: Marion Boyars.

Williamson, M., & Dawtrey, A. (1993, December 27). Gatt spat wake-up on yank market muscle. *Variety,* 45.

Wills, G. (1993). *Lincoln at Gettysburg: The words that remade America.* New York: Touchstone Books.

Wilson, A. (1994). The betrayal of the future: Walt Disney's EPCOT center. In E. Smoodin (Ed.), *Disney discourse: Producing the Magic Kingdom* (pp. 118–128). New York: Routledge & Kegan Paul.

A world view. (1997, November 29). *The Economist,* 71–72.

Wright, R. (1986). Genre films and the status quo. In B. Grant (Ed.), *Film genre reader* (pp. 41–49). Austin: University of Texas Press.

Yacowar, M. (1986).The bug in the rug (pp. 217–235). In B. Grant (Ed.), *Film genre reader.* Austin: University of Texas Press.

Yoshimoto, M. (1994). Images of empire: Tokyo Disneyland and Japanese cultural imperialism. In Smoodin, E. (Ed.), *Disney discourse: Producing the Magic Kingdom* (pp. 181–199). New York: Routledge & Kegan Paul.

Young, S., & Concar, D. (1992, November 21). Secret life of the brain. *New Scientist Supplement,* pp. 1–8.

Zettl, H. (1990). *Sight sound motion: Applied media aesthetics.* Belmont, CA: Wadsworth.

Author Index

Subject Index

Woo, John, 47
Wyatt Earp, 44

X

"X-Files, The," 48
Xuxa, 117

Y

"Young and the Restless, The," 4, 36
Yrrol, 43

Z

Zimbabwe, 139, 176